Unconventional Romantic Love Story between
Astronaut from Mars (Egyptian Immigrant)
and New

ture,
man

Girl
With a Blue
Diamond
A NOVEL

ASHOK Y TAMHANE

outskirts
press

Outskirts Press, Inc.
http://www.outskirtspress.com

ISBN: 978-1-9772-2101-8

Cover Photo © 2020 Shutterstock and Pixabay Cover design - Kerrie Robertson Illustration, Inc. All rights reserved - used with permission.

Outskirts Press and the "OP" logo are trademarks belonging to Outskirts Press, Inc.

PRINTED IN THE UNITED STATES OF AMERICA

*I dedicate my book to Mrs. Florence Silber, without her inspiration
and tremendous help I would have not been here.*

*To my mother Pramilabai Tamhane, who thought me to
face the world with courage, intelligence and truth.*

*I also dedicate my book to my high school teacher late Dhundiraj Dixit
who praised my essay writing and generated great confidence in me.*

AGAINST ALL ODDS, HOW DID I START WRITING?

It is the god's gift to write. But what would you call someone inspiring me to write a novel and commit to help me to correct my grammar and spelling? I think god sent angel would right adjective to describe. This is what happened. After a few years of experience in engineering field my challenges to handle my projects became easy and I thought of writing something. I did not know what to write. I knew I could write. I just started writing in my office time and wrote a few random pieces. My secretary at that time was Mrs. Florence Silber a sweet and smiling lady, I recognized her as a book gobbler. Any work especially typing, with her super fast speed she would have plenty of spare time in the office. She used to take out a book from her pocket book and start reading. When I asked, she told me she used to finish three to four books in a week. So, I thought she would be the right person to make a judgement on my writing style. After reading my one write-up, she asked me "Where did you copy this beautiful literature from?" "I wrote it." "I can't believe you wrote it. Do you have more write-ups I can read?" I gave her two more randomly written write-ups I had written. After reading those, she said to me "These are beautiful writings. If you can write so well, you can write a novel." I told her my English grammar was poor and spelling was horrible. Can you believe, her instant response was "Don't worry. I will help you. Start Writing." And my stupid brain accepted the challenge. I told her I did not have any story line, but I could develop one. And I started writing from beyond square zero.

Florence kept her word and checked my writing all the way to the end. Florence met Steve Levinson at a vacation resort in Poconos in Pennsylvania. Steve was a high school English teacher in Queens, New York. He asked Florence when she was checking my write-ups. Steve read my write-up, had very good comments and suggestions. He liked my writing style. I always discussed with Florence. She advised me on different events, where I had a dilemma. Without Florence I won't be here and I wouldn't have met you, my readers. She also suggested a title for the book. I am extremely grateful to Florence.

I still think it started when I was in ninth grade. Our Marathi teacher (Marathi is a major Indian language spoken in West region of India), Dhundiraj Dixit used to praise my and another student Ashok Joglekar's essays so much that he used to read our essays in other classes where he also taught Marathi. Since then I knew that I can write. One of my bosses in New York gave me his letters to rewrite because he liked my writing style.

Along my journey, I started giving my typing work to temporary secretaries to keep my project secret from the office people. One of them, Jody T. gave me good suggestions to improve my writing. The other young temp liked my writing as romantic. After she left our office, one day during lunch time I was walking with my friend. She came from the opposite direction and can you imagine, she kissed me on a street of Manhattan. The only other person who knew about my writing was Etta Ward, a sweet, smiling and always happy receptionist we had to say 'Good morning' to everyone in the mornings. She wanted to read more and more of my writings. She always said "Ashok, finish the book so I can read."

As I had no support from home, only less than ten percent story was written at home, my sweet home. The story was mainly written while traveling on Long Island Rail Road, on plane, during spare time in various offices I worked, staying late in the office, in Knoxville, Toledo and Littler Rock where I was stationed for long term office work.

Because of no support, my manuscript was sitting on shelf for many years before we moved to Florida. After coming to Florida, I converted my typed manuscript into word document, rearranged the events, gave another finishing touch. The revised manuscript I gave to our new friend, Vasantha Iyangar, to review. She liked the story, character development, humorous and romantic writing style. She encouraged me to publish it.

You must be anxious to know why I selected my hero as Egyptian immigrant. I am an Indian immigrant. I wanted my hero to be an immigrant to US. So, it was easy for me to make one main character easy task - the new immigrant facing the initial settling issues, cultural differences. I could not select an Indian hero, as I myself is born and brought-up Indian. I know how conservative Indians are. Every step I would have held my thinking saying a young Indian would not think like this or would not do such a thing. My thinking freedom would have jeopardized. I could not say that my hero was exception to Indians mentality with open mind. The time I started writing, my office cubicle mate was Khaled, a young Egyptian immigrant, very friendly young guy. I started asking him questions about Egyptian life and culture as a curiosity. Then my questions became more inquisitive and more detailed so, I told him my intentions and he told me so many things on his own. He really helped me shape my hero. Khaled's father was in our company. He helped me set Egyptian dinner menu and cooking recipes.

I was very lucky to get a good editor and herself a well-known writer Elizabeth Ridley. She did excellent job of editing and made number of suggestions to make my book better. But I was still disappointed in her comments and told her so. I had expected her to tell me to remove this scene, this does not belong here, this is bad and so on. Instead she had praised my writing in so many places that I was again riding on cloud nine. She liked my sly humor, romance, poems, excellent detailing, tension/conflict, mystery creation, cultural insight, strong atmosphere, horrifying scene, sad and sweet events etc. She said it is a great job, touching and poignant story. So, you can be assured that my first-time adventure is worth reading.

Now I know you want to know how I created my heroine character. When I was in my high school years, in my town in India I had heard two ladies, one young in her twenties unmarried and other married in her forties that could be called to my heroine's type. Then in US I saw a documentary on national TV channel that depicted full life story of a girl of this kind. And through the English literature I learnt more of this kind of girl. So, when Florence convinced me to write a novel, first thing I thought of this type of character. Total character development of the heroine is my imagination.

Again, I am grateful to Florence, without her inspiration and tremendous help I would not have done anything. I am grateful to Vasantha Iyangar for their help and support. I am grateful to Steve for praising my writing style and giving me helpful suggestions. I am also grateful to Jody T., Etta Word. I am extremely grateful to Khaled, who helped me to create Said's character and number of Egyptians I met in different offices to make Egyptian back ground in my story. Thanks to my cousin, Ajit Tamhane who is a professor at North Western University, for his valuable editing and giving finishing touch.

Ashok Y Tamhane.
December 22, twenty-eighteen.
Revised November 11, twenty-nineteen.

CHAPTER ONE

Never expected, I would ever meet her. And now I was standing at the south east corner of Thirty-Fourth Street and Seventh Avenue anxiously waiting for the traffic light to change so that I could cross the seventh avenue hopefully to meet her at the opposite corner.

I saw a girl, standing right at the corner that was also a front entrance to the Bowery Bank. I did not think that was her. She was facing Seventh Avenue in the direction I would be coming from. This particular spot was exactly between the subway entrance that was closed for many years and a corner of the Bowery Bank. She was hardly noticeable amidst the peak hour crowd passing in front of her. The time was precisely five forty and I was ten minutes late. This girl I was looking at was the same height as she, but much slimmer. She was wearing a light blue satin dress with a navy-blue spring jacket folded on her left arm and a pocketbook in her right hand. It was mid-April but an unusually warm day. I was looking at her. She looked nervous. I had said that I would be there by five thirty and you know the New York subway as usual kept its reputation as late. Maybe she thought I was not going to come. While I was crossing Seventh Avenue, she switched her pocketbook from her right hand to her left hand and rolled her right palm over her hair. That particular action of hers made me more certain that it must be her. How the hell could I recognize her? With her bulky size, she used to look like she was in her mid-thirties while this girl looked sweet sixteen. I used to see her as over two hundred pounds. What I was looking at was a beautiful figure of about hundred and thirty pounds. And this girl had an altogether different hairstyle, like Dorothy Hamill's. The new hairstyle emphasized her slim neck and beautiful shoulders. Previously she had shoulder-length hair that curled at the ends. Now I was closer to her. I could see her eyes. Those big greenish-gray, liquid eyes could not deceive me; they simply could not belong to anybody else but her. She looked confused as she spotted me approaching her.

With hesitation I said "Hi, Kaif Halat?" For a moment she was stunned, just gazing at my face. Then slowly she said, "Hi, Said. I would have never recognized you unless you had said those magic words. You look so different and handsome without your mustache and beard, and you have short hair. I'm fine. And you?"

You would be surprised that I still remember every detail of that meeting because that meeting started a new era in my life. I took her hand in mine and kissed it.

"Oh, my! You have changed so much. If not for your eyes, I would not have recognized you. You really look different, gorgeous and sweet sixteen; I like your new hairstyle. It's cute."

"Thanks. My brother suggested that it would look great on me. So, I told him I had no money and asked him to pay for it and he paid. Thank God, my sister-in-law wasn't there. It is my natural hair color, auburn. My new hairstyle seems to go along with the changes I have been going through myself. I have changed a lot otherwise." Now she was relaxing a little bit.

"What happened? What made you come back to New York?" she asked me.

"It is so simple—my heart started singing all the time, day and night, even in my dreams. 'I had lost my heart in New York!' So, I brought my shadow back to New York. I missed New York. I should wear a big sign, 'I love the Big Apple.' Right?"

"Ha, ha! New York did not miss you. I missed you for a few weeks after you left for Ohio."

"That's good."

"In your absence the city improved its crime rate. The subway graffiti artists expanded their business. They came out of the subway and took their art work on street walls of the city."

"Great prosperous news."

She was smiling and I noticed a slight dimple on her right cheek, which I had never seen before on her chubby face.

I had already selected 'Cafe Gathering' for our dinner and had made a reservation. This mid-Manhattan restaurant was not crowded in the evenings. There was a relaxed atmosphere. One can enjoy a really large drink.

We got a nice corner table. As soon we were seated, the waitress took our drink orders. "I stopped drinking, except on special occasions, I drink a glass of white wine. I will drink today my favorite Pinot Grigio. I welcome you to the Big Apple and I am glad you remembered me. So, it is a special day to me." She ordered a glass of Pinot Grigio and I ordered my favorite.

We had hardly a chance to talk when all of a sudden, I found myself dumbfounded. I simply did not know what to talk about. Then I noticed that she was wearing a ladies' watch and that too, she had put it on her left wrist. I remembered she used to wear a man's watch on her right. She had changed a lot, I thought.

That 'Diamond' ring looked beautiful on her delicate right hand. Yes, those hands, once upon a time were fleshy, looked so delicate now. Can you imagine someone losing more than seventy pounds off her body? I was not going to tell her that I liked her ring because I had said it before. And I was sure she was going to say it was her birthstone. Maybe a long cigarette would decorate her hand as it used to do for Lynda. It reminded me that I had an old cigarette lighter belonging to Lynda. She had left it in my apartment, and I found it in my belongings when I was unpacking my stuff last week. I had brought it with me to give to her.

"Here is something for you. It's not new. I found it in my belongings. Somebody had left it. It's good. You can use it."

"I can't. I don't smoke anymore."

I started playing with the cigarette lighter. Now I started understanding what she meant by saying that she had changed. She had mentioned it a few times.

I saw a round white spot about size of half the diameter of a nickel on the back of her right hand. It was barely noticeable on her white skin. I noticed it.

"What is that mark? Is it a birthmark?"

"No, that is my after-birthmark."

She spread her hand in front of me and I touched the spot with my finger.

"This is a cigarette burn. The doctor said it will go away in a few months."

"Is that the reason you gave up smoking?"

"No, not really. But that prompted my quitting. I don't want to talk about it now."

Our meal was served.

"Hey, your steak looks great," she commented, looking at the dish in front of me.

"Do you want to switch?"

"No way, mine looks good too. Hey, you speak much better English now."

"Thanks. And you know I understand you much better. Do you know why?"

"Why?"

"I employed my ghost to teach me English."

"Cute, I knew you would come up with something like that." And she laughed.

"How was life in Cleveland?"

"Oh, nothing like New York! Cleveland was a quiet, steel city on Lake Erie and overall life was also quiet. The life was so slow in Cleveland. I got bored. There was nothing much to do. New Yorkers are so smart and well-dressed compared to the people there. And you know most of the women smoke."

"I always thought New Yorkers are big smokers."

"Nope!"

"I met a few girls of interest, I mean girlfriends. I was bored of being alone." As soon as I said this, I realized that I should not have talked about lonesome life. She was in the same boat. Anyway, she did not show any emotions.

I told her the joke about the contest and prizes to stay in Cleveland, the one I had heard on the radio. She did not understand it. So, I explained to her that the prizes were punishments to stay in Cleveland. And she laughed freely.

"That makes me feel like visiting that city. Tell me more about Cleveland."

"Well, people are friendly. At the same time, some of them were skeptical towards a foreigner like me, as if they had never seen a brown-colored man like me. It is not like New York where you see people from every country in the world. And you know, we say 'Hi!' here in New York. There they would say 'Hello!' or even a no answer was acceptable. There is one Broadway and one Main Street, as every city in America has to have. Besides that, Lake Erie is beautiful. I used to enjoy driving around the lake in the late evening when there was not much traffic on the road. Especially I enjoyed driving in the moonlight. I had spent hours at the so-called Lake Erie beach in the moonlight evenings, sometimes alone, sometime with my girlfriends. I really enjoyed that part."

She was anxious. "It's interesting, you had more than one girlfriend?"

"I had two girlfriends."

"Wow, two girl friends that makes this boy interesting! Were they beautiful? What happened to them? Did you bring them to the big apple or ran away from them?"

"Oh, well, I didn't run away from them and I they did not follow me here. People in small city are scared of crime rate in big cities. The second one was good looking, better than average looking. You know one thing I did not like about this girl, she would do anything for me. She did not have strong opinions of her own." I was talking about Nancy. "And the first one was beautiful, very aggressive and ambitious. She was a bank manager. I liked her. She found a big officer in her bank organization and she left me for him."

She was interestingly listening. I wondered what she would think if I had said I wanted to kiss her. Instead I just looked at her face.

"Why are you smiling?" she asked.

"I was remembering how different you used to look the last time I saw you. You have changed a lot. You know, you look pretty and younger."

"Thanks." She smiled.

"My friend, Julie Anne, did I ever tell you about her?"

"Oh, yes, I think so. What about her?"

"She got married two months ago. I am happy for her." She told me about Julie's husband, John, who was one of many assistant sales managers for the Northeastern zone of 'Goodyear' tire company.

I asked her "How is your family?" And she replied, "All are fine and enjoying life."

She told me she had changed her apartment and her lifestyle after some scary incident. "Now I live in Brooklyn. It is a nice, big and bright apartment."

We exchanged small pleasantries. She thanked me "For the dinner and an enjoyable evening" and kissed my cheek. I said "I enjoyed your company." In fact, I had enjoyed this memorable meeting with her. Her kiss seemed a little warmer than the one earlier in the evening, or maybe it was my imagination.

I dropped her at the subway platform. I had to take the uptown 'F' train to Queens and she was going downtown to Brooklyn on the 'F' train. Both these trains were coming on the opposite sides of the same platform. The only thing I did special was when my 'F' train came before her train. I let it go and waited until her train arrived.

When her train arrived, she thanked me again for the dinner before saying good night. I said, "I will call you during the week. Good night!"

She stood in the door waving good-bye and I did the same. She was smiling. As soon as the train moved, I saw her smile was gone and she became serious looking. Her face had the same expression when I first saw her almost three years ago. Maybe she was thinking about the outcome of this meeting. I was wondering what exactly she meant when she said she had changed.

It was the first week of April 1976 and I was back in New York.

Some past memories, you just can't forget, as if they happened to you recently. My first meeting with her was of that kind. A lot of water had flowed between my first encounter with her and now. My memories flew back all the way to the time since I met her for the first time. It was a torrent of memories.

CHAPTER TWO

This was how my life started in America.

On the eighth of May 1971, I was reborn in America. I mean I landed at JFK Airport in New York. It was a Saturday.

My mind was very fragile. Coming to the United States as an immigrant was the greatest adventure of my life. There was an anxiety for the future. I was worried about the job situation over here and my employment prospects as Mokhtar had already explained to me in his letters was bad. I was homesick, physically and mentally tired. Since I changed my flight in London, I could not stop thinking about the events during the last year. My whole world had changed so fast, I could not believe it myself. Those were strange circumstances that pushed me to this adventure.

While the plane was landing, I saw the Statue of Liberty and the gorgeous skyline of New York City. I was overwhelmed. My emotions were mixed. With all my courage, I closed my eyes and prayed to Allah. "May this land bring me happiness, peace, and prosperity?"

I forgot all about my mental fatigue while going through the immigration authorities and the U. S. Customs. Mokhtar had told me not to worry about customs; it would take a long time because the U.S. Customs thoroughly search everyone coming from the Middle East for drug-related products. It was some experience!

Karim and Mokhtar were waiting for me. As soon as I came out, they embraced me. "Ahlaan bik iilaa America w jayid haz (Welcome to America and good luck)." I had the greatest relief seeing them in this completely unknown country.

I was going to share a two-bedroom apartment with Karim and Mokhtar. Karim was my classmate and roommate at the dorm when we were studying in engineering college in Cairo. Mokhtar was staying in the same dorm and a year junior to us. We three were great friends. Imran was going to join us in early September when colleges were going to open for the fall semester. Imran was Mokhtar's cousin and graduated from the engineering college at Alexandria. We three were U.S. immigrants and Imran was coming as a student for further studies. Karim and Mokhtar were taking evening courses towards their master's degrees at Brooklyn Polytechnic Institute in Brooklyn besides their full-time jobs. Their wives were in Egypt and both of them were planning to bring their families next year when they would be close to finishing their studies. Both of them were in the States for the past two years.

On our way, we were constantly talking. None of them had a car. So, we were riding in a yellow cab. I was sure the cab driver must have gone crazy listening to our conversation in Arabic. After arriving home, we also talked a lot. I was tired from the journey but did not feel tired while gossiping.

The next day, Mokhtar bought the *New York Times*. I was overwhelmed to see the amount of paper in his hand, so, I asked him, "Did you buy the whole week's newspaper?" I was literally shocked when he told me that it was only Sunday *New York Times*. I searched through the classifieds for a suitable job for my kind of experience. Mokhtar gave me a big list of companies and job agencies. Both of them trained me how to look for a job and how to travel around the city by subway.

During the week I was busy visiting employment agencies. "Do you have U.S. experience? We don't take applications unless you have at least one-year U.S. experience." "If you don't have U.S. degree, we don't have a job for you." I had one of these two standard answers from agency to agency. At the most, someone would take my resume. I had filled a few applications with a few agencies during the first two weeks. All the agencies told me not to call them. If there was any possibility of a job, they would contact me.

I was fascinated by the colored television, which used to occupy me all through the evenings. Colored television was a new experience for me. Three nights a week Karim and Mokhtar had their classes. They had their examinations in June. So, they were busy with studies during the other evenings and during the weekends. Either I would keep myself busy with the TV using earphones in my ears or would stroll around outside in my jacket. Yes, I used to feel cold without a jacket during my first summer.

That formed a routine for the first few weeks. Every evening both of my friends would ask me about my adventures and different experiences during the day. They would boost my morale by saying that those were real bad days and I had to have good patience to wait a few months before I could find any job. I might not get one until the summer was over. They did not tell me all the facts of the situation. Karim had sponsored my immigration. They told me to 'Keep faith in Allah and only your luck could help you' and assured me not to worry about anything.

I was prepared for anything. During the week after I came, one evening both of them got bored of studying and the three of us went to see the movie *Butch Cassidy and the Sundance Kid*. I was thrilled to hear the famous song 'Raindrops Keep Falling on My Head,' which I had loved forever.

After two weeks I started getting beautifully written regret letters from different companies. 'We are very impressed with your background and talents. Unfortunately, at present we do not have a position to match your experience and qualifications. We will keep your resume in our active file and will let you know in case a suitable position becomes available.' All of them were of the same nature. My friends told me their active files were wastepaper baskets. At least I was optimistic enough not to believe them. 'Said, you can make a big file of those regret letters.' Their suggestion interested me and I started filing those 'Regrets'.

Both of them would go to college right from work and would come home late and tired. Every evening I would cook food for all of us. I had very little cooking experience. Whatever I used to cook, all of us enjoyed. They had absolutely no time to comment and had nothing to complain about. I thought the situation was perfect to develop and experiment with my talents as a chef. After they finished their semester, we started taking turns cooking. I learned better cooking from them.

Karim and Mokhtar finished their exams in June. That Saturday they were excited to go to the racetrack, for some excitement, for some fun and of course with a great hope to make some money. I was going with them. I had become a part of their lives. Our apartment was in Jackson Heights. We started around ten thirty. We took a subway to Kew Gardens and from there we had to take a bus to Aqueduct racetrack. Karim and Mokhtar bought 'Daily Racing Form' at a newspaper stall at the subway entrance. Both of them kept busy going through their newspapers and discussing among themselves to find the winners throughout the journey.

As soon as we reached the stands, both of them rushed to the booking office and bought winning tickets. I mean always winning till you loose. I was thrilled to look at the racetrack and the whole atmosphere. People were discussing with their friends or neighbors nothing but the horses and races. It looked like a train station during rush hour. There was still time to start the first races and a few horses were still warming up on the tracks. When the horses came to the starting gate, everyone was busy watching the horses and there was total silence. As soon as the horses dashed out of the gates, the whole scene changed like magic. People started calling for the jockeys and the horses to "Go, go." The whole atmosphere was electrified. The chaos went on increasing till the horses crossed the finish line. Some hands went up in the air. Winners were happy and losers were hopeful for the future. No one showed emotions. It was just the first race. Almost everybody started walking to the booking office.

Win was a dead hit. Both my friends won for the place. The payoff was mediocre and they were not happy about it. For the next few minutes they fought among themselves for not selecting the winning horse suggested by one of them. The first and third horses for the triple were unexpected. The triple paid big money. Mokhtar taught me later, "It is not unexpected. It is called a long shot. Learn something new from us, Dumbo!" Both of them were mad till the next race started. Karim was more matured. He told Mokhtar to "Forget it; it is not yet the end of the day." I thanked Allah when both of them won the next race. Everything was forgotten and was history by then.

The last race, they said it was a chance for the losers to win. Only the losers clung to their hopes till the last race in a big hope to win. The real winners had already fled with their winnings in their pockets. And I had one more chance to learn new thing that the last race was the race for the losers to win.

I prayed to Allah—though I had very little faith in him—to make all the losers' winners, including my friends. I imagined all the people there were mainly losers. Well, their faces were showing that. Though it was not funny, it thrilled me. They, I mean my friends, bet a lot of money. You should have been there to watch their faces. I was watching their faces rather than the horses and knew the progress of the race from their faces. They were just lucky that out of their many horses, one came second and they won some money besides total loss. "So, if you bet on a horse and it comes first, second, or third you still win, right? I don't understand why don't you bet on every horse? You would be always a winner, right?" Karim answered me, "Shut up, Said." I realized; I must have said something stupid. Well, at least my process of learning was winning. I had learned so many things in such a short time. I sealed my mouth. I remembered someone had said that men learn new things in life till the end of his life, I mean women too.

I did not know how much they had lost. All three of us were quiet. I felt sorry for my friends as if I had lost my own money. They must be mad at themselves. I felt myself a bit stupid because I was the one who had almost no feelings among almost all the losers. I was the only winner by not losing any money. I was enjoying watching all the others.

Well, so far, I had learned a lot of new things from them. The first one, on the first day of my arrival, on the occasion of starting my new life in this country of opportunities, they welcomed me and wished me prosperity. They had toasted me with champagne in a real American style. It was against our religion to drink alcohol. They were drinking. They never thought that I had never drunk. Trust me, that was my first introduction to alcohol and I did hesitate in the beginning. Karim encouraged me, "It is OK, Said, to drink on special occasions. Just don't get drunk." And I started drinking. I did not even think that was against my religion. All my senses had died more than a year before I came to the States. My whole world had closed on me and I just remained a human beyond human emotions and couldn't even convince myself that it was Allah's wish.

After the races, we took a bus not going to Kew Gardens, instead we sat in a bus going to Flatbush Avenue via Atlantic Avenue. I had no courage to learn about this. None of us was talking. The bus started and they started talking. I was curious to know about where we were going. Karim told me to watch and enjoy. I was doing it anyway for the past few hours, so I continued doing it.

We went to an Arabic restaurant on Atlantic Avenue in Brooklyn. They ordered the food. I was little gloomy thinking over my future in this country. Karim said to me, "Come on, Said, and cheer up. It is not the end of the world. All the things will turn rosy for you in a matter of time. And don't feel bad about our losses. We have good and bad days at the track. We had won good money in the past. Don't think of anything and enjoy the food." I calmed down and enjoyed everything. We bought Egyptian spices for our cooking from a nearby Arabic store on our way home.

I was so excited over the horse racing and the whole atmosphere that I dreamt that night about horse racing and me betting on the horses and winning a big money.

We would go to the race track both Saturdays and Sundays. I had a lot of temptation to bet but I had no heart and no money to gamble. Afterwards it started to bore me watching the same things again and again without participating, I mean without betting, there was no fun. So, I would stay home watching TV or strolling in Flushing Meadows Park. The only condition I had to obey was to join them at the Arabic restaurant on Atlantic Avenue. Sometime in July the races moved to Belmont in Long Island and we had to take the subway, the Long Island Railroad, and then a bus to go to Belmont. Except the place, a few structural and scenic differences, other things were the same, the same horses and jockeys, the same breed of people raising their hands and talking to the horses.

In August, Karim bought a used car. It was a beautiful sky blue 1967 Impala with black vinyl seats and it was nicely maintained. The car was owned by a family who sold it after their children grew up and had their own cars. It was so big that three of us would sit comfortably in the front seat. On that Impala I took my first driving lesson on American roads. I had learned driving in Egypt just before coming to the States, on Karim's advice.

I accompanied them to Belmont a few times after Karim bought the car and then I stopped going to the races. I used to feel gloomy. My adventure to find happiness in this country was not working. Four months had passed since I came here and I had no job. I was depressed and homesick. There was nothing much of any attraction I had left back home to feel sorry for my coming to the US. I was young and I could certainly wait without getting frustrated. I started looking for jobs outside New York City area that only fattened my 'regrets' file. At least I was enjoying cooking for my friends and was getting better in my cooking day by day.

My friends suggested looking for an odd job like a clerical job or a bank teller's job. The bank teller's job was a longshot because my foreign accent and difficulty in understanding all the people in general. I sincerely tried a few banks without any success. And secondly, all these kinds of jobs that were odd jobs for me were taken by students working for the summer. I had nothing but disappointments. During that period, my friends really did a great job of cheering me and convincing me that both of them went through the same situation when they came two years ago. They kept my spirits high.

After four months, a strange coincidence occurred. One of Mokhtar's colleagues left his job to take an assignment in Saudi Arabia. Mokhtar talked to his boss and arranged my interview. I was given the job and a reasonable salary. I was lucky! It was not exactly an engineer's job but in the engineering field. The job title was mechanical designer. My friends did not think it was a great salary. They told me how much they were making. Anyway, I got a job. It was a great relief. I was happy and my friends also felt happy for me.

It was Wednesday when I learned about getting the job. Karim and Mokhtar took me to a bar and they celebrated my good news, and my 'Achievement.' We drank liberally. Well, all the credit for this occasion went to Mokhtar. I thanked him again and thanked both of them for bearing with my boredom. "Don't say that, Said. We are all friends."

Thursday after they came home from work, they loaned me some money and we went shopping. They fitted me in new clothes to make an American out of me, suitable for my job. Being Thursday, the sale day, I got good bargains.

On Saturday, they went to the race track. I did not go with them. I had to write two letters, one to my brother and one to my childhood chum Husen from my hometown with whom I and my brother played since I could remember. In the evening I joined my friends at the Arabic restaurant on Atlantic Avenue. After that we went to see an Egyptian movie in a nearby theatre. When we came home at night, I had a surprise for them. I had champagne for all of us in order to toast myself good luck for my first job in this country.

Sunday proved a great day for me. It opened a new era in my life. I went to Belmont race track with my buddies and betted on horses for the first time in my life, on borrowed money. I had watched my friends and had learnt how to bet on horses. I played right from the beginning. First, second, and third races went in great anxious moments of hope and my borrowed money went from my pocket to someone else's. I thought I had learnt enough to pick a winner. After the third race, I realized for the first time in my heart how the other losers really felt. So far, I had just my imaginations of the losers. It was bitter, especially on borrowed money. In the fourth race, my heavy favorite with eight-to-three odds finally won by one and one-half lengths and my hands went in air and unknowingly words escaped from my mouth "Albengho!" (Bingo). I felt so embarrassed for a moment. I got two dollar and forty cents over my investment of two dollars. My friends congratulated and patted me on my shoulder; that made me more embarrassed as I realized that a lot of people were looking at us. Anyway, I had a longshot winner in the seventh race. And at the end of the day, I had won a little over six dollars. 'Beginners luck,' I thought.

In the evening we went to a Chinese restaurant in Jackson Heights. The whole weekend was on me, on the borrowed money from friends. I was glad that my friends enjoyed with me.

Sunday night I was really tired, physically and mentally. All my tension for more than four months was over. I felt homesick and lonely.

In the beginning of September Mokhtar's cousin Imran joined us. He was going to study at New York University as a full-time student towards M.B.A. He was from a rich family. Karim and Mokhtar started their evening college in September. Imran used to be at home in the evening. He always had to study. I used to get bored. Karim had strongly suggested me to enroll in evening school towards a Master's degree. I had no heart to go back to school. I resumed my job of cooking. It was happy arrangement.

In the evening I would go to some movie or would go to Roosevelt or Yonkers race track for the evening trot races. I was not a 'Regular' there. My gambling was under my control.

One evening at Roosevelt, I mean at Roosevelt race track, I was busy figuring horses for the fifth race exacta. A medium-built young guy came to me. I had seen him a few times at the race track. You see so many usual faces at the race track every day. The same people come to the betting windows at a particular time that you can keep the attendance and you would find 'All present'.

"Hi! How you doing today? Any luck? I see you regularly, man. I am Vassily Harris." He extended his hand for a handshake.

I really did not want to get into any kind of conversation or friendship. I thought it would be rude otherwise. So, I extended my hand. He shook my hand and raised his hand upward and twisted his palm to shake hands brother-style.

"I am Said. How are you?" I did not even add "Vassily." I said it a little curtly. He did not notice it. He was a stranger to me.

"Glad to meet you. You know, shit, I lost the fourth in the last leg. The fucking longshot pushed three horses and shit won big money, man. How you doing today?" He was persistent to know how I was doing.

"Not well! I played two so far. No luck!"

"Some days you start shitty, man. Are you from Egypt or the Middle East?"

I was surprised at his accuracy. I didn't wear any kind of button on my dress that said either 'I love Anwar Sadat' or 'I am from Pyramids' country'.

The guy was not ready to quit. I was not interested in making friendship with him, he was unavoidable.

"Yeah!" I said.

"There is an Egyptian in our office. He has goddamn features just like you. Typical features, right man? Sharp nose, black hair, same color like yours. Well learned, smart people!"

There was nothing I could say to get rid of him.

Then Vassily continued, "Bet I got a winner for the fifth race. That is the best jockey on mud, man, but shitty horse. Horrendous combination! This guy does the trick. Today he is riding a lousy horse. Ten-to-one odds. I bet shit, he is going to win. Same two did bloody well last time, man. You know in the seventh race; the fifth horse is 'Son of Jack' that is the son of 'Jack Daniel'. That was shit terrific horse. Won number one money for two years. I played on him many times. This rider 'Jose' wins two, three races every night. Would you like to play on it, man?"

"I always play exacta on fifth." Of course, that was not my rule. I tried to avoid him.

"That's fucking bullshit, man. Just two dollars on win? Be a sport. Want to split a bet?"

I could not deny him. Splitting two dollars was too cheap. That was the real gambler's way. Finally, we settled four dollars to win between the two of us. I put four on my own selected exacta.

We came back in the stands to find that we lost. I had also lost my exacta.

"Shit. Don't you worry, man? So, we don't have beginner's shitty luck for our partnership. So, it is going to be lucky. Some you win, some you lose, and you don't win them all, man."

He suggested we go for a drink and then paid for my whisky. We hung around, played a few races. We won a few races with small money.

Next time I met Vassily at the race track, it was a week later. He was in a terrific mood. It was his payday, he told me so. He also told me that he works as a messenger boy distributing company mail in a brokerage firm on Wall Street.

We played quite a few races but did not share a bet. Only for one race we had selected the same horse and it won a good pay-off. Overall, he won one race and lost the others. I also won an exacta and made some money for the day.

One thing I realized was that Vassily was a seasoned gambler. In the following months our friendship grew thicker. He used to tell me funny stories of the Wall Street brokers and their different tempers depending on the market situation. He would listen to my stories with equal interest. He appreciated my judgements and my selections at the race track. A few times he won from my selections. Sometimes we would go to the restaurant together. I liked him as a friend. He was a nice guy.

In due course of time, Mokhtar and Karim rented their own apartments and established their families. Mokhtar's wife's name was Mona and Karim's wife was Nafisa. Imran went to stay with his college friends. Karim and Nafisa had a daughter, Shakila, three years old and a one-year-old son, Abdul. I was left alone. I moved to a one-bedroom apartment in Jackson Heights. I bought my first car, the first in my life. It was a brand-new Monte Carlo, silver gray with maroon interior, fully loaded. I loved it. It was a beautiful car. I paid half of the price from profits from those lovely Arabic horses at the race tracks and some overtime money. I had won two thousand dollars on a double bet of six dollars in a big triple. I had losses also. Overall, I was winning. I was just lucky and always said it was the mercy of Allah that I was winning.

I enjoyed going to the races, to a bar for drinks, going to movies and Broadway plays and enjoying Arabic food at my friends' homes with their families and enjoying the food at the Arabic restaurants at Atlantic Avenue in Brooklyn. One of my thrills was visiting Jones Beach on weekend evenings. I would park my car in number four parking lot at Jones Beach, which used to be open till midnight. Then I would go to the beach, would find a quiet spot and sit down in the sand with my legs half folded and arms around my knees clapped together. The sun would be still lingering behind the evening clouds with the sun's rays exploding in bright streaks through the clouds, giving them silver lining. Within a few minutes the west sky would be golden yellow then orange and then red. It would be a beautiful sight to watch. It would be mind-soothing to watch the dancing of the waves and the heavenly music they would be playing with the mild breeze in the air. I had come to Jones Beach in the evening so many times. I enjoyed the atmosphere during the twilight. It used to be so quiet. A few couples would linger hand-in-hand, a few would just lie in the sand. I would lie on the sand looking at the darkening sky and waiting for the stars to appear one by one and listening to the music of the waves. Just try it yourself and I am sure you would forget everything around you, just like I used to feel as if nothing else exists besides you and nature. I would recall the old days when I was in college. I used to go to the bank of the Nile in the evening alone myself. I would run as a part of my soccer practice and then I would sit in the sand. Those were the days when there was nothing but happiness in my life. My life song was singing the happy tunes in those days. That was the period when Helen came in my life.

I was in my second year of engineering. I distinctly remembered the day, the first time I met her. The whole scene was pictured in front of me as if I were participating in the live events of the past. The Engineering College was playing against the Commerce College in Cairo University soccer championship semifinals on common ground of the Arts and Commerce College. We won by three to one and I was unanimously acclaimed hero of the match because I had scored two goals. One of the goals as I remember resulted from a sixty-foot-long kick over the heads of the players and straight in the net. The goalie had no chance to jump and save the goal. After the game my teammates carried me to the pavilion. As soon as they put me on the ground, a girl came running through the crowd and kissed me. I have a picture of that scene. I was stunned. It was very unusual. And that was Helen (Helen of Alexandria not of Troy), deep blue eyed, sharp Egyptian nose, a beautiful dream girl with smiley face. The news photographer did not spare this unprecedented event. The next day our picture was in every newspaper.

In my imagination, I was floating in heaven that night. I saw her again and again in my dreams. I did not want to end the night.

You met me, touched me, touched my heart.
You smiled, opened showers of flowers.
Did magic on me, made my life.
My mind is flying wild in dreamland.

Helen's parents were living near Alexandria. She wanted to be away from her parents for college. She convinced her father that the Arts College in Cairo was much better than any other college in the country. And Helen came to Cairo for her college studies and thus met me. Her father was half English and was an officer in the government service. Helen's mother was Egyptian.

We became great friends and lovers. She was in the first year of the Arts College. Our friendship was the talk of her and my colleges. She became my heartthrob. We used to stroll on the banks of the Nile. She would take off her hijab (a scarf covering lady's hair) when no one was around. Her reddish brown, below shoulder length hair would dance on her forehead and ears in the breeze. She had thin and large ears. Listening my simple jokes, she would burst into laughter. She was bubbly. We would walk hand-in-hand when it used to be dark, I mean we were not married and it was Egypt in the sixties, this kind of closeness was not acceptable to the society.

My whole world was filled with green and pink colors in those days. My life was full of music and my heart used to sing tunes of love. It was like a romantic poem. We would sit in the sand at our favorite spot looking at ships and barges sailing through the Nile. In the darkness of the evening, their lantern lights would cast streak of light on the dancing waves. Those sailors would entertain themselves by singing songs in their voices. That used to be melodious to listen to. No, Helen and I never sang any love song. We just listened to love songs. Sometimes someone on the other side of the bank played a flute, the basic flute made of bamboo with nine holes. Those soothing heavenly tunes in the evening were filling the whole atmosphere like a magic. That music was out of this world. The whole thing used to make us high, as if we were drugged. I did not have any experience with the drugs. I should just say the music used to make us high. We had to leave, breaking our trance before the curfew time at Helen's dormitory.

We had talked about our future dreams of marrying. Our marriage would not be accepted by our families. Me marrying a Christian girl and her marrying a Muslim boy was not common in those days and it was not accepted by society. My father would have condemned me and would have abandoned me. We had to live in big cities like either Cairo or Alexandria, where people did not care about mixed marriages. We had accepted those situations.

Our romance continued till the end of the college year. When we left for the summer break, she cried that she would miss me for a long time. She told me her family was furious over the photo they saw in the newspaper and sent harsh letters to her after that. She had kept it secret from me for a long time. In fact, I also received angry letters from my home. But I did not tell Helen about it.

I do not know what happened to Helen. When I came back from summer break, there was no Helen. None of her friends knew anything about her.

Life went on. I got over my frustration in course of time and decided never to fall in love again. A number of girls showed great interest in me. I was a hero in those days. Love was not my kind of sport anymore. I kept myself busy with soccer and my studies.

Many times, I had come to Jones Beach in the early morning to watch the sun rising from the ocean. It was a beautiful sight. I loved nature and had love affair with Jones Beach. The only thing I did not want and tried to avoid was drifting in the past memories. That could have become an obsession. Then I bought a Raleigh ten speed bicycle. I would ride my bike in Flushing Meadows Park after coming from work. Sometimes on weekends, I would put my bike in my car and go to bicycle paths in Little Neck in Nassau County. A few times I went on a chartered fishing boat and gave my catch to Mokhtar. One weekend, I went to Niagara Falls with my friends and their families and enjoyed the amazing thrill of the big waterfall. I visited Niagara Falls a few more times, every time I enjoyed it as if I was watching it for the first time. I used to watch tennis, soccer and ice hockey games on TV. Most of the time I would stay out of my apartment during the summer. I really enjoyed my being single.

My lovely Jackson Heights neighborhood lovers once did love me so much that someone did a lovely job on me. He or they loved my color TV and my newly bought Sanyo stereo system so much that they accepted them without my permission in the name of love and for the sake of love and gave me their lovely memories forever. That was a short love story from our neighborhood, loving burglars with love. One evening I came home and realized what they did to me.

I could do nothing but accept their love deeds with shock and sadness. I called the cops to report the theft. They told me that they had no time to investigate such a small burglary. They made a report and told me to claim my losses from the insurance company. People from my office had told me to have apartment insurance and I bought one. Bob from my office told a story that a one of his friends who lived in the Bronx was burglarized a few times and he had multiple locks on his front door. Finally, he started keeping a few locks unlocked and that worked. The feeling that somebody loved my situation, the way they did, was not acceptable. I was all upset. After the cops left, my mind felt the gloom of it. The whole day I was thinking of going for a movie, not to the race track. My betting was already at the OTB (Off Track Betting). I was hungry but did not feel like eating. I was not going to deepen my gloom in booze. So, going to a bar did not seem like my choice. How about calling my friends and talking with them? I did not feel like doing that either. I preferred talking to Vassily. That was a good choice. He would listen to me and cheer me. So, I drove to Yonkers. I did not find Vassily. Played a few races and lost each of them. It was not my day after all.

I came home after the races. I felt unsecured, threatened of my privacy. I came to America to establish a new life and forget my past in Egypt. I wanted to stay single and enjoy my life and be happy. The burglary in my apartment disturbed me.

A week later when I met Vassily, he was in a good mood. "I bet Ronny's Palmer got to win this damn race, man. Last time he won three months ago on shitty, muddy track. Then he started shitting and was dropped. Today it's raining. A damn muddy track and shit loves mud. That horrendous Tommy is riding him. He got to win, man."

"That B horse looks good to me. I am going for B, putting ten to win. This muddy track is very uncertain."

"That's a favorite. Won't win. I won't go for that shit. I'm going for the big gravy. Hey, doc, you want a side bet? My horse is winning and paying big shit. I am putting twenty to win. Want to share, man?"

When the race started, Vassily's horse was doing well and he was happily saying, "Wasn't I telling you?" What happened to my horse? Maybe he was in his romantic mood, dreaming about his lover. Well, my horse stayed almost last most of the time. The horses were running the last turn before the finish post. Vassily's horse was still out front and Vassily was shouting and waving his hands. The horses were close at the finish line. At the last few seconds, his horse pulled back and finished second. What happened to my horse? I did not even bother to check.

"Shee ... t, man. That sucker Tommy fixed the race. Sucker pulled that horse last minute." He crumpled his tickets and rapped on the floor. He started walking down the steps.

"I am sorry, Vassily. Wait a minute, I am coming with you."

"You, shitty dope, you stay there, man. I am going."

He did not look back. I was also not interested to stay. I followed him to the parking lot. He was almost running. The next I heard his car lurking with screeching noise.

Next time I met Vassily at Yonkers, just a few days later. He greeted me, "How you doing, doc, my buddy?"

Vassily was working a weekend job at some store and a few evenings at the same store. He was trying to save money to fulfill his fantasy of owning a Toronado. He had told me.

After a break-in in my apartment, I felt unsafe in Jackson Heights. I decided to move out of the area and started looking for a new apartment in Queens itself in a better area. I had no knowledge of different areas in Queens. I got advice from my office friends and started searching for a place in Forest Hills.

The job situation in the engineering field started improving. I directly sent my resumes to all the companies on the list Mokhtar had provided. I did not go to any job search agencies. I got interview calls from two companies, accepted a job with Custom Engineers. It was not a designer's job that I had before. It was real engineering job. I had found a nice apartment in Forest Hills. My life changed so fast. I got a good job and I was going to change my apartment. I was happy. Before moving to the new apartment and joining the new job, I visited Egypt. I was happy to meet my mother and my family.

After coming back from Egypt, I moved to my new apartment in Forest Hills, met that girl, and that started a new experience in my life.

CHAPTER THREE

Whe I came back from Egypt on Friday afternoon, after visiting my family, my friend Karim picked me from the JFK airport. It was June of 1973. My third year in America. Karim had rented a garden apartment in New Jersey. I was going to stay with him for the weekend. And on Sunday I was going to move to my apartment in Forest Hills. Before going to Egypt, I had left all my belongings and my car with Karim.

Karim had invited Mokhtar and family and Imran and his wife, Rehana, to spend the weekend. All four of us could meet and reminisce about our old college days and the initial days in the States. Imran and Rehana could not make it on Saturday due to a previous engagement. I learned good news from Karim. His wife, Nafisa, was pregnant. They already had a girl, Shakila, four years old, and a son, Abdul, two years old. Mokhtar and Mona had a one-year-old son, Khalid.

The three of us spent half the night gossiping and recalling old memories. None of us had any sweetheart memories of love affairs from the past, except me. We talked about some college girls. In our college days, it was a big deal even to talk to a girl, forget about any further friendship. We just had the luxury of looking at the girls in our college days if they were not wearing veils that would cover their whole face. Among my friends. we used to call it 'bird watching.' Some of the college girls did not wear veils but always wore a hijab. I mean, I am talking about Egypt in the sixties. I was tired from the journey and jet lag but enjoyed meeting my friends. Their wives didn't participate in our three musketeers' gossip. They used to get bored.

On Sunday morning, all the others slept late. I could not sleep and got up early because my internal clock was still set on Egyptian time. Imran and Rehana came before noon and the four us had a ball, talking over barbecue. Mokhtar and Karim became teetotalers after their wives joined them in the states. Both of them still enjoyed drinks only at restaurants and office parties. None of their wives ever drank any form of alcohol, with the exception of Rehana, who would occasionally drink wine. She was from a rich and modern Egyptian family and was a college graduate.

That Sunday evening, I collected my belongings from Karim's home and drove to Forest hills. Being Sunday, there was plenty of street parking. I parked my car in front of the building. I had to make three trips carrying my TV and belongings to my apartment. On the first trip I took my TV set. I opened the front door to the apartment building with my key. There was a big lobby with big glass windows facing the street. Two passages, one on each side, were running to two wings of the building. There were A to H apartments on one side and I to P on the other side. There was a bamboo design wallpaper on the front wall of the lobby. This wall was easily thirty feet wide. They had a bricked planter-like thing about two feet high next to the front wall. Maybe you could call it a flower bed. The bricks were painted with brick-colored oil paint. There were remains of different plastic plants in that planter. They must have been put there a long time ago. I was sure that at one time it must have looked pretty.

A plump girl was sitting there on that planter wall. She was wearing a pair of jeans and a closed-neck T-shirt. She was sitting resting her right elbow on her thigh and her chin on her fist. She had a blue diamond ring on her left ring finger. She had a ponytail. She was 'Ms. Nowhere.' Well, she was completely lost in her thoughts.

A blue diamond! Yeah, a blue diamond!

The blue diamond story goes like this. In those days, my knowledge about precious stones was simply vast. And with all of my knowledge, I used to recognize any kind of shiny stone as a diamond. Later someone explained to me about the different kinds of stones and their names. That time I really felt embarrassed to call a diamond a 'stone'.

When I made the second trip, she was still there in the same state. I tried in vain to figure out where her eyes were focused. One more thing I noticed, she had a wristwatch with a wide, silver-white band and a big watch, which I did not think was ladylike. And it was on her right hand.

When I approached the door for the third time, she got up to open the door for me. That girl had accumulated a lot of fat on her approximately 5' 5" body. She could be 200 pounds. She had smaller hands compared to her body. The hands were fleshy. Maybe the hands were proportionate when she had a proportionate figure according to her height. Now they looked a little too small. Well, sometimes I feel I act like a critic. I was watching her hand that came forward to open the door. She had light brown hair.

She opened the door and gave me a sweet and innocent smile, showing her pearly white teeth that brightened her whole face. I was not looking at her teeth. My eyes were glued on her eyes. She had beautiful greenish-gray eyes. I saw the same innocent smile in those eyes too. She said "Hi!" and I said "Hello." Quite a few moments passed between the "Hi" and "Hello." I was just trying to figure out the whole figure in front of me. I thought those eyes, no question, they were beautiful, somehow did not belong to that chubby face or that body. The eyes, I thought, were mismatched, just because of her chubbiness.

And that was my first encounter with that girl, 'Ms. Nowhere.'

The next day was my first day at the new job. This was my third job in the United States. Still there was an excitement!

It was a hot summer Monday in the middle of June. I reached the reception desk about five minutes early. The office opened at eight forty-five. There was nobody there. I sat there a bit nervous. I started going through some of the periodicals that were lying on the table. Fifteen minutes to the hour, a middle-aged, nicely dressed, good-looking lady appeared at the receptionist desk. She appeared to be extremely tired from the weekend.

"Good morning! I am Said Ahemed, starting to work here from today." I had gotten up and was standing next to the receptionist.

"Good morning! Are you the one who is joining us today? They had given me your name. I can't find the papers." I was sure she did not understand me clearly.

She was still sleepy. "I am Mary ---------, the receptionist." Mary -------. One of those terrible names you never really want to remember because they are extremely hard to remember and hard to pronounce.

"Please, be seated. Let me see if I can find somebody from personnel."

She walked through the lobby. Within a few minutes, a young man dressed in a three-piece suit walked towards me and shook my hand.

"Good morning! Mr. Said Ahemed, Ahemed I guess is your last name, is that right? I am Robert (something), assistant Personnel Manager."

You will pardon me for not mentioning all those names. It is my weakness to remember the names. This Robert had already murdered my simple name by pronouncing it wrong.

"How do you do, sir? That is right, Ahemed is my last name."

"Please, come with me. I want to get a few forms filled out. John Gordon, our personnel manager, will talk to you after you finish."

Standard forms! I always hated some of those items. They were clumsy. I was sure they also didn't understand why they needed some of that information. I finished the clumsy ones first. Now this particular one was a record of education right from the moment you stepped into grammar school till you passed the college degree. I could never understand why they want to know about your grammar school. I only remember the year I passed my degree in mechanical engineering. That was the lucky year 1967, I meant that had to be a lucky year for me, I got my degree. Then I started counting the years backward, the high school and the grammar school and so on and when I was born. I checked the manipulations with my birth year that was year 1944, a leap year. This must be the holy year. I was born!

The second clumsy section was your 'Experience.' Every time I filled out those forms, I decided to prepare a complete record of my experience and education. So, the next time around I could use it without any agony. It had never happened so far. The next one I really hated to answer. My blood pressure suddenly shot up. That Inquiry was always there: 'Marital status.'

Then I filled in U.S. Immigrant, country of origin, height, weight, and so on. And finally, I wrote my name that was actually the first item - 'Said Ahemed.' I loved my name and I loved myself, because there was nobody in my life to love me besides my mother. At last I put the date and signed my name.

After this, there was fifteen minutes of initiation session by Mr. personnel manager, Mr. John Gordon. The same stuff from office to office. "We have such and such benefits and they are really better than the other companies and blah – blah - blah"

Thank Allah, it was over. He called my boss, Mr. George Bryant, the chief mechanical engineer. Mr. Gordon himself took me to Mr. Bryant's office. "This is your new boy, take good care of him."

On our way to George's office, right in front of his office in corner of the hallway, two tables were arranged at right angles to each other. There was a typewriter on the table facing the partition. A shapely young girl was sitting in the chair facing the partition. We passed her on our way.

George's office was well decorated for a chief mechanical engineer of Custom Engineers, a consulting firm specializing in all kinds of jobs in industrial plants. They had engineered and designed small fossil power plants. I was joining them as a mechanical equipment engineer.

Again, fifteen minutes of another lecture. Something like, "… If you work hard, there is always an appreciation. You will get good raises. We are a nice group of twelve engineers and so on and on."

I was more interested in looking over the street where I was able to see the front of Grand Central Station. Well, this office was located at 1023 East 42nd Street, right in front of Grand Central Station. We were on the sixth floor. I was thinking in the meantime, 'Someday I will be the chief engineer and I will be sitting in his chair.' I was sure they must have some kind of tape-recorded introductory lecture or they must be conducting classes for these big bosses. 'How to bore the newcomer on the first day.' "If you have any questions about the job, feel free to ask me. Best of luck. Hope to have a long association."

"This is your office." George led me to a partitioned cubical down the hallway. "Now I will introduce you to other engineers in our group."

In the cubical next to me was a busy engineer. He was looking at some drawing. He got up from his chair as soon as he saw us. He was not very tall and had already started to gray and go bald. He must have been in his late forties. George introduced me to him.

"Glad to meet you, Mr. Ahemed. I am Eddie Fisher; I am related to the great singer Eddie Fisher no more than the name."

"Well, I am glad to know at least one Eddie Fisher in person." He laughed. He had a funny style of standing.

The next cubical was occupied by one Mr. M. Schmidt! Who was busy talking on the telephone. "That's Mike. He is busy." If you want to learn how to talk into a telephone so that not even your own ears could listen to your voice, then you must listen to our Mike when he talked to his girlfriends. Yeah, he had more than one girl-friend, well, he told me so later. You should watch his face. He used to whisper in the mouthpiece during those singsong-type love calls. I did not notice his telephone habit on the first day. Later on, as I started passing my life with 'Custom Engineers', I learnt it.

There was one engineer named John. He had a European accent. To me he looked like a bunny rabbit, who might get scared for no reason. He might have felt a bit relieved to see one more foreigner in the company.

There were at least three Bobs, two Mikes, John, and Eddie, Bill, and so on in the electrical and mechanical group. And there was one Indian engineer with Allah bless his name. They used to call him 'Sam.' Thank Allah he was 'Sam' for everybody.

Finally, we came to the secretary. Now, she was busy on the typewriter.

"This is our secretary, Ina."

She stopped typing and leaned over the typewriter. A girl in her mid-twenties, she was wearing a light green plain dress with short sleeves. Her hair was just touching her shoulders. She had a round face. She smiled.

"I am Ina, Ina Zabriskie. Welcome aboard and good luck. How do you pronounce your name? Is it Sed Amed?"

"Oh, no!" It was a sheer murder of my name.

"It is Saa-ee-d U-H-MU-D. Thanks for your good wishes."

She shook hands with me. She did not get up from her chair. She had blue eyes.

She repeated my name, "Said Ahemed. Where are you from, Said?"

"Egypt."

"That's interesting."

I went back to my desk. George had brought a bunch of company standards. For a couple of days, I was supposed to study them.

Ina's blue eyes reminded me of Helen. Though Helen had deep blue eyes like the Mediterranean Sea. It was certainly not a happy reminder.

My job was fantastic and the salary was good. The whole day I was walking six inches above the ground.

I came home from the first day of work at my new job. Well, that apartment was my home, sweet, unsweet whatever it was, it was my home. This apartment was fully furnished with wall-to-wall carpeting with lots of sunlight and tons of fresh westerly wind. This happened to be a corner apartment, 7-H, means apartment number H on the seventh floor. I mean there is no need to tell you if you happened to be a New Yorker, somewhere in America it could be apartment number seven on floor H. I was happy with the seventh floor.

My apartment was facing west and I already had enough heat from the sun. When I came home, it was burning hot and I felt an urgent need to buy Venetian blinds that could block some sunlight. I heard they were expensive. I did not know how much they cost. Anyway, I had to go for the shades at least. My bedroom was my joy. It had front and side windows facing the open sky on the west and the south. I could keep them open. And my drawing room, well, you could call it a living room, had a twin window facing the west sky and yes, the setting sun and the moon and the stars and the birds. Right across the street from the apartment building there were two blocks of private houses, maximum two stories high. I used to see Flushing Meadow Park and Grand Central Parkway as my backyard.

The view from my window was simply gorgeous. The whole world in front of me was green with a blue sky. The traffic on the Grand Central Parkway was active. The same world was still blanketed in the morning fog when I had left for the office that morning.

I was lucky to get this apartment. It was certainly worth much more than 'the gift.' And I was also lucky to get that job, of course without any kind of gift. The building super, super-man as I used to call him, promised me and fulfilled his commitments by giving me new furniture in exchange for my hard-earned thirty bucks. That also was an extra gift for him. To get this apartment, I had paid him half a month's rent of $125 as a gift. He had asked for fifteen dollars gift for a new refrigerator, which I declined for two reasons. The first, my refrigerator was in good condition; at least it was not a roach haven. The second reason was more important to me. Could you believe those fifteen dollars in the name of a new refrigerator could win fifteen hundred dollars at the racetrack? Would you deny? By the way, 'H' horse at racetrack was lucky for me, giving me good payoffs.

I was so happy that I felt like worshipping the Allah. I was not very religious. According to my Muslim religion, I am supposed to pray to the Allah five times a day but I hardly used to do so in a year, though I am a firm believer of the Allah that is our God. That day I did my 'Salat,' that is a Muslim prayer.

I still had to unpack all my belongings and though the apartment was clean, I won't be happy unless I cleaned it myself. And I had to do my laundry. I wanted to go grocery shopping. All I had in the refrigerator was a half-gallon of milk, four cans of beer from the six-pack I bought yesterday along with one hundred Lipton tea bags and a pound of Domino sugar. I was strictly a tea drinker.

After coming home, I mean whenever I used to come home directly from the office without going for either a movie or a play or if I didn't go to Yonkers or Roosevelt racetrack, I used to cook my supper. I didn't like to cook and nor had any ambition to be a super chef. Basically, I was tired of eating out. This way I used to know exactly what I was eating; I would eat to my taste—a bit spicy was the type of food I had eaten throughout my life. Besides, it was money saving too. I had no groceries and thus I was not going to cook that day.

I was sitting on my new sofa sipping tea from my favorite mug (Yes, it had a broken handle). The TV was on. The picture on the TV screen was hardly visible because of too much sunlight in the room. I finished my tea and started on a tall glass of beer. Right, I did not have a beer mug at that time.

The time was ticking as the beer was filling my stomach. The sun had set and the west sky was colorful. The whole world was drowning in the evening gloom. From the window I could see active traffic on the Grand Central Parkway. That was the only sign of life. I was able to see the whole west sky from one end to the other. And I had lots of chances of seeing a rainbow, nature's magic, as I always called it. I was fascinated to see a rainbow so often in New York. In Egypt it was an extremely rare sight. Mostly I had seen full rainbows only in the movies or in pictures before I came to the States. And I had never seen a double rainbow before.

Sometimes I wonder, Why the rainbow is full of colors?

Why it is called the bridge of lovers?

It's true. The rainbow is beautiful enough to be called the bridge of lovers. Love is beautiful.

Slowly I drifted into thoughts. I started feeling homesick. Just three days ago I had come back from Egypt after visiting my family for fifteen days.

My eldest brother, who was helping my father with his grocery store, gave me information of Nadia, which I was the least interested. My father was getting old and still working hard as he did throughout his life. I must say that age had consumed his temper. He was keeping good health though he had lost his strength. I was glad my eldest brother was putting his heart in the business. My other two brothers, who had cloth stores in our town, were doing well. All my sisters were happy with their families. They had plenty of kids among all of them. I had four sisters and three brothers. The last I remembered, was my mother. As a matter of fact, I could never get her out of my mind. She told me again to get married. I never liked her suggestions of that kind. Believe me, she was absolutely right. She loved me, her baby son. She was the only person who really understood my feelings. I loved my mother and I could not fulfill her wishes.

Oh, I see you are interested to know that story of 'The Gift,' the one I said earlier. Well, it is simple - a gift to get an apartment, I mean a gift and not an agency fee. A gift to the man who is in a supreme position to award an apartment to you on a rental basis and offer limited favors to you from time to time in return for more gifts. This supreme man is the so-called superintendent of the apartment building. His philosophy is simple. 'You have to pay a month's rent to the agency to get the apartment. You pay me half; the apartment is yours.' And if you are in real need, you could not deny his simple request.

This is how the story goes.

When I went in search of an apartment, these super-men did not recognize me as a foreigner. They thought I got a nice tan. As soon as I opened my mouth and said something, they knew I was not 'One of them.' So, "They ain't any apartment" and thus I would make an 'About-turn' and would go to the next super-man.

When my friend Mokhtar was looking for an apartment, one super asked him to help him to fix the transmission on his car. Mokhtar said he was not an auto mechanic and never worked on a car. The super said, "I am looking for someone who can help me to fix my transmission. There is no empty apartment right now. You help me, I will help you to get an apartment." Mokhtar did not get his message and insisted he could not help him. Finally, he wound up paying a month's rent to an agency to get an apartment. When I started getting replies like "There ain't any apartment," I remembered Mokhtar's story of the super who was looking for help to fix his ever-broken transmission on his car. And I strongly suspected that all these supers wanted some extra money from the new tenants. So, I started wearing my expensive gold watch, a gold chain, and a few gold rings on my fingers when I went in search of an apartment. This way the super knew that I could pay him his 'Gift.' And it worked. I got this wonderful apartment.

I had a strong urge to see Vassily, to meet him. I was going to look around some of those places where I was sure to find him. So that was my task for the evening. I did not have his telephone number. When I went to Egypt on vacation, I discarded his number saying that I just did not want to see him again, did not want to meet him again, I wanted to forget him. His number was not listed. The reason was a bit weird. He got his apartment from his buddy who moved to San Francisco for more fun and more freedom. And this fellow Vassily never bothered to change the telephone number to his name. Well, the next day I met him at Yonkers Racetrack. He was happy to see me. He was just the same. Vassily lived in the Bronx.

On Saturday, I had to do my super-wash laundry with lots of bleach. All my clothes, which had a few washes in Egypt, had caught a yellow tinge from Egyptian water. My shirts and pants that were washed in Egypt already had been sent to a laundry.

Even one load of laundry used to take me one and a half hours. Not that it was a waste of time. On the contrary, it used to be a 'Pass time.' I used to load a washing machine and go back to my apartment and then come back and load a dryer and go back again and so on. When I was in Elmhurst, somebody did a job on me, took out all my clothes from the dryer as soon as I went to my apartment, and threw my wet clothes all over the floor. Since then I used to watch my laundry. For a better 'Pass time,' I used to read *Time*, of which I was a fan since my college days. When I was living in Elmhurst, Queens, my fertile brain took this as the great opportunity to study English literature. So, the body and mind of the boy named Said went to Barnes & Noble and bought *Rebecca, Gone with the Wind, A Farewell to Arms*, a couple of Agatha Christie's, and two volumes of *War and Peace* and yeah, and the Oxford English Dictionary, which was absolutely essential to read the English literature. This Said could not progress beyond a hundred pages of *War and Peace* volume one in the following years. The other books were completely read in due course of time. Sometimes I used to take my most favorite *Alshaer* Ahmed Rami with me; I mean his *Aghanith* book. By the way, *Alshaer* means poet and *Aghanith* means poetry/songs in Arabic. Ahmed Rami was a great Egyptian/Arabic poet who had written beautiful romantic poetry. Umm Kalthoum, number one singer at that time, had sung those songs to make them famous. Depending on my mood, my choice used to fall on either *Time* or any other of those famous books or Ahmed Rami. My friend Husen from Egypt had presented me a new book of Ahmed Rami's poems when I visited Egypt. 'Rami' was the winner that evening. After loading the washing machine, I started reading my book. I had read that book earlier. This time also I had same interest as if I was reading it for the first time. It was pouring rain outside and that was the right kind of atmosphere for reading poetry.

My deep meditation with the book was broken by "Hi there, how are you?" I closed my book and looked at the speaker of those sweet words. It was that girl in the laundry room at about ten. She was standing in front of me.

"I am Lily O'Mara. How are you?" She extended her right hand to shake.

For quite some reason, I had sentimental feelings for the name 'Lily.' I liked it. She actually had said her name as 'Milly O'Mara' and I heard it as 'Lily' and later it created an awkward situation, based on my inability to understand an American accent and a Brooklyn one at that time.

"I like that name. How are you? My name is Said Ahemed."

She loaded a washing machine.

"I live on your floor in apartment seven A. I saw you when you came to see the apartment about a month ago."

Good memory, I thought. What could I say to her? I kept quiet.

"I've lived in this building for the last year and a half. I like it here," she said.

"Yeah, it looks like a nice neighborhood. My apartment faces west and I can see Flushing Meadow Park from my apartment."

"I know, I know. My apartment is exactly the same as yours facing west. It is on the other side of the elevator."

I thought that was enough introduction and she would leave me alone, so that I could go back to my book. I started singing the poetry in my mind as best as I could. I could not spare myself from watching her, such a huge body moving relatively swiftly, and it was a funny sight to watch her. She loaded two washing machines. She had a shopping cart stuffed with clothes. I heard her whistling. Her actions indicated that she was quite young.

After she finished loading the washing machine, she sat on the same bench as I was, right next to me, keeping only two feet distance between us. I did not make any attempt to ignore her. My body shrunk when I saw her so close to me. It just happened that my washing machine stopped. So, I got up to transfer my clothes to a dryer.

When I came back, she was looking at my book. I wanted to sit on the other bench away from her. It would have been intentional rudeness and I didn't mean it. Not that I disliked to talk to her. This girl was not a girl but a married woman. Her diamond ring was telling me that. I was scared, that her husband would catch me talking with her like that. I sat down on the same spot and noticed those big beautiful eyes were sizing me up. She had smooth skin. It was like an apricot.

"Hi, may I ask you, what language is that? I never saw it before."

I had to explain to her about the language and told her that I was an Egyptian. I did not tell her that Arabic was written from right to left, contrary to the English language, and Ahmed Rami was a poet whose poetry I was reading - unnecessary information, I thought.

"Oh, so you are Egyptian." There was no sound of any kind for a while. So, either she was satisfied or was scared that I was an Arab. So, I tried to get absorbed in my book. She was constantly watching me and I was self-conscious and could not concentrate. What a situation! I wished the dryer would stop for any reason, even if it broke down, I would run away with my wet clothes. The time was killing me. She was neither unpleasant looking (for that matter I would put her on the beautiful side), nor she was verbally attacking me. I was feeling uneasy because she was a married woman. She found something to talk about.

"Did your wife and son like the apartment? I saw them when you came to see the apartment. I was going out when all of you came."

Oh, my god, what a conclusion!

This was what happened on Friday evening: Karim and his family came to pick me up at JFK airport when I came back from Egypt. On the way to New Jersey to Karim's house, we stopped here to show them my apartment and drop my suitcase that I had taken to Egypt and to check if the super had fixed the apartment properly. Karim dropped us first and went looking for a parking spot. That was when this big girl saw me, with Karim's wife, Nafisa, and their son, Abdul. Karim's five-year-old daughter, Shakila, did not come with them. She went to play with her classmate in the neighborhood.

"That was my friend's wife and son. My friend dropped us and went to park his car," I explained to her.

"Oh, I am sorry for misunderstanding."

I had no reason to explain my marital status to her and I was sure she would not ask me. She kept quiet for the rest of the time. All this conversation we had was literally face to face. I was watching her face and she was watching mine.

She did not have straight teeth, though they were white and shining like pearls. A lot of fat was accumulated on her cheeks. She had no makeup on her face except lipstick. She had pink on her nails, a mediocre choice, I thought. The same color was on her lips.

My dryer stopped and I picked my clothes and left the laundry room.

"Good day."

"Good day, I got to wait for a while."

Of course! Yeah, I wasn't going to keep her company until she finished. She had a funny American accent and was hard to understand. I had to ask her 'Pardon' a few times. She used to put Rs at the end of words for no reason. I felt like asking her what part of the country she came from.

In the elevator I laughed to myself. I should have wished her "Have horrifying nightmares." Well, she needed some means to lose calories. She looked quite different compared to the first time I saw her on Sunday evening. Today she looked quite happy.

In the afternoon I went to 'Greenwich,' a gift and a card shop at the corner to buy a birthday card for my friend Husen's six-year-old son, Ismail. Promptly I used to send him at least a birthday card and some money as a gift on his birthday. They loved American greeting cards in Egypt for the simple reason that they were beautiful. I was surprised to see that girl, Lily at the cash register. She was in a jolly mood, munching chewing gum.

"Hello, how are you?"

"Hi, surprised to see me here? The regular cash girl is on vacation. So, they called me. Whenever they need extra help, they call me. I pass my time making extra bucks."

"Hey, that is nice."

That evening I went to 'Boodles' on Northern Boulevard in Jackson Heights. I used to visit this bar frequently and stayed loyal to it. The bartender, Randy, was happy to see me.

"Welcome back, Said. The whole place missed you. How was your trip back home? And how is your family?"

"Well, I am glad that you missed me. My trip was wonderful and family is fine. Thanks."

He gave me a drink on the house. I gave him a brass ashtray I had brought for him from Egypt.

Randy, a young guy, was known as a weatherman. He had a degree in meteorology. He could not find a proper job in his field in those days. So, he worked as a bartender and hoped to find a right job someday. Patrons of 'Boodles' would ask him the weather forecast. Many times, his weather forecast would be more accurate than the TV forecast. He had a reputation of forecasting snowstorms correctly and to his credit he had forecast the big snowstorm of January 1972 when no TV forecaster had even mentioned snow flurries.

The next day evening, I went to the other bar, in Forest Hills, with a fancy name, 'Pink Panther Drinks Here.' I started visiting these two bars in Forest Hills when I was in Elmhurst. A couple of bars there, those I had visited, were not good and the patrons were tacky. They would drink a lot and start cursing others loudly. Someone would get into fist fights. 'Pink Panther...' was decorated in pink, including carpets and furniture.

John, the bartender, greeted me as usual and asked me about my vacation. I sat on the bar stool and chatted with him. After a while, I went to my favorite table, which was next to the window.

I saw Frank talking to somebody. This was a regular sight at 'Pink Panther.' Frank always used to walk from one end of the bar to the other end with a drink in his hand. He would sit down and talk to the people whenever he wished. You could always expect his round in approximately half an hour. He sat in front of me. "How are you, honey?"

"I am pretty good, and how are you, Frank?"

"I too am good. I am Frankenstein today. I am not Frank. I am Frankenstein, you understand."

"Oh, yeah, I can see that. But why?"

"Why? .... Why? Don't you see I feel like Frankenstein, that is why?"

I did not want to say anything to that. After a while he said to me, "Don't you fight with me. I am Frankenstein." Then he looked at me carefully and must have recognized me. "Where were you, honey?"

"I went to my old country."

Frank got up and sat next to me, held my chin, and brought his mouth close to mine.

"You live here, honey, how come this is not your country? You said you went to your country?" A repulsive stench of alcohol erupted from his mouth. Frank was not going to understand if I explained him that I had been to visit my family in my old country Egypt. So, I said, "I was on vacation." He was satisfied and went to another table.

Thursday evening when I came back from the office, I saw that girl sitting on the same spot as she was on Sunday evening. She was smoking. As soon as she saw me, she smiled in recognition. 'Must be waiting for her husband,' I thought.

The following Saturday, two weeks after I came back from Egypt, we had our summer picnic in New Jersey. In fact, they were waiting for me to come back. Every year since 1971 we used to go to Jones Beach in summer for a party. This year Karim was able to convince us to have the picnic on the other side of the state line. I had to pick up Imran and his wife, Rehana. I started at about seven fifteen. As soon as I came out of the garage, I saw that girl was walking fast on the other side of the sidewalk. She had a small suitcase with her. I stopped the car.

"Good morning. Want a ride?"

"Nice of you. I am already late." She sounded bit nervous. I opened the door for her.

"Thank you very much. It is a beautiful car."

"You're welcome and thanks."

"I am going to a single's picnic. We are going to Albany. They have a state fair. The train starts at eight from Grand Central station. And I am already late."

I had nothing to say. I did not quite understand that she said 'Single's picnic.' I did not want to tell her that I was also going to a picnic.

"I hope I find a boyfriend."

What? She was looking for a boyfriend?

"I thought you were married."

"Nah, I am a widow."

"I am sorry about that." I looked at her; she certainly did not feel sorry.

"Thanks. It is certainly better than a divorcee. At least I get sympathy from people."

We came to the subway entrance. I wished her good luck in her search for a boyfriend. She thanked me and wished me good weekend. I was wondering about her ring. I thought that was her wedding ring, my un-American knowledge. I felt sorry that such a young girl was a widow and she lived alone. I wished she would find a boyfriend.

All of us enjoyed the picnic in New Jersey. I was sure everybody missed Jones Beach. At least I missed it. We, all four of us used to go to Jones Beach as bachelors in those days when the other two had their wives still in Egypt and Imran was not married at that time. It used to be a different kind of fun, filled with old memories.

The next day, Monday, in the office, around ten o'clock in the morning, I heard a cuddly female voice saying, "Hi, guys, I am back from my vacation," and then a lot of different male voices, "Welcome back, we missed you," "Hi, Janet," "How was your vacation?" "Hey, Jan, you look great, look at that tan." One voice said, "Hey, you look sexy," which was followed by a flattery voice, "Thank you." Then I heard voices coming from one of the cubicles. This Janet had gathered the boys around her and was telling them exciting stories of her vacation. I heard Ina's voice also.

"Hi, Mike, you look very busy."

Mike was busy on the phone as usual with his girl. He put down the receiver and said, "Hi, Jan, how was your vacation?" I never heard Mike speaking so sweetly.

"Oh, short as usual, but wonderful."

"You got a beautiful tan."

Mike and Janet began whispering. I could catch words even though they were not clear. They were mostly talking about her vacation, how she enjoyed it and how she met somebody of interest and his father had a big tobacco farm in Virginia and he himself was a professional photographer. "He is going to mail me the pictures he had taken. I can't wait to see the pictures and talk to him. He will be calling me in a couple of days." There were a lot of whispers and laughter for the next few minutes.

Then she came in my cubicle and said, "Hi, there! I am Janet Snyder. I was on a wonderful vacation for the past two weeks. Aren't you the new engineer?"

I told her she was absolutely right. "My name is Said Ahemed." I shook hands with her and proceeded to ask her about her vacation. She told me she had gone on vacation to the Bahamas with her parents. "You see, I am not married yet." She played golf and tennis, went to the beaches, surfed a lot and so on. "I am like a novice in golf or tennis," she told me.

"Let me go back to work. A pile of papers is waiting for me on my desk." She was the project aide.

"Hi, Eddie. Good morning."

And I heard Eddie saying, "Hi, hon, nice to see you back."

Then silence set in our area. For the past few minutes, the whole atmosphere was charged with a kind of electricity. I felt everyone was trying to listen to what she was saying.

She must have been about five feet three inches tall with brown hair and glasses. She was wearing an attractive dress and nice-smelling cologne and had a sweet voice and walked sprightly.

That evening when I came home, a little late because I happened to be on the subway that got stuck for forty minutes. I saw her sitting in the foyer at her favorite spot. She had a cigarette in her hand. She did not look at me. I saw a cigarette butt on the floor. She was lost. Her world was upside down. I wanted to ask her about her picnic and if she found someone of interest. From her state I realized that her picnic was a "Doom."

The same evening, I met Vassily at Yonkers. Both of us were happy and excited to see each other. He told me that he was working an evening job with a printing press for the last few weeks. No wonder I didn't see him at the racetrack. Vassily was holding a second job. He always had to supplement his income to recover the losses at the racetrack. He never showed remorse for his poor performances with the horses. And he wanted to own an expensive car, particularly a 'Toronado.' He always wore expensive clothes and used expensive colognes. According to him, that was one of the pleasures in his life.

I played a couple of races won a few lost a few. It was not big loss or win, and I did not bet heavily.

We went for a drink. At the race track we never got drinks of our choice. So, we always preferred to drink beer on tap. "Doc, it's on me." And Vassily paid for the beer.

We went back in the stands. He asked about the welfare of my family and my trip in his own style.

"Hey, doc, you know when you were on vacation, that goddamn

Armando won a big race for me. Kenny was the rider. Shit, it paid eighty-seven to win. I had twenty down. Big fucking money, doc."

The next race was finished and both of us were losers. "Goddamn! What a fucking day! C'mon, doc, let's go."

It was more than a month after I moved to Forest Hills. One evening I came home, she was sitting in the lobby, her reserved spot. While I was struggling to open the front door, she got up and opened it for me. She looked happy and said "Hi!" to me.

"Thanks. How are you, Lily?" So far, I had never called her by her first name.

"Did you call me Lily? That's not my name. My name is Milly; that is short for Mildred. Milly O'Mara."

"Oh, I am very sorry. I heard it as Lily when you first told me. I am sorry about it." I felt so embarrassed. *Allah knows when I am going to learn this American accent.*

She walked with me. I said to her, "Milly O'Mara. Like MO."

"That is what they called me in school. O'Mara is an Irish name. My mother is Italian. My parents live in Brooklyn." She told me that she was going to see *The Sound of Music,* her all-time favorite movie. It was playing at the movie theatre on Queens Boulevard.

"I got to go. I have to cook and eat before I go to the movie." And she went to her apartment.

I was going to Yonkers race track that evening.

One night I came home late, usual time after the races. As the elevator door opened, I saw that girl standing in the elevator smoking and totally drunk. She was wearing a workman's overall. Her hair was pretty much scattered. She did not recognize me.

I said "Hi, Milly."

She said, "I forgot to press the button." I did not know how long she was standing like that. When we reached our floor, I said to her good night. She started walking towards her apartment. After a few seconds she said, "Night, mister." I could not sleep for a while. I kept seeing that girl standing in the elevator smoking and drunk.

CHAPTER FOUR

Five nine, 165 pounds, sharp nose, black eyes, and eyebrows. Five-feet-nine-inch height was considered tall among his countrymen. His friends sometimes used to call him 'Rajul Tawil' which means 'Tall Man' in Arabic. The eyebrows were thick. The eyes were calm. Nothing special about the forehead, lips were on the thicker side. Ears were proportionate. That long, not well-groomed hair was hiding those ears. The hair was thick, curly, jet black, typical for Egyptian. Those cheeks were masculine. For the past few years the chin had elongated and had become black. Well, the man had appreciated Russian premier Bulganin's beard so much that he had adopted it for himself. It was a French beard and someone told him it was called a goatee. And yes, he had a Hitler-style mustache. The whole face would have looked handsome on that well-built body, if it had been shaven and properly groomed. This man did not smoke. Not that he never did, in general he did not like to smoke. The expression on his face was calm and there was no smile on that face. Just a little bit of a smile would have made a big difference.

Well, that was me in those days till I joined 'Custom Engineers.' I did not change much after joining them, except there was an addition of a little smile. I was truly happy for joining this company.

The happiness started showing on my face and my body. I put on ten pounds in the next few months.

"Would you mind if I sit here?"

"No, no, not at all, be my guest."

She was a beautiful young girl. I just had a glance at her. To me she looked very much interested in talking to me. I pretended as if I was listening to the music. For a moment I thought I should have been smoking. It would have helped me to ignore her. I was not interested in her.

"Looks like I have seen you before some place?"

There was nobody else at the table. So, it was for me and I had to answer her. It was my meeting with some girl one evening at 'Pink Panther Drinks Here.' She was a total stranger to me and happened to be a patron of this bar.

Some drunken guy had raised his voice and started shouting, "Shit man, you don't understand my old lady. Her head is full of shit. She is all fucked up. Oh Lord, give her some brain in her shitty head."

"He is a jerk. He always gets drunk and accuses his wife." Then she addressed to me, "No, honey, I am not talking about this place. I mean some other place I saw you before, somewhere in the city. We might be working in the same area."

"Maybe!"

She started asking me where I worked and what kind of work I do and things like that. I was basically trying to cut her off by speaking rotten English with a bad accent and asked her pardon for not understanding what she was saying. She did not deter. Finally, I said, "You know, I got a bad headache."

"Too much booze? I know how to treat you. I myself will be your cure."

"No. I must go home and go to bed. That will be the best." And I ran away.

She was looking for a guy to give her company that night in bed. Well, I was quite sure about her intentions. I had met this kind of girl from time to time in bars. She certainly met a wrong guy like me. She should go to a single's bar. Some creep would pick her immediately. She had a beautiful body.

When I used to enter the lobby of our apartment building in the evening, sometimes I would see that girl Milly sitting at her favorite spot in the lobby as if it was reserved for her. Sometimes she would get up and start walking with me to her apartment. We would gossip for a while about the office, movies, weather, cooking, grocery prices, and even politics. Between my and her activities the frequency of these meetings was limited to either once or twice a week. Sometimes she would go to a movie in Manhattan directly from the office and she would tell me about it later. "You must see this movie. It is fabulous." If she herself was in a fabulous mood, she would add, "Mr. Did Say."

If I met her in the morning that meant she was late for the office and she would just run ahead of me, sometimes making big noise with her footsteps. On such particular day she would not say "Good morning, Said." Either she would not say anything or she would just say, "Hi!" Some days even in the morning she would give me a big smile saying she was late and she had to go and then she would walk fast floating in the air spreading a fragrance of her cologne.

One day in the morning, in the elevator she said, "Good morning." As a matter of fact, I myself was late that day, which meant she was super late.

"I forgot to set the alarm last night and overslept," she said. "And must have forgotten to wind my wristwatch also." She wound her watch and asked me the time.

So far in the first two months, I had learned quite a bit about her. Her parents lived in Brooklyn. She had one brother, who lived in Hicksville, Long Island. She used to spend a few weekends at her brother's place. "I would love to visit him more often. I don't want to bother him and mainly his wife," she had told me once. She liked to watch movies; I mean in the movie theatre. "That is the best pastime to spend the evening," she had once said. Dustin Hoffman was her favorite hero and she had seen his movies repeatedly. Watching the same movie again was a common thing for her. "Did you see *Love Story*?" I asked her once. "Oh, yes, I liked it. I don't want to recall it. It is a sad story. It made me cry."

I had told her that Rock Hudson was my favorite and my sweetheart heroines were Marilyn Monroe and Elizabeth Taylor. I also loved to watch movies and so far, my favorite evergreen tune was from the movie *Come September*. I was in my evergreen college years when I heard it the first time. She thought for a moment and said she remembered it and she also liked it.

I had told her that I loved to see plays and I had seen most of them. On that she said, "I love to see plays. I can't afford it. It's too much money. You know, for the price of one play, I can see at least four first-run movies. It is a lot of entertainment. Right?" She looked at me for an answer. I just nodded.

"Did you see that play *Same Time Next Year*?"

"No."

"I am going to make reservations. Would you like to come with me? I will buy your ticket."

" I can't afford it. I won't be able to pay you."

"No, you don't have to pay me. I will treat you." I thought that I lost forty dollars at the race track. What difference did it make? At least that girl would be happy. She refused my offer by saying, "I appreciate your generosity. Thank you for that. But I would not like to accept it." I was just nice to treat her as a friend. But she refused. I felt sad.

She had an associate degree in accounting but she worked as a secretary with some small accounting firm. So far neither of us had asked personal questions. So far so good!

"Hey. Said, I like your hair and your eyes. They are jet black." That girl, I mean Milly, said to me as she looked into my eyes. I felt like raising my eyebrows and scaring her. But I didn't. We were riding the elevator one Saturday morning. "It is Egyptian specialty."

"Can you believe I had soft, golden-blonde hair when I was a kid and now it has turned brown? You know men like blondes." She sounded sad about her hair.

"Well, I don't know if there is any preference." I thought I should make a comment to help her feel better. "I liked your light brown hair. And your eyes are beautiful. Would you like a ride in my car?"

"I am just going down the corner. I prefer walking. Thanks anyway."

Honestly, I liked her straight, light brown hair that looked so soft. And of course, I always liked her eyes.

Once I caught her in good mood, so I asked her, "Kaif el hal?"
"What does that mean?"
"How are you in Arabic?"
"It's interesting. How do I say, 'I feel rotten as hell' in your language?"
"Oh, no, I won't teach you bad words."
"Don't you worry, Mr. Did Say? I promise I won't use them on you."

"Still, I won't tell you."

"Okay, okay, then how should I answer that thing whatever you just said?"

"I asked you 'Kaif el hal?' Means 'how are you?' Then you say, 'Hamdulellah,' which means 'I am fine, thank god.'"

Then she memorized it. "'Kaif el hal?' and you answer 'Hamdulellah'. 'I am fine, thank god.' You know, Said, I still feel rotten when I say it."

"You're kidding! You certainly don't look so. You look very happy today."

"You are right. I am really 'Hamdulellah.' How are you? 'Kaif el hal?'" To that I said, "Of course, 'Hamdulellah.'" She laughed.

Thereafter sometimes I used to ask her 'Kaif el hal?' instead of "How are you?" Sometimes she would ask me in Arabic. Sometimes before I could ask her anything she would say, 'Hamdulellah' and she would laugh. Once she said she felt rotten. So, I said, "You're kidding," and she replied, "I am not." She sounded mad.

Sometimes she would talk about her boyfriend. "You know he is tall and handsome, a terrific guy," or, "He is average looking. He gets irritated if I tease him. He is an OK type."

After a month or so, I would ask her about her boyfriend she had talked about and she would say, "We broke up. It did not work." She would always feel sad for any of her boyfriends breaking up. "I am all alone, independent. I don't have any boyfriend at the moment. Men don't like a girl like me."

Next time she met me in the laundry room she had almost finished her washing and drying when I came in. She stayed for a while, talking with me after she finished.

As soon as I entered, she asked me, "Kaif el hal?"

I replied, "Gamil geddan. Shokran," and explained the meaning of it as "Very good. Thank you." She spoke after me and tried to remember it. After some formal talks, she asked me how I came to the United States, as a student or as an immigrant.

"I landed here as an astronaut from Mars." After a pause I said, "I mean from Egypt."

"What, did you say astronaut?"

"Yes, astronaut."

And she laughed and laughed for a while. I told her that my immigration to the States was as great adventure as landing on the Moon to my people in Egypt. The whole town came to the airport, 40 miles away from my hometown, to give me a send-off. My family had rented a bus for all the people.

"You are so witty, Said! How old are you?"

"Who, me? I am not old. I am young."

"I see that. What is your age? How young are you, boy?"

"Well, let us assume if I die at eighty, I should still have fifty-one more years to live."

"Oh boy, you are real smart, aren't you? Why should this young boy ever die? What makes you so complicated?"

And she started counting my age with the help of her fingers.

"Is this twenty-nine-year-young boy married? Maybe I thought your wife is still in Egypt."

"Well, once upon a time, he was married. Not anymore."

"I am sorry to hear that."

"Well, you should not feel sorry. I don't anymore."

Now I realized her great understanding. "Oh, no, she is alive and healthy. She stays in Egypt. We are divorced."

"Oh, my goodness, I am sorry that I misunderstood you. My husband died. He was killed in a car accident."

"Sorry to hear that."

"That's okay. It is better to be a widow than divorcee. Do you have any children?"

"I had a daughter."

"You mean she lives with your ex-wife?"

"No. God loved her more than anybody else. She was just two years old."

"I am sorry, Said. It must be hard on you."

"It was really a sad thing to happen. She was cute, like a doll."

My entire happy mood was gone. I thought she also felt sad. She was engrossed in her own thoughts for a moment. We passed a few seconds in silence.

"Well, these things do happen in life. That's the way life goes."

"I am sorry, Said." She put her hand on my shoulder.

She looked furious one morning. I said "Good morning, Miss."

"Hi!"

"How are you, Milly Mo?" That was one morning on the way to the office.

And she did not say anything. When we reached the lobby, she waited for me. She did not run though she was late.

"It's good that I met you, otherwise my whole day was spoiled. You know I met my neighbor just now. He is a crazy and obnoxious man." She circled her finger near her temple and gave a long whistle. "That guy is cuckoo! He always gives me dirty looks. His dog is also crazy. Sometimes his dog cries at night and that spoils my sleep. He puts him right near his front door."

"Well, I am sorry for having such a neighbor."

"I can't change the facts." She did not speak for a while, then finally she said, "Isn't it a gorgeous day? They are calling for a nice weekend."

"Oh yeah. Do you have nice plans for the weekend?"

"Nothing for this weekend. Do you?"

"I will be working in the office the whole day Saturday. On Sunday I am going to my friend in New Jersey."

"How lucky! I wish I would have worked on Saturdays too. I have nothing to do."

"Well, you can go shopping."

"No, I can't. I have no money for shopping. And I just don't like to spend time window shopping. I have plans for the whole day sleeping Saturday and Sunday." And she sneered. I did not like the idea that she had nothing else to do and that was why she had to sleep away the whole weekend.

"Don't you like to watch TV?"

"I hate TV. I mean I can't watch it the whole day. Maybe I will go to a movie. I have seen most of them. I will have to see one over again."

We could not speak on the subway until both of us got seats next to each other at Roosevelt Avenue. "You know the summer is going to end soon and I haven't found a boyfriend." She sounded sad. It was the third week of August and the summer was almost over. "Okay, bye." I had to get off at Lexington Avenue station. That was my stop and I had to walk from 53rd Street to 42nd Street. She would get off either at 34th Street and 6th or 8th Avenue station depending on whether she took the 'F' or 'E' train.

"Have a nice day, honey."

I liked her calling me 'honey.'

This was the story of one of those mornings, when I used to meet Milly on my way to the office.

Some mornings would start like this. When I turned in the hallway on my floor, I saw her waiting for the elevator and of course she was late for the office. At first glance something hurt me. Something was not quite right. She heard my footsteps and ignored me. She was not ready to face me. She had worn a gray skirt suit with a black blouse, a gray-colored scarf and a black pocketbook. She was not in a good mood and avoided looking at me.

I said, "Good morning, Milly."

She just said "Morning" in a low voice. She was serious. Her face was either reined by a sort of rage or maybe a sort of sad look or maybe a mixture of both. There was nothing except silence till we reached the lobby.

She almost snapped, "I am late. I got to run."

And she almost ran, making a loud sound on the pavement that kept ringing in my ears till I reached the subway.

Later, whenever I saw her in that dark gray suit, and in a bad mood, I knew she had a bad night before. I felt sorry for that version of Milly.

It was Thursday, our biweekly payday, and thus I had an extra fifteen minutes for lunch. I never cashed my check during that time since I dealt with the local bank close to my home. These extra fifteen minutes I was going to wander around looking for enjoyable, beautiful things of any kind. So, I always kept my senses ready to accept and appreciate beauty.

I went inside Grand Central Station and stood in front of the immense picture; the one Kodak sponsors monthly. I had seen the same picture a couple of times during the last two weeks. That day I had leisure time and I was going to let the beauty fill my eyes and heart. Whenever I used to see that picture at Grand Central Station, I always felt love for nature and Kodak. All the colors from the picture would come alive and touch my heart. If you want to enjoy that picture, you just put yourself in it and you would enjoy it more. You could get lost yourself in it. Those Kodak pictures are simply amazing. They used to display them, a new picture every month according to the season. I was trying to put myself in the picture.

A well-dressed gentleman in a suit and bow tie disrupted my concentration as his voice rose and fell and his hands waved back and forth. He was in one of the corners attracting a small crowd. He started speaking. "All my brothers and sisters …" I started looking at the people around him to see how many of them looked like his brothers and sisters. Well, I was just kidding. I knew this impressive way of addressing the audience. I myself was a victim. When he said those words in his high-pitched voice, Automatically I went close to the man and started listening to him.

"If we don't unite together and don't act together, we are going to destroy this beautiful world. We are going to destroy our own lives. Just read the newspaper with your eyes open. Look at the crime rate in this city and all over the world. We are bent on killing each other for our selfishness. We must control this selfishness. We must cut down the crime. We are all brothers and sisters. We are all one family. We must love each other. The youngsters of today have no direction and family love. They are distraught. They get involved in drugs and crimes. We the parents must love them. We are all the children of the God. The youngsters must trust god, and god only can lead them out of the trouble.

"All my brothers and sisters, we must act right now. The whole world is sitting on a time bomb. The bomb is ticking and we are all going to explode, if we don't act now…" The crowd was expanding. I was absorbed in his philosophy and his oratory. People were listening to him with great interest. He had a good training. He looked like an educated person himself. I saw a badge on his pocket which read 'One Family Under God.' He had a pile of booklets on a stand nearby.

I remembered a few lawsuits against his church from a couple of parents for brainwashing their teenage children. This church had a large and constantly increasing number of young followers. I thought his philosophy was appealing. Frustrated youngsters were surely going to join him to create a larger 'One Family.' I enjoyed the whole thing. I had no need to become a member of his 'One Family.' I said to myself if the whole world went to hell, I would be one of them.

If you are in Time Square area, you can't miss them. They are there, on the scene of New York City, Times Square three-card monte thugs. When NYPD (cops) were not around, they were there to prey on the city visitors. The main guy, the dealer, handles the whole show. He would take three cards from a pack of playing cards, two of them one color say red and one black, and lay face down on a cardboard box used as a table. The dealer shows you all the three cards and then quickly switches the cards. You bait money and recognize the single card that has a different color. If you win, you double your money. If you lose, you lose all your bait. They do not need any speech or mimicry to attract their customers. The dealer's assistant shows the crowd how easy it is to win by winning every game. Actually, the dealer had made a fold mark on the different color card for his assistant to recognize the correct card. This trick lures the people who are mostly visitors to the city. The dealer would make the players win the first few games. This would wake up confidence in players to make quick money and they would play more games to lose. The dealers are expert with their hand tricks. The players have no chance of winning. If at all you win, the dealer would tell you, "You can't take our money; you keep playing." If the cops come, the dealers would run without collecting their box or cards. This used to be the usual scene around the Times Square area. I was tempted to play but I did not. This is still a part of the culture of New York City.

It was kind of slow in the office and I did not have much work to do that afternoon. So, I was thinking about my neighbor, that girl, Milly, and I used to think of her as Lily, like a white fragrant flower of lily, when she was in a terrific mood.

Her face was made of different kinds of roses, white, red, pink, yellowish pink, and peach. Her eyes were simply beautiful and her eyebrows were thin. The color of her eyes was wonderful. You take a drop of a green color and a drop of a true gray color and mix them with four drops of water. That is what I thought her eyes would look like, grayish green. Well, I am not an artist. But I must say, it was a rare color of her eyes. The eyes were large, almond shaped. Anybody seeing her for the first time would look at her a second time to look at her eyes. Her eyes were simply beautiful!

She, I thought was about five feet six Inches tall. The whole mass must be more than two hundred pounds. If she would trim down say about 60 to 70 pounds just by a butcher's knife, she would look gorgeous. I thought so. I mean by not using a butcher's knife and sparing it. Well, if you had seen her you would have certainly agreed with me.

Her nose nothing special. The tip was blunt, as if someone had tapped it with a small hammer, like a goldsmith's hammer. If you drew a straight line joining the tip and the beginning of her nose, the middle of her nose would be about one sixteenth of an inch higher. The mechanical engineer in me was scaling her nose.

I did not understand myself why I was analyzing that face so minutely. I thought maybe I had free time that day.

Both her ears were hidden by shoulder-length hair. I had caught a glimpse of her ears whenever she would wear her hair in a ponytail. Her large-size, thin ears looked elegant.

She had beautiful hair, all straight, touching her shoulders, and curling. They looked silky soft. The color was between beige and chestnut brown. Have you seen a dried leaf of an oak? That was the exact color of her hair, brown! Later that girl herself told me that it was auburn color. It could have been dyed.

Her lips were thin, maroon-colored, bright and shiny. Later in my life I was taught to recognize that as cherry color. And yes, I was addressed as 'Dummy' at that time by one of those smarties. So, her lips were made of cherries.

Her cheeks were on the plump side due to the accumulation of fat. The color was rosy pink may be with the help of cosmetics. I knew her real skin, without any aid, was fresh, milky peachy rose and no freckles, slightly conical chin.

The whole face was like the moon and the whole figure was like a pumpkin! The face would glow when she would flash a smile showing her pearl-like teeth.

Big news that day on the evening news was an incident in Brooklyn Canarsie; a synagogue was set on fire the night before. The same kind of hatred I had experienced during the 1967 Arab-Israel war. A result of religious hatred resulted from the war between friendly people. I lost Moses, my Jewish friend. I always wished he was happy. His family had to leave our town.

"Did you see that movie *Midnight Cowboy*? That was on TV yesterday and of course your favorite Dustin Hoffman was in it."

"Hanh!"

She was not in a mood to talk, red nosed, red eyed, and late for the office.

"Did you see that girl, Milly, the one that lives in apartment 7A? I did not see her for some time." I was asking an old lady from our floor.

"Oh, that one, I don't remember seeing her for a while," she replied, putting stress on 'her.' "She rarely talks to anybody. She is kind of weird. I saw you talking to her sometimes. We (A special 'We') think she uses bad stuff." I did not want to ask her any more. I did not like her tone. I kept quiet. But she did not; she continued, "I think she is on drugs. She is a slut."

I did not know the meaning of the word "Slut." I realized that it must be a bad word. I just did not want to check it right away in a dictionary. She was not on drugs. I was sure about that. I would not swear.

A couple of weeks later I checked the meaning of the word 'Slut.' My heart throbbed. One small corner of my heart sadly admitted, my heart knew about her. I wished it was not true. I wished that that lady had not known about her. She should have never said something like that.

Every time thereafter I saw that lady, I thought she was saying the same thing again and again to me. I hated that old lady for no real reason.

There was a sound of TV so she must be inside. I knocked on the door. I was thinking as soon she opened the door; a delicious smell of her cooking would hypnotize me for a moment. She would give me that innocent smile. Maybe she might be waiting to go out with her newly found boyfriend. She would open the door thinking that her boyfriend was there at the door and she would open the door with a big smile ready to burst into laughter. Now seeing me there, the colors from her face would drain. That would certainly amuse me.

Her door was chained. She saw me and opened it. I peeked through the open door. I could not see much. Whatever I saw, I could say her apartment was in a mess. Her face was blank. "HI, Milly, how are you?" And I thought, let me tell her right away why I was there because that was the wrong Milly in front of me.

"I did not see you for almost two weeks. I thought, maybe you were sick. Are you, all right?"

"Yes, I am here and I am all right."

"That's good. I am glad to see you."

"Thanks."

I said, "Good."

I turned away. Of course, I did not expect her to call me inside for a cup of coffee. Maybe the other Milly might have done so. I mean she would have called me for a cup of coffee. Anyway, I was on my way out.

As soon as I turned my back, my face was upset just like hers. "Why in the hell was she so upset?" I felt sorry for her.

It was half past one o'clock in the morning. I was returning from Yonkers race track. I had the company of Vassily at the track that evening. For some reason I always liked his company. So, I was in a good mood. While I was in the elevator in my apartment building and waiting for the elevator door to close, I heard somebody shouting, "Will you please hold it for me, honey?"

My god, who was calling me honey at that time of the night?

I heard running steps and waited for her to come. There came Milly. I had not recognized her voice and was surprised to see her that late, and even more so to see her appearance.

"I saw you entering the elevator. How are you, Charlie?"

"I am fine. How about yourself?"

"Me? I am too good."

I agreed to that. She was too good and drunk. She was wearing beige corduroy pants that had big front and back pockets and shoulder straps, the type mechanics and farmers wear. She had an open-neck T-shirt with 'Love me, I have heart for love,' written on it and a heart symbol in the place of the word 'Heart.' The neck opening of the T-shirt was so big that I could have a nice and sexy view of her big bosom. I did not care to look at them. Her hair was in a ponytail and her face was glowing with sex appeal. I was surprised rather than shocked to see her dress, her mood, and the whole Milly as such. After a few moments of quiet, I told her I had been to Yonkers race track where they have nightly harness racing. I also told her that sometimes I go to a late movie. I didn't mean to ask her whereabouts. I felt pity for her. The silence was getting to me. We had reached our floor. I opened the door to let her go first. She did not want to go to her apartment. She wanted to talk to me.

"I went out to entertain myself. You know I am single. I am independent. I am free to do anything I like to do. "

"Aren't you scared of going out at night, especially on the subways and walking on the streets at night? It is not safe. The crime rate is so high in the city."

"Hey, Charlie, why don't you ask this to yourself?"

She sounded offended and started staring at my face. The poor thing was so drunk that she could not recognize me and took me for someone by the name of Charlie she knew in our building.

"I am not Charlie. I am Said, Milly, I am Said."

She sneered as she said, "Oh, come on, Said. What is the big deal in the name? Said or Charlie. After all, all men are just the same."

She was still staring into my eyes, disgusted, lost in her thoughts for a few moments in between. Then she realized what she was saying.

"So, you, Mr. Said, why don't you ask this question to yourself?"

I felt this conversation was futile. She was high. And after all, it is a free country. Still, I tried to defend myself.

"I always take my car at night and I am pretty safe in the car."

She was still looking into my eyes with steel hardness. I felt extreme pity for her, such a young girl spoiling her life. Then she remembered something to say.

"Don't you know I don't own a car? And don't you remember that accident in Manhattan? The bus ran over the sidewalk, killing nine people. Hey, mister, you can get killed at any moment. What if somebody kills me? I am not scared of death. I am a bionic woman. Nothing could happen to me."

I lost. There was no point in arguing with her. She would not understand.

I said, "Good night, Milly."

She did not answer and walked away with heavy feet on the floor. I just stayed watching her figure. *Poor thing!*

Someday this Milly will get married. There will be someone in her life who will love her next to him. And she will be happy then. I mean I hope this to happen. And she will have her own babies. I wish she should have such mischievous kids that this Milly in growing them will reduce to half her present size. She will look beautiful then. Maybe, someday?

That early morning, I had that scary nightmare for the first time that woke me wide awake and I could not sleep thereafter. The next day I kept recalling my encounter with Milly and that nightmare.

I did not see her for a few days after that night. When I met her one evening in the lobby, she talked to me as usual. I wondered if she remembered anything from that night and getting mad at me. She was quite drunk that night.

First thing in the morning, Janet Snyder was in our area. First stop she had with Ina, then with Bob and then Mike. With both of them it was a secret talk because her voice was coming in whispers. Both those stops lasted for a long time. Then she came to my cubicle.

"Hi, oh, Jesus, I forgot your name?"

"Said."

"Hi, Said, how are you?"

"Fine, fine. How are you?"

"I am fine too! Thanks."

She was wearing a sort of weird dress, black, shiny, with a black-spotted leotard and black, shiny, full-sleeve tight top. She had become a black cat for Halloween. Ina had a pink dress with a large skirt and a big red bow under her neck. She was a flower that day and was floating in air instead of her usual walk.

She asked me, "How long are you in this country?" I answered her.

"Does your wife like to live here?"

"I am not married."

"Me neither!"

She told me a few things about her. Someday she would like to visit Egypt. She was going to arrange a Halloween party for her friends that evening. She had occasionally organized our office parties. And since I joined this office, she had organized an 'End of Summer' party. She was a good tennis player. At least she was a good gossip, I thought. She was popular and tried to present herself attractive by wearing good dresses.

Vassily asked me one evening at the races, "What is your apartment number, Doc?"

"7H. Why?"

"I am going to put four dollars on goddamn H in the seventh." And the idiot won eighty-six dollars and forty cents on four-dollar bet.

How lucky was Mike! He had three girlfriends and he was going to get so many Christmas gifts from them. Of course, he also had to buy them gifts and that was part of love. Sometimes he would discuss the Christmas gifts for his girls with me. Sometimes he would show me what he got for someone. And every time I used to think how lucky he was.

We had two Bobs in our mechanical engineering department. One had a crush on Ina, well, that was my conclusion based on observed facts. At least he used to have a lot of sweet talk with her. My boss, George, once casually mentioned to me about his sweet talks with Ina and suggested if I wanted to get a girlfriend, I should learn to talk like Bob. And we had this other Bob, always fascinated me. He was extremely slim, tall, and light weight. Sometimes I used to wonder if this Bob tried a parachute jump from a plane, instead of coming down to the ground, he would keep floating in air because of his featherweight. Anyway, that was my imagination; I never had any experience with a parachute jump. This Bob had one girlfriend and was faithful to her. They were planning to marry after a definite period of courtship. Someone must have either convinced him, or he might have read someplace about the enjoyments of long courtship.

I hardly saw that girl, Milly, during the Christmas season, sitting in the lobby in the evening. I saw her more frequently in the morning rushing towards the subway on her way to the office. In general, she avoided talking to me during that period.

I did not find her even to say happy New Year. By the time I met her, it was January 5th, in the morning and in the elevator.

"Happy New Year, Milly."

"Same to you, Said." We shook hands.

She looked exhausted. "Were you on vacation?"

And she plainly replied, "I wish."

"You smell fantastic!"

"What?"

"I meant you smell good today."

"Thanks, sweetie."

CHAPTER FIVE

I woke up late at about ten on that Saturday morning. A big snow was predicted by our bartender Randy. All the TV stations forecasted a clear and cold weekend. No one had indicated any snow. Randy had predicted a big snow was approaching our area. I loved snow. I should say I was crazy for it. I used to drive to Jones Beach whenever it was snowing. I would put chains around the wheels of my car for perfect safety on snowy roads. They used to keep a limited area of the beach open during the winter.

You would be surprised to know how many people used to come there to enjoy the snow just like me. I would sit on benches of the boardwalk and watch the snowflakes coming down like white flowers. There would be nothing but the white stuff all around me. Even the blue ocean would look white due to fog from falling snow and that would remind me of the cotton fields in Egypt. I loved to roll in the snow. I would drink the scenery through my eyes. As soon as I heard of the snow (the TV stations changed their forecast during the night) I thought of going to Jones Beach. Then I realized that I had to go to the supermarket at least to buy milk. When I came down, I saw her in the foyer playing with a couple of babies that were playing in the foyer while their mothers were looking after them. She was quite engrossed and happy with them. She did not notice me and I did not say good morning to her. On my way back, she noticed me and we talked about the big snow.

The snow was so heavy that I could not go to Jones Beach. Instead I walked to Flushing Meadow Park.

At the beginning of March, the harsh winter started taming and the weather was getting warmer day by day. One evening I met Milly. "Hi Milly, looks like you are not well."

"Yeah, got a cold! I was caught in the rain the night before."

"I see. You know you should treat yourself to a large hot toddy, your own recipe, the one you had told me about. You need some rest. You should stay home, relax, sleep, and watch some afternoon TV."

"I can't sleep in the afternoon, and those soap operas are boring. My going to the office would be certainly better than staying home. Thanks for your suggestion."

"Hope you feel better."

I remembered when I had a cold sometime back in October for almost a week, one evening she saw me while coming home from the office in exactly the same kind of situation. When I said, "Hi, Milly how are you?" she said, "I am fine. But you are not. You look sick and look at your eyes." She touched my cheek and said, "You have a fever, my dear." She asked me if I knew how to fix a hot toddy. I said no.

"Let me give you my recipe." And she gave me the instructions to make a toddy.

"Drink a hot toddy. Eat one slice of bread and go to sleep with a warm blanket and don't throw off the blanket if you feel hot. Drink a lot of orange juice. Hey, you might catch pneumonia if you don't take care of yourself. Don't you know that? Be a good boy!"

"Thank you very much, Milly."

"You are welcome and feel better."

And you know, I followed her advice exactly and felt better. The next couple of times whenever she met me after that, the first question she asked was how I was feeling.

It was the last Saturday of April. I woke early in the morning due to nature's blaze on the east side. I had decided not to wake up early, but outside brightness through my bedroom window would not allow me to sleep. I went near the window. The trees had just started budding. And it looked like they were sprayed with light green cotton. Some of the early flowering trees had started blooming. I saw a few colorful birds chirping and dancing through the trees. All of them were calling me, inviting me. I could not resist. I had to go out to Flushing Meadow Park to enjoy the outdoors.

She was in the elevator on my way to the office. What? You call it a slave house? No, I loved my office and I loved my job too. There were a few other riders in the elevator with us. When I came out of the elevator, she gave me a happy smile.

"Good morning, Said, how are you?"

"Hi, good morning, Milly. I am fine, how about you?"

"What a beautiful spring day. Winter is gone with the wind and spring is here."

I was surprised by all this.

"I envy you, Milly MO."

"Why? What did I do wrong to you?"

"You are so happy today, that I envy you."

"Ha, ha, I got it. Anyway, thanks for your compliment."

And we walked to the subway talking all the way. She was not running or rushing even though she was late. She even mentioned, "Matter of fact, I am already late. I should be running. But what the heck. They are not going to fire me. Right?"

"You said it."

We saw a cherry blossom tree in front of a house. It had just started blooming.

"Look at that tree. That's a cherry blossom. That is my favorite. I wanted to see a cherry blossom in Washington. Maybe someday! Every year I and my friend Julie go to the Brooklyn Botanical Garden to see cherry blossom. They have plenty of these trees. It's a beautiful sight. And you see flocks of Japs there as if they have nothing else to love in this country."

"Why Japanese?"

"Don't you know cherry blossom is a Japanese tree?"

"No, I did not. Now I know."

We were talking on quite a few topics like that the weather had suddenly become nice. "Hope this summer is beautiful." That was her. We talked about grocery prices going up.

"Hey, how is your cooking coming along?"

"Well, I am doing fine, I guess, still healthy and alive."

"No kidding. I thought I was talking to your ghost."

"No, mister did say. I am still alive."

I had not seen such a terrific Milly before.

In the subway she pointed to some fat lady sitting there.

"Look at that fat one. She is my twin. Whenever I am late, I see her sitting there at the same spot as if it is reserved for her. One of these days I am going to stand in front of her and I am going to laugh at her. We are of the same size and height." And she started laughing.

My station had come, so I said to her, "Good bye, Milly. I got to go. Have a sparkling day."

"Enjoy your day too, Said," she replied.

My whole day was wonderful. Of course, my day itself had started on a happy note. I met a happy Milly, that morning. I kept remembering her face.

"Hey Said, you got beautiful flowers. Are they real?"

"Well, sure. They look unreal. Smell them. Aren't they beautiful?"

She already smelled them. I was coming back from Karim's home after spending a weekend and I had picked a few rosebuds from his garden. When she saw me with those flowers, she got up from her spot and started walking with me to go to her apartment.

"They are beautiful. I love flowers, especially the roses. Someday I will have my own rose garden. Where did you get them?"

"From my friend's garden. He has a house in New Jersey."

"I remember when I was a kid, we had a few rose bushes in front of our home in New Jersey. My father had a hardware store in Elizabeth. A big shopping center opened nearby and my father lost his business. On top of it, his store was robbed. This caused him to have a nervous breakdown. After all that, we moved to Brooklyn and I lost all my friends. I was ten years old that time."

She sounded upset. The way she said 'I lost all my friends', I felt as if she was saying, 'I lost all my happiness.'

I asked her, "Would you like to have these flowers?"

I knew she would like to have them. She hesitated for a while.

"They are yours. What would I do with them?"

"You can keep them in your room. Please, take them. "

"Are you sure you don't want them?"

"I am positive." I offered the bouquet to her, which she took and smelled them with pleasure.

"They are beautiful. How nice of you. Thank you so much. I will take them to the office tomorrow. Thanks, Said."

Since I had given her the flowers, her mood was lifted.

My next meeting with her was completely different. I stepped out of the elevator and was taken by complete surprise, same as she. I hardly saw her face. She was waiting to go up. I even forgot to say either "Hi" or "Good morning, Milly."

Well, it was 'Good night' for her. It was about four thirty a.m. on a summer Saturday morning. I was on my way to Jones Beach to watch and enjoy the sunrise and then I was going to ride my bike.

In the hazy, foggy early morning hours, a mystery girl is wandering on the streets of New York.

Allah only knows where she is going,

because she does not know.

Looking for her fantasies and happiness,

in mysterious places.

"Oh, I am happy. I enjoy my life," once she had said.

Allah only knows the truth.

And 'She is not happy,' that much I know.

'She was quite good looking. If she trims down by 60 pounds and changes her lifestyle, she would look gorgeous. Some decent person would marry her. She had no reason to go out at night like this. What kind of life was she living?'

I came to Jones Beach. The rising sun had made the whole beach scarlet red, the color of blood, the color of anger. That was the color of war. There must be a war going on in her mind.

I stopped thinking about her. The sun started getting hot and I was getting hot too. There was no point. I was unable to help her. It is a free country. I did not enjoy that trip to Jones Beach that day.

Mike was upset over something as if it was the end of the world. I casually asked how he was. And I thought he was waiting to open his heart to somebody.

"Oh, God, a terrible thing happened to me, Said. Are you in love with anybody?"

"No."

"You are lucky. You would not understand my feelings." I thought one of his girlfriends had died. I mean he was really sad. "My girl Linda walked out on me. She is getting engaged to someone else next Sunday."

"Come on, Mike, you don't have to worry about it. You have plenty of other girlfriends."

"Said, you won't understand; I had liked her the most. I thought she only loved me."

I wanted to tell him, 'Why the heck you care for one Linda? You have plenty of them to fool around. She just did the same thing you would have done to her. What is the big deal?' Instead I said, "That's how life goes." He did not say anything except he sighed.

The whole day I saw him completely lost. He did not call anybody; I mean his other girlfriends. That was the first time I thought, 'Hey Mike, I did not realize you have any kind of heart in you'. It was the first time I ever felt sorry for Mike.

That morning I felt uneasy. Being Monday, the office was slow and I could not concentrate on my work. I phoned both Karim and Mokhtar and talked to them. After yesterday's picnic, there was nothing much left for gossip and whatever we talked failed to elate me. I wandered around the office talking to people and asking them about their weekends. Ina was chirping like a bird, which was a sure sign that she had a terrific weekend with her boyfriend. She was too happy to describe and that made me more upset.

Mike was in a great mood. He had recovered from breaking from his girlfriend. That made me envious. Here I was back from one of the year's thrilling events with all my buddies and instead of being in a happy mood, I was upset. I tried to find out the reason for it and could not get to the core of my feelings. My best bet was to keep myself busy at work.

I had decided to go to the race track for the evening after going home. When I left the office, I felt like going to a play. The one I had not seen so far and which was a 'Must-see' type was *Sticks and Bones*.

There was plenty of time to accommodate one movie until the play was going to start. It was hard to find my favorite Marilyn Monroe on the silver screen in Manhattan in old dollar theaters. Her movie would have cheered me. At least my second favorite, Elizabeth Taylor, was visiting New York screens. The name of the movie was either *X Y and Z* or something like that. I was too concerned myself to know what was happening on the screen. Elizabeth was as lovely as usual. The movie was too complicated and needed my full attention. I did not understand the movie.

The play *Sticks and Bones* was serious and started getting gloomier every minute. It coincided with my mood. I started getting involved with the drama. The play was too serious about a family facing real problems in coping with their son who had returned from the Vietnam War. It was a sad situation. The play was good but overall, I did not like it. I thought I did not want to know someone else's problems.

I did not go to my apartment. Instead I went to a nearby bar. I sat in a corner and had two martinis, got drunk, came home. I did not sleep well that night.

The next day in the office my gray mood had not lifted. Nothing special happened in the office except I was irritated with some people in connection with the job, which was surprising and unusual.

On my way home in the evening I had a strong feeling, to meet a happy version of Milly in the lobby. I could talk to her a little bit and that could help me to cheer up. She was not there. I tried to concentrate on local news on TV and had a couple of beers. I drank like crazy. I felt bored. I walked to Flushing Meadow Park and strolled aimlessly. And then I was at the gates of the race track. I was dressed in my formal attire so that I could go to the clubhouse. I wished to meet Vassily that day. He was no show that day. It was immaterial if I won or lost. I was killing the evening and trying to get some thrill to uplift my mood.

On my way home, I ate two hamburgers and had to take the help of booze to calm down to sleep.

The next day I decided to take a different approach to get to the bottom of my feelings.

As soon as I came home from work, I changed my clothes, washed my face, had a cup of tea, and jumped into the car. Through the traffic I headed to Jones Beach. By the time I came to the beach, a half moon was slowly going down the west sky. Her rays were adding to the dim light coming from the lights on the boardwalk. A few couples were strolling on the beach in that romantic atmosphere. A few mooning couples were busy in their romance lying in the sand. I could spot them in that heavenly moonlight. The waves were playing romantic music.

I went to the same spots and sat on those benches where we were sitting last Sunday. The place had started filling slowly and slowly with darkness. It was getting eerie. I came to the beach, sat on the sand. The sight of the sea hypnotized me. I always loved this beach. The mild breeze, sound from the waves, those I always enjoyed as if I had come there for the first time. I had a feeling that something happened during our picnic that upset me.

And my mind started playing with the pleasant romance with Helen's memory. How I met her at our college soccer tournament and the romantic evenings we spent together on the bank of the Nile. Someone on the other side used to play beautiful tunes on a flute. I started feeling as if those flute tunes were coming from the waves at Jones Beach. My life song started humming the love tunes again. I recalled those days as if I was enjoying them right now with Helen. Those tunes of flutes were singing in my ears coming from the waves at Jones Beach and my Helen was sitting next to me. Well, my fantasy! Helen's memory made me sad. We could not become one.

I tried to think of sweet memories from the past to cheer my mood. My graduation from the engineering college was a big, happy moment in my life; it was a great achievement. My brothers gave a big feast for our family friends and whole town to celebrate my graduation. My whole family was proud of me. Matter of fact, the whole town was proud of me. I was the first engineer from my town, and I remembered my mother had cried in happiness. I can never forget that scene.

All those memories, sweet and sad, went through my mind while sitting at the beach. Now the waves from the ocean were roaring and were making irritating sounds. The moon had gone. The darkness was eating my heart. The stars in the sky were no more my friends. They were mocking at me. There was nobody around me. A light from a fishing boat was slowly disappearing and going away. The time was close to midnight. I felt my loneliness, more so emotional than physical.

I came home in the same irritated mood. Today I was not going to eat hamburgers. I had no appetite. I had a hard time sleeping. I had decided not to booze myself to sleep.

This was how our picnic had started.

On Saturday evening, I called Mokhtar and went to his apartment to help him with the preparation for the picnic and to taste the food his wife had cooked for the picnic. He told me all the food was already prepared and nicely packed.

"I want to taste your preparations."

"My friend you have to hold your horses till tomorrow."

Anyway Mona, Mokhtar's home minister, I mean his wife, served me delicious 'Kebab and spicy chicken she had prepared for the picnic with the supper. They always welcomed me to have supper with them.

After the supper we chitchatted for a while. Mokhtar had stopped drinking. He always had beer for me in the refrigerator. Their year-old son, Khalid, reminded me of Elham.

On Sunday, Mokhtar picked me up around ten in the morning. He had to wait in a long line for half an hour to get gas. He had a full tank of gas in his car the night before. But someone did a job and emptied the tank. Those were the days of the oil embargo. And stealing gas was routine in New York in those days. The lockable gas caps were only for name sake.

The picnic was as usual. Mona, Nafisa and Rehana enjoyed teasing me about the girls as usual. Mona used to be the aggressive one in this matter. This time she went a step further saying I had a secret girlfriend that I won't tell them about. She had said, "At least invite us for the wedding. We will definitely come for the wedding unless you want to marry her in a nudist club, then we won't." And everyone laughed at that. I thought to myself that for an Egyptian girl, she had become American very fast. All my friends and their wives suggested I get married and straighten my life. I would make one girl's life happy. That was like a ritual when all of us would be together. And I always questioned them that I might not make the girl happy, and on that they would laugh at me. The wives would suggest me their marriageable relatives and friends from Egypt. I had always told them that I was enjoying my single's life and they were envying me. This time it was not different.

Karim and Mokhtar advised me from time to time to quit racing and my night life of visiting bars, which would not put me anywhere in life. I was not the man for that kind of life, according to them. They always suggested I get married and be happy. I used to tell them, "Who wants to get married? Am I not happy as a single? I had enough of pain from my first marriage and I would not like to try again." They did not know the fun of being single. I never listened to them. Now for the first time I thought that they were right. My buddies knew me well; especially Karim knew my every heart bit.

For the next couple of days, I was still upset, not as much as I was during the first three days. And all of a sudden it struck to me and that thought made me uneasy. It could not be true. It could not be the reason of my getting upset. I brushed it off. Wasn't I happy single?

But I had to accept it. It could be the reason for my agony. Could you believe my loneliness was eating my heart? I always thought that I was enjoying my loneliness. Now I realized I was not going to enjoy it anymore. I felt a need for companionship.

When I reached the elevator, I saw Milly was waiting for it. It was right there and she was continuously pressing the button mumbling something.

She had a half-burnt cigarette held between her lips. She was just holding it as if it was stuck there and about to fall. I opened the elevator door and she almost jumped in it. The cigarette fell from her lips and also fell a crumpled pack of cigarettes from her hand. She did not notice any of these things. I picked the pack of cigarettes. It was so badly crumpled that none of the cigarettes in it was worth smoking. I was not going to give it to her. She was not in a condition to understand anything. She was standing in a corner pressing against the walls. I stood in the other corner. She noticed my existence in the elevator and clutched her wallet tightly, as if I was going to snatch it from her.

She did not recognize me. She was completely drunk. She was wearing light-colored sunglasses and a large, open-neck blouse with

'I am lovelorn. Love me.' written on it. The top button of her blouse was open. She was wearing hot pants and those too were not properly put on. It was noticeably twisted. Her fat-laden flesh was bulging out from different parts of her limited garment. Her face was happy and looked as if she was engrossed in her deep thoughts. For sure her whole world was upside down. Was she high on drugs? I had no way of knowing. She looked so pathetic.

I wondered how she came home without stumbling. I thought of giving her a hand up to her apartment. So, I held her arm and said, "I will walk you to the door."

"Don't you dare touch me! I don't need you," she snapped and almost jumped away from me.

I just stood watching her. She was hardly walking. When she came to the front of her neighbor's door, she stopped and stamped her left foot twice. Then she stood in front of her door and did the same. Slowly she raised her right fist and punched the wall a few times. Then she took the key from her wallet and started struggling to open the door. It took her a long time to open the door. I was watching her. The whole thing was pitiful. My heart ached. *Why is she like that?*

Why did I meet her like that that night? I could have been a minute late and I would have missed her. I would have stopped for one traffic light and I was sure I would have missed her. I had seen her coming home late, but not like this. I knew the nice part of her. I knew a happier version of her. She was such a nice girl. I always loved to meet her happy personality and was scared to face the other part of her. I wished someday only happy Milly would exist. At present she was living a horrible double life and that was the unfortunate truth. Why was she like that? Why did she live a sort of double life like Dr. Jekyll and Mr. Hyde? What was wrong with her?

One good thing was that I did not give her back the pack of cigarettes. Imagine if she would start smoking in bed in that condition. I was sure she would set her apartment on fire. She might have another pack of cigarettes in her apartment and she might start smoking and then...? Only Allah could save her. I felt like asking her why she did things like that. But I could not do that. It was a free country and none of my... A girl like that was an easy victim of any kind of crime. Someone could stab her to death. I didn't remember what time I fell asleep. It was quite late, and even then, it was not a good sleep. I was half asleep for quite some time. And finally, whenever I slept, I had that dream for the first time.

The next day I could not remove Milly from my mind. I was seeing her jumping in the elevator, standing in the corner, stamping the floor and punching the wall. And those were all the images from last night's realities.

When I came back from the office, she was sitting in the lobby. She had a cigarette in her hand. When I passed, she was not smoking. She was doing nothing. She was miss 'Nowhere.' When I opened the lobby door, she looked at me, so I said, "Hi, Milly." She really had not seen me. Her world was still upside down. At least she was good. For sure she had gone to the office that day. The people from her office must be noticing her different moods. I wondered what they might be thinking of her. A nice, loving man in her life could make her life straight. Who would marry a girl like this? Will she ever be happy?

The featherweight Bob was reading during lunchtime as usual. So, I asked him, "Would you like to have a walk outside with me? It's nice and warm outside. Let us get some fresh air." And he started giving me a lecture on how this air in New York City was polluted with auto exhaust and how it was poisonous and harmful to human beings. He gave me some statistical figures from some survey. I did not want to waste my time with him. So, I told him, "All right, you are right, Bob. Let me have a boost of outside air. At least it is beautiful outside."

Could you believe, one day I found him reading Dr. Spock's *Baby and Child Care*. So, I said to him, "Congratulations, Bob. Looks like you are getting ready for marriage and to start a family right after marriage!"

"Not really, some day."

"I thought it is soon. Because you are studying Dr. Spock's *Baby and Child Care*."

"I thought after getting married, I won't have time to study this. This knowledge is necessary for raising babies. What do you think?"

"Bob, you are a great planner."

And to that he even said, "You think so? Thanks a lot."

I felt like crying for poor Egyptians who were never and would never be qualified for raising babies according to this "Babo."

I was sure this Bob, after getting married, was going to read *The Kama Sutra* in bed and going to execute it step by step.

All the things around me started looking old and not lively. I felt like I was missing something in my life. And I felt like seeing my mother. I wanted her to tell me the same thing again that she had told me every time I visited Egypt. She used to cheer my ego.

One day I met Frank at 'Pink Panther Drinks Here.' He had a little more than usual. He started telling me, "I got to tell you something. I am going to fight. You know. I don't have a heart to fight. Don't look at me. I am going to fight. I know I can't fight. It is not going to work. I can't win. I got bifocals. Don't you believe me? You want to see? I am old. I am fifty. I can't fight. Don't laugh. I know I can't win. I am not going to hang myself. Don't look at me. I am not lying. My daughter is thirty and I am fifty. My daughter says, 'I love you, Papa.' My son is twenty-five. He walks like Jesus. You know Jesus? I know Frankenstein. You know Frankenstein? I am going to fight my wife. She is a bitch. I don't have a heart. You know, I don't have a heart. Don't you laugh? Don't shake your head. I am not going to fight with you. Do you know I am fifty years older than you? I got bifocals. Don't look at me. I am going to fight with my wife, my wife. She is a bitch." That was a continuous monologue.

There was another guy with a beard and hair like Jesus at 'Pink Panther...' He always wore a T-shirt saying 'Jesus is Coming.' Or 'I am Jesus' and the second line said, 'I am the Superstar.' He walked continuously all over the bar with a drink in his hand.

I used to get a laugh from those scenes at the bar. All those people were my friends because I was one of them. Though I only had one or at the most two drinks and never got drunk. And now I felt that I did not belong there. Now I started to realize that I was taking shelter from these things to hide my loneliness and I was getting pleasure from that kind of life.

The days seemed to melt into one another. I turned the pages of my calendar without notice. Nothing seemed to change. That was my life in those days. A doldrums existence!

I kept myself busy every evening doing something or other. Sometimes the TV was enough to keep me happy. Going to the racetrack was a big excitement and a lot of fun. Now it was no more a pleasure just a pastime. All the charm and thrill had vanished. Even winning big money stopped thrilling me.

I used to see some young drunk girl carried by her friends, literally dragging her. This used to be a regular scene at the track. It never bothered me. Now I started feeling irritated by these kinds of scenes. I did not want to see these things and the sad faces of those losers. And there was not going to be any end to these things unless I stopped going there instead of being a part of them. Recently I started feeling aloof at the track. I started feeling as if I were standing in an empty circus tent. The circus was over for me.

I started playing hide-and-seek with Vassily. So far, I liked to meet him. Whatever was his lifestyle, it did not bother me. He truly respected me, respected my education and respected my judgement. And I think that was what I always liked about him. Now our friendship started making me feel sick because of his lifestyle.

One of the best things I used to enjoy was going to the Broadway plays. The last couple of times, I did not enjoy it. I felt lost and lonely. My last visit to Jones Beach also failed to cheer me. It only brought me the memories of Helen, and that tortured me.

While coming home late at night, I started getting gut feelings that I might meet Milly, in a drunken state in the elevator. I did not want to see her like that again.

I started visiting Mokhtar and Imran more frequently. Mokhtar was certainly smart enough to notice a change in my attitude and he talked to me about it. At least I was glad that someone cared for me.

The fast life of New York was getting on my nerves. I used to enjoy my loneliness, but not anymore. It looked like I had come to the end of my lonely life. I started facing the realities of my own feelings. My life song was playing blue tunes. I had to respect my feelings and fulfill them. That would be the only way to become happy in life.

Sometimes I wonder, why I am not a butterfly,
free like wind. Why I am not a bird,
free to sing as I like?
Why am I like me, having no future for me?
Sometimes I wonder why the rainbow is so beautiful.
Why it is so full of life and love?
Why there is no love in my life?

There was no love, I was lonely and needed a companion to share my life with me and to bring some happiness and love. Unless I got out of this city, I felt, I was not going to find any of those things and peace of mind. I decided to move to a small city away from New York where I would start my life fresh. I would try to find someone to marry me and that would make me and my family happy. It was the winter of my life. Soon there would be the spring. There would be flowers again in my life. I must bring that spring.

The starting point on the road to my new life started with preparing a new resume. This time I did not waste time, and within a week I personally handed my resume to a few job agencies that had a nationwide operation. A couple of weeks later, two agencies called me for job openings in Houston and Los Angeles. I did not want to go to either of these places and had decided to stick to the northern states because I loved the snow and preferred the winters to hot summers in the South. About a month later, a lady from one of the agencies called me for suitable jobs in Boston and in Cleveland.

"I am still scared of that strangler in Boston. So, I guess I will try for the Cleveland job." The lady at the other end got confused for a few seconds. Then she laughed. Of course, I thought the job in Cleveland was better and more challenging.

It took two more weeks to get an appointment letter in my hand from Ross Bros, Incorporated. In the interim I had gone to Cleveland for an interview and they had offered me the job.

Quitting my job and winding up everything in New York was just a matter of time and formalities. I had no furniture of my own and I was going to sell my car. There was another most important and beloved thing that was certainly going to happen in between this changeover. I was going to Egypt to visit my family and friends.

As soon as I received the appointment letter I went to Milly's apartment. She opened the door and stood there; she did not ask me to come inside. I told her that I was going to Cleveland for good and before going there I was visiting my family in Egypt.

"I got bored and lost in a big city. I want to have a new life in a small city."

"I am sorry to see you go. You had mentioned moving out of New York. I did not expect so soon. We have become good friends. I will miss you." She felt sad.

"I will miss you too. You know something. Milly; I would like to see you happily married."

"Ha ha, who knows? Someday maybe... Thanks, Said. And you too."

"Well, the world is round; maybe we will walk into each other someday somewhere."

"Nice to know someone like you."

"I must say the same. Take care of yourself. Good luck to you and all the best."

"So long! Have a fun and nice vacation and wonderful trip to Egypt."

She shook my hands. I kissed her hand and she hugged me for a long time. "I will truly miss you, Said." Her voice was heavy with a touch of sadness and her eyes were wet. I shook and kissed her hand again. I felt extremely sorry for her. "Good luck and all the best, Said."

"You too! Bye now." I walked into the passage and did not hear the door closing. She kept watching me. I turned back and waved my hand. I got emotional.

Somewhere deep in my heart, I felt sorry for that girl. Such a nice girl ruining herself. Maybe loneliness was also her problem. And one thing, she never asked me to come inside her apartment, as if there was some ghastly thing in there. That mystery was going to remain as a ghost of past in my mind as if never to be solved.

CHAPTER SIX

B y the time I came back from Egypt. it was almost the beginning of October. From JFK, I took a flight to Cleveland. I did not stop in New York. I had joined this company 'Ross & Bros' in Cleveland. I had to start a new life in America all over again. I had groomed my hair short and shaved my face clean before I went to Egypt. My new look made me look younger and handsome. I was quite a different person that night at the Howard Johnson in Cleveland. I really felt homesick as always happened to me after coming back from Egypt. It was hard to remove my mother from my mind. She was getting old.

My first day on my new job, for sure I did not go wrong; it was the same story as the last jobs. I had to fill out multiple forms and many signatures for Human Resources. There was similar introductory speech from the HR manger and my boss.

This time mechanical engineering department's secretary was probably in her fifties. She kept looking at my face for a long time. I told her my name twice. The second time I had to say it really slow and she rehearsed it. For a moment I thought she was going to ask me 'What kind of name is that?' or 'What country do you come from?' But she did not ask. Her name was Elizabeth and everyone called her Betsy for short.

When I got my first monthly paycheck on the fourth Thursday, I decided to open a savings and checking account with the local bank and transfer my New York account. The paycheck was drawn on 'Farmer's Bank of Cleveland,' and that was my natural choice for banking. I went to the bank on Friday to avoid long payday lines. This bank, or rather this particular branch, was quite different from any bank in New York. The whole building was the bank only and it had its own parking lot. The total office area was spacious and old-fashioned. They had four tellers, one male officer 'Assistant Manager' and his name underneath on a wooden sign placed on his table, and an attractive and smart-looking lady 'Assistant Manager' and many customers, nothing like the long lines in New York during lunchtime.

Both the officers were busy so I had to wait. I was looking around. There was a grandfather clock in the bank. The whole floor was carpeted and was clean. My concentration was on the lady assistant manager. Her name was 'Ms. Lynda Smith'. I hoped I'd get my turn with her. And luckily, it happened.

She was tall. Her hands were slender with long, artistic fingers. She was smoking an extra-long cigarette, which enhanced her hands showing long, lean, beautiful fingers. Her chestnut brown hair exactly matched her eyes. Whatever hairstyle she had; it was suitable for her face. She wore large glasses with 'L' imprinted in gold in one corner. She was wearing a beige-colored pleated skirt with a plain, off-white, full-sleeve blouse with a simple collar with a brown ribbon neck bow and a beige jacket. I wished she had greenish eyes and light-colored hair like Milly had. She had fine grace and walked with perfect use of her height. She was almost gliding when she walked. I should say she walked with the grace of a swan and it was not an exaggeration. From all her actions, from her style of walking and talking, anybody would notice that she was a different breed.

She had a sweet, firm voice. After listening to my situation, she said, "I am glad that you opened your account at our bank. We have a special low-rate auto loan for this month. Do you own that beautiful car I saw you parking?" She pointed to my car in the parking lot. "We can transfer your loan from the other bank. I am sure it will be cheaper in long run." I wanted to tell her, 'No, my ghost owns that car.'

The smile on her face was just a normal commercial type. Those eyes! As if they were spreading wine. They were sexy. A line of mischievous smile was in her eyes. I must say she was beautiful and smart. Her whole face was charming and was made quite attractive with all kinds of cosmetics.

My new car was a G 11 S6 Porsche coupe, 1972 model, and I had bought it as soon as I came to Cleveland. It was secondhand, I mean a used car, well maintained. It cost me more than 9 grans. I had saved all that money since I came to the States. With my home-cooked eating, drinking, and gambling habits, the saving margin was good. I must say I was lucky with horses. In general, I was always on the plus side. And my brother in Egypt gave me five thousand dollars cash as a gift from our father's business with his consent.

You know something, when you are all beaten up in life, your ego hurts and you get a kind of vicious satisfaction when you do the things the majority of people simply cannot do. I thought I was not like that. Now I realized it was not true when I bought a fully loaded Monte Carlo with cash in 1973. I enjoyed the same kind of satisfaction then and I enjoyed the same feeling when I bought my Porsche. I loved it. The lady manager was impressed when I told her that I bought the car with cash. When she learnt that I came from Egypt, she told me how she was fascinated by Egypt and wanted to visit Egypt someday. I liked her because she was charming, attractive, tall and held a managerial position at the bank. She also talked nicely with me and was fascinated by Egypt. She liked my car and I liked her. In the following week I received an invitation from the Farmer's Bank to attend a Christmas party.

When I went to the bank to deposit my next pay check, Ms. Lynda Smith came to me and did me a favor by depositing my check directly instead of me standing in line. And then she simply started talking to me.

After asking me how I was and how I liked this new city. She asked, "Did you receive the invitation to our Christmas party?"

"Yes, I did."

"It is only for our distinguished customers and you are my special customer."

"Thank you."

"Do come, Mr. Ahemed. It will be a nice party and a lot of fun." And she gave me directions to the place. "I am sure you will enjoy it."

I felt a little embarrassed because the customer she had been helping was waiting for her. I was impressed for myself that someone like Lynda had honored me as a special customer by inviting me to the Christmas party.

There was one Mr. Rajani Patel working as a structural engineer on our project. He was introduced to me along with the whole project group during my first weekly project progress meeting. I did not know what country he came from. Surely, he was an astronaut, I mean an immigrant like me. He had a thick accent. Later I learned he was from India.

During the week we met each other a few times for the job chores. He was short and dark with straight black hair. He had black eyes with thick eyebrows. For some reason, I did not like him in the beginning.

The next week both of us had a long meeting about the job. And after some time, I got annoyed by his constantly asking me "Did you understand?" after every few sentences.

"Do you get it, Mr. Patel, that I am not a dumb person not to understand what you say? Would you please stop asking me every time, 'Did you understand?' I am not stupid."

"'Shanti, Shanti,' I am sorry, I am very sorry. I did not mean it. Do you understand?"

"And now you are cursing me in your language?"

He literally fumbled. "Oh no, oh no. I mean, I am very very sorry, Said. I was saying 'Shanti' means peace in my language. I was not saying anything bad. Do you understand?"

"See, you are still asking again and again if I understood. Do you think you are extra smart or what?"

"Said, please, calm down and try to understand me."

He paused for a few moments to think straight. "It is just a habit of saying ... I really don't mean anything like you said. Do you understand what I mean? Oh, I am sorry, I said it again. It is just a bad habit."

I had calmed down and accepted his explanation.

The next week when we met again, he was really scared of me. He apologized again and said that he seriously thought over his problem and his habit was from a lack of fluency in English. I accepted his reasoning, which was quite logical. Both I and Rajani were immigrants and were facing similar problems. Later we became good friends. He even invited me for dinner. I was sweating while eating spicy, tasty Indian dishes. One of the dishes was an Indian version of Baba Ganoush. Rajani and his wife, Sonali, both were vegetarian.

I was undecided whether to go to the bank's Christmas party. There was nothing else to do anyway and Lynda had insisted that I must come. I had no reason to refuse except, I did not know anybody there except Lynda. And she would be busy with her own people. Finally, I did go and never regretted.

The Farmer's Bank of Cleveland's Christmas party was on Friday, December 13 at The Hilton. Lynda greeted me at the entrance. She looked gorgeous in her party dress. She was sweet with an extra sweet smile.

"I like your dress and your new hairstyle."

"Thank you, honey. You look sharp too." I was wearing my favorite three-piece, navy blue, pinstripe suit.

What could I say to that? I just said, "Thank you."

She introduced me as her friend to her colleagues and a few others from her head office. In general, she was friendly with me.

And for the first time in my life, I found out that my Egyptian nationality had potential to be a good topic for party conversation. Many of the people who talked to me were fascinated because I was Egyptian.

"You don't look like you are from the Middle East. Are you an Arab?" someone had asked me.

They asked me so many questions about my religion, traditions, the pyramids, and other things about Egyptian life. Even one elderly lady asked me about superstitions and Egyptian beliefs. No one showed much interest about Egypt when I was in New York.

"Do you believe that thirteen is an unlucky number?"

"Did you ride a camel?" someone inquired.

I told her, "Oh, yes, many times. My family had a camel and two horses."

"Is it enjoyable to ride a camel?"

"Not quite. It is not like riding a horse. It is bumpy. It feels great when the camel is running."

"What an ugly animal," she commented.

I wanted to tell her that, 'For sure the camel is an ugly animal. But it is a civilized animal. To my belief, no one had seen a camel making love in public.' I did not say anything. I told her that camels loved music, especially the flute.

Lynda was with me during most of the conversation. When the dancing started, Lynda asked me for a dance.

"Who, me? I don't know American dances. I only know Egyptian dances."

"Come on. It is simple to dance. I will teach you. I am not an expert. I need to take ballroom dancing lessons." And she taught me the basic steps and danced with me. We enjoyed dancing. "You dance quite well," she said to me.

She asked me if I could drive her back to her apartment. She had not brought her car. I had no reason to say no.

She examined my car with great interest before she got in. On our way, she praised my car and then she said, "I wish I had this kind of machine." Basically, she was impressed by my car. Then she asked me if I had any plans for New Year's Eve and if not, she invited me to join their party. She used to celebrate that day with her friends. Again, I found no reason to refuse her.

While driving, Lynda sat close to me, putting her arm on my shoulder. When I stopped at her apartment, she kissed me slowly in the beginning, then forcefully. She had her arms around my head as her fingers played with my hair. That kiss was wonderful and full of desire, passion and fire. Her response excited me. I did not want to part with her lips. We held the kiss for a long time. We kissed again. We could have kissed all night.

She asked me for a cup of coffee.

"Thanks for asking. My stomach is all messed up from booze

and food and all that dancing. It can't take anything more. I just need to lie down. I will take a rain check on that."

"All right then. Thanks for driving me home. Good night." She sounded a little disappointed.

Just before Christmas, I received a handwritten thank-you card from Milly. Her handwriting was neither that great nor bad either. It was a slant script. She must have laughed after she finished it. I could picture her face. I read the card again and this time I thought she was standing in front of me saying the whole thing and oh boy, she laughed mischievously. I stored the card in my dresser drawer.

I had sent her about a four-inch-diameter brass head of boy King Tutankhamen. The card said, "I appreciate your thoughtfulness and remembering me at the time of Christmas. I like the wonderful gift you sent me. Thank you very much for sending me somebody's head. And thank God it was not real."

"Enjoy the holiday season with your head (mind) in the right place and have a very happy New Year! Ho, ho, ho!"

That was it. I was not going to reply her. I did not expect ever to meet her again, though I had sympathy and good wishes for her. I had said good bye when I left New York. I would go back to New York to meet my friends. I won't visit her.

The New Year's party was arranged at Lynda's friend's place. He was married and he had his own house with a basement. Two more couples were married and the rest of them were singles. The total population expected if everybody showed would go to sixteen, Lynda had told me. By the time we got there at nine in the evening, half of the crowd was already there, drinking, listening to the loud music and "bullshitting" (that was exactly what Lynda had said). To my shock, this was how Lynda introduced me to her friends, "Oh, hi, guys and birds, this is my newly found boyfriend, Said Ahmed. Are you surprised? He is an engineer and he comes from the great country of Pyramids. He owns a Porsche. He is absolutely fantastic." I could not understand what she meant by my being absolutely fantastic?

The basement was decorated with lots of balloons and "Happy New Year" banners. There was one banner that had a bleeding heart and arrow saying, 'Good luck next year for fishing singles' and then a big happy moon face.

There were lots of balloons on the floor. Lynda asked, "What are they doing there?" "You step on them," someone said. We did.

The others gathered there were Big Al, Joe R, P.J., Bob H, Dennis, Carol, Mindy, Pam, and so on, and then joined later by those with names like Joe T, Bob M, I mean a kind of parade of names. I had difficulty in remembering their proper names after a couple of drinks. One name sounded quite familiar to me and that was Dennis. I knew Dennis for a long time from the Menace family. I told him, "I knew your name since I was in Egypt." He was surprised. "Dennis the Menace, the world-famous cartoon boy," I explained to him. He laughed loudly, the effect of the drinks. "He is a real menace," Lynda said. After a while, Lynda told me that this boy Dennis was her ex-boyfriend and they broke up long ago. They are just friends now. They were all talking in spite of the loud music. One by one they started telling jokes, mostly ethnic and X-rated jokes.

"A guy used to go see a movie every day. The doorkeeper at the theater asked him why he was coming every day. The guy replied, "There is scene where a lady comes out of a river and a goods train passes in front of her. When the train passed, the lady has changed her dress. One day the train would be late and I would see the lady changing her dress."

"Hey, guys, do you know the XXXXX people in America go to

see a movie in large groups. The group must be at least more than eighteen." And he stopped and waited for a few seconds then he said, "That is my joke." Everybody was so intent that for a second there was no reaction and then they started booing him.

"Wait a minute, do you know the reason."

Someone said, "You coonie, take a dip."

"The reason is that in case the movie turned out to be 'Under eighteen not allowed.'"

Lynda told me, "He himself is from that country. And his name is 'Richard;' if somebody calls him 'Dick,' he gets mad."

"In America golf is played like you put a ball in a hole. In my country, we play golf a different way too. We put the stick in the hole and the balls stay out." He was born American, though, according to Lynda's commentary.

"It is customary among American Indians that the chief of the tribe names every newborn. Once a young boy got curious and asked the chief how he finds the names. The chief answered, 'It depends on my mood and the circumstances. If it is showering when the baby is born, I give a name 'Rain;' if the sun is setting, I call a name 'Sunset', if I am in a romantic mood, I give a name as 'Love,' 'A dancing cat,' 'Flying angel,' and so on. Why are you so interested in the names, Fucking dog?"

Everyone was insisting that I tell some Arabic jokes. Lynda said, "Come on, Said, be a sport."

"OK. This is it. This happened in the big city. In a big grocery store, a big old goat entered and got his way into a storage room. The goat was enjoying feasting on the grains. The customers tried to get the goat out. But no one could stand his odor. Finally, a XXXXX customer went in the room and the goat came out."

"Shame, shame," somebody shouted.

"That is enemy action," someone yelled. Immediately after that someone told another Arab joke.

"One Arab from Ohio went to North Dakota to get a driver's

license. The inspector who was conducting the test asked the Arab, 'Suppose you are driving a twenty-two-wheeler truck down a mountain. The road is winding. And you are going at sixty miles an hour and suddenly you notice the brakes have failed. What will you do next?' The Arab replied, 'I will wake up my co-driver. He would never see such an accident in his life again.'"

I said, "I already got my Ohio driver's license."

"One American went to the Philippines for a job assignment. One evening, he goes to a call girl and had sex with her. All the time the girl was shouting 'Maling bhutas,' 'Maling bhutas.' The next day this guy tells his colleague about his adventure and says, 'Oh, this girl was enjoying it so much. She was constantly screaming 'Maling bhutas, maling bhutas.' The Filipino colleague says, "'Maling bhutas' means 'wrong hole.'"

Lynda's comment was, "His girlfriend's mother is Filipino."

We danced, drank, and a few people smoked pot. I did not smoke, not even a cigarette. Lynda did smoke pot.

When I woke up the next morning, I found myself in one corner in a blanket with Lynda next to me. She was facing me and her arm was around me. Somehow, she had to show that I was her boyfriend, I thought.

She had spelled her name 'Lynda.' So, once I asked her, "I was wondering, what is a difference between 'Linda' and 'Lynda'? You spell your name as 'Lynda.'"

"'Linda' is commonly spelled. I didn't want to be a commoner. I changed it to 'Lynda'."

"How old are you, babe?" she asked me.

I told her my age. "You look young for thirty-one," she said.

After the New Year's party, Lynda called me at my office. She was inviting me for dinner with her on Friday evening.

"I am not going to treat you in a lavish restaurant or so. I am just inviting you to taste my cooking at my place."

"That would be nice of you. Is it going to be an experiment on me?" I asked her.

"No experiments. I am not a bad cook, by the way, and I will make it more enjoyable for you, I guarantee."

What reason could I find to deny her? Wasn't I looking for a friendship? And here Lynda was offering me one. Didn't I like Lynda at the first meeting? Still, I was hesitating to say 'Yes'. She asked me if I had plans for Friday.

"No, not really. Well, I shall come."

What should I present her on my first visit to her place? How about a bouquet of flowers? I thought it would be too intimate for the first visit. For the same reason I discarded a bottle of perfume. Then I thought of a box of chocolates. Maybe she might say, 'I am sorry, dear, I am on a diet and don't eat any sweets.'

I recalled that Milly had once said to me exactly in the same words that she was on a diet when I had offered her candies for the first time. And I had taken Milly's name as Lily when she first told me her name. Her thoughts feathered my memory with a flowery touch. And then I clearly remembered the second time when I offered her candies. That was the day of Halloween. I was coming back from the office and saw her sitting at her favorite spot. I stopped by her and offered her candies.

"Would you like a trick or treat? Even if you want to trick me, I will treat you. Take a few. These are for the trick-or-treating kids."

"I am not in a mood for a joke."

"Today is Halloween. Are you tired of this trick-or-treating business? Maybe you must have enjoyed it too much in your childhood."

"I went with my brother for trick-or-treat when we were in New Jersey. He is ten years elder to me. When he became seventeen, he stopped going for trick-or-treat. One year my mother watched me going around the houses and one year my neighbor's mother was with us. We needed some elderly person to watch and protect small children and girls from somebody playing mischief. We moved to Brooklyn when I was ten. The other girls of my age went for trick-or-treat. My mother did not allow me."

She was upset. To show her sympathy I had said, "Maybe she was overprotective."

"Yes, she was. She did not trust anyone. You don't know my mother. I was not allowed to play like other children after we came to Brooklyn. We had to sell our house in New Jersey. She was upset due to my father's problems. Then she became strict with me. I missed many things in life." She got up and walked out of the building.

So, the question of what should I give Lynda, was not solved yet. Finally, I decided on a bottle of 'Madera,' a famous Portuguese wine. I had never tasted it before, I had heard it was a good wine.

Lynda was well dressed, looked sexy, and was pleased to see me. She kissed me on my arrival. She put on the music and offered me my drink and fixed a screwdriver for herself.

She asked me about Egypt and expressed her desire to visit the country and learn about Egypt's glorious past. I realized that she had expressed her desire to visit Egypt a second time so far. Was she expecting me to say, "Someday I will take you there?"

Naturally, I was pleased. Then she asked me if I would like to join a ballroom dancing class with her. I was looking forward to learn dancing. So, it was perfectly agreeable to me. Matter of fact, I thought myself lucky that things were finally working as I wished. So far, I liked Lynda at least enough to develop a friendship and relationship and may be more.

For dinner she opened the bottle of 'Madera', the one I had brought. "How do you like my cooking?" she asked me.

"Fantastic. I am enjoying."

Then she told me, "I didn't cook that rice. That is the only thing I can never cook right. I had asked my mother to cook it for me this afternoon. She lives in the neighborhood."

"Well I am only expert in cooking rice. Of course, I can cook lots of other dishes, rice is my expertise."

Believe me, I was thinking of Lynda's mother looking over us through the rice. In short, I was getting a little high and felt she too was getting high because she kissed me hard for no reason. And in general, she was bursting into laugher for practically no reason.

We were still drinking after the dinner was over. "I like you, Said. You are such a handsome young guy, with a bright future.

"I am a modern and liberated girl. Aren't we living in the later part of the twentieth century? If I like someone, I would ask him for a date. If we like each other, we would stay together, and if we develop an intimate relationship, we could get married. The time is changing, honey. When it comes to dating and matrimony, the girls are still at the whim of the boys. I am not going to follow the traditional pattern. If I ask somebody for a date and if he feels I am too arrogant, then it is his choice to deny me. If I don't like someone after a while, I quit on him. I met all kinds of boys, some of them were too immature, and some with thick heads on their shoulders and not competent. I quit quite a few boys and a few quit on me too. I have no remorse for anybody. All gone with the wind. I am still looking for the boy of my choice. I like you and asked for a date." My head was cleared. My first reaction was, I did not like her liberal views she had. After all, I was from an old country, Egypt, a traditional Muslim country. It was a cultural shock to me. I felt very conservative myself. I must say, I agreed that we were in the world of changing times and this was a time for equality between men and women, at least in a country like America. Whatever she was saying was not wrong after all. I partially agreed with her. I liked her frankness and for those reasons I liked her. "I like your frankness and I like you. I think we can be good friends," I said.

"Good! I am glad," she said and she kissed me passionately.

The music was on; she turned it a little louder. We started dancing to the tunes. Then all of a sudden, she stopped, hugged me, and started kissing me violently. Her hands were moving on my back. Slowly the speed slowed down. She started caressing me with a magic touch. I was shocked with pleasure. She was excited and she had excited me along with her. We could not control it anymore and made vigorous love. Lynda had a beautiful body. I had not made love in a long time. She was terrific in bed.

We made love again.

And that night I had that nightmarish Dream. That dream woke me and it was hard to sleep again.

I was supposed to pick up Lynda in the morning and we were going to the shiny slopes for skiing. When I reached her apartment building, I called her through the intercom. She called me upstairs to her apartment to see if I was properly dressed.

"Let me see your gloves." I obeyed her order.

"They are not good for anything and never for skiing, my boy. You are gonna buy new gloves. Now put on your hat. Lemme see how you look."

Just before the first winter in this country, Karim, Mokhtar, and I went winter shopping. The main purpose of this shopping was that they were going to outfit me properly for the winter. That is when I had bought that fake bear cap.

"Oh, shit you look like a monkey."

"That's good, isn't it?"

"Why so?"

"No girl would look at me except you."

"Not even me, you smart kiddo. Spend some money. Spoil yourself."

Lynda drove her Camaro. She had fitted a ski rack on top of her car. It took us more than an hour to reach 'Mansfield' ski slopes. Before we went to the slopes, we had to stop for shopping for my ski gloves and a cap. Lynda had her own ski gear and she helped me to select my rental equipment. She even helped me put it on, at the slopes.

"I will get you started on the bunny slopes. I will give you your first lessons in skiing and then I will go on my regular slopes."

"What will be my first lesson, my teacher?"

"How to fall and how to get up."

"You must be kidding?"

"No, kid, not kidding."

She showed me how to fall on the sides. She said, "Never fall on your back and never on your front. Always relax while falling. Don't be stiff. Always fall on your sides so that all your bones will be in their places and don't act smart." She showed me how to fall and get up after a fall, how to stop and how to control the speed. "Now stand firm on your knees. Bend forward a little bit and push off with your poles." She spent almost an hour with me. She helped me to get up after falling. I never thought that it would be that difficult just to get up without her help in the beginning. She gave me basic lessons in skiing. Then she went on slopes of her level of skiing and I started risking my own life with how to fall safely and things like that. I had no knowledge of skiing. I could say that was the most difficult experience of my athletic life. Lynda was a good skier. It was great fun. From time to time, Lynda came to see my progress and corrected my mistakes. Within a few hours, I was totally exhausted.

The next day, late morning Lynda called me. "How is your body? Is it fit to make me happy?"

"No way." I explained to her the state of my almost broken body, which was luckily still in one piece.

"No kidding. Aren't you a great athlete?"

"No more, I guess. I thought I was!"

"Don't you worry. You will be there like a hero after some practice."

"How are you, my dear?"

"Don't ask me. I don't think I am any better than you. Take a saltwater hot tub bath."

"What is that? Put salt in the water. Are you joking?"

"No, I am not."

And she explained to me about a saltwater bath. "That will make you feel good. Relax the whole day, and drink lots of water so you will be fit for the office tomorrow."

I did what Lynda had told me to do. I slept in the afternoon for a long time and was barely fit for office on Monday.

Rajani Patel asked me directions to go to the immigration office for some errand. I happened to have been there a few weeks ago. I told him, "As soon as you enter the building, you will face a bank of elevators, turn left, go all the way down, then you will find a narrow hallway."

After an hour he came back to me saying that he could not find 'Bank of elevators' in the building. He searched the building directory and there was no bank by that name in that building. So, he came back. I felt like laughing. But I did not laugh. Instead I felt pity for him. The poor guy was searching for a bank with the name 'Bank of Elevators.' It was a real practical joke of one foreigner giving instructions to the other foreigner in a language foreign to both of them.

Lynda always asked me about my past. How I came to America. Would I like to stay here permanently? She was fascinated to visit Egypt.

Once we went to a quiet and expensive restaurant. Lynda had helped the owner to get a loan for opening another branch of the restaurant and he had offered her dinner for her and a guest.

"Do you still love your ex-wife? Do you still remember her?"

"Nope, I don't. Well, it is not that. Sometimes I do remember her. I have no feelings for her. I hate her."

"Can you tell me why you divorced?"

"Uh, well, I really don't like to talk about it. Why? Are you really interested to know about it?"

"Yeah, in a way, yes, I am."

"Oh well. I guess I will tell you."

And I told her the circumstances that led to my divorce.

"Hey, Said, kiddo, cheer up. I didn't know you would get so upset. I did not mean to. Did you have a crush on any girl in your school days?"

"Yeah, I had a sweetheart in the engineering college."

"Tell me about your romance with her, my romantic boy."

I told her about Helen and how we met. She was enjoying my story.

"Did you make love with her?" I did not know why she was asking me all these details.

"I had so many chances of making love to her."

Her face was delighted. After a pause I said, "I loved her, but I did not make love to her. She trusted me. We were in Egypt, where our society had conservative standards. I would have not engaged in sex with her and I am glad for that. I had sentimental feelings for her." (I did not tell Lynda that our love was pure and holy. Otherwise that would have opened the door for more questions.) "Well, in those days it was extremely difficult for a Muslim boy to marry a Christian girl. The society is very conservative and religious."

She was listening to me seriously.

"Now you are in America."

"Yes. It is a different society. Time and the place have changed and I have changed like a Roman in Rome. Am I right, dear?"

"No. You are American in America. And kiddo, you are all right. You know, when I was in high school, the boys teased the girls who started wearing bras. From behind they would pull the elastic strap and snap it. It would hurt badly. All the boys would laugh and would say 'Bunny Rabbit Associate'. I did not get much experience of it, because the first boy who did it to me, I turned around and slapped him good. Since then the boys always stayed away from me and all my friends.

"I want to wrestle with you in bed, Said. Let us go home," she added. She was really strong, believe me. She was a good swimmer and was on the college swimming team.

"Said, you have a wonderful body. You are like a tiger."

"I am glad you think so. Thanks. I enjoyed you too."

To me Lynda was certainly like a tigress. We enjoyed sex to the full extent. Once she asked me what were those striped scars on my back? I explained what they were. She felt sad.

One Sunday morning we decided to go a park to stroll there, jog, run a little bit and then go to a café for a brunch. I liked the idea.

We were getting close and trying to know each other better. Both of us were well dressed for the occasion, in shorts. She had beige short, I had light blue denim. Her light pink tee shirt read 'BORN TO RUN' with cartoon of running young girl with boxing gloves, mine olive color said 'HAPPY MAN' with a happy moon face. Our white sneakers were worn out. We started strolling with hand in hand on the park track, then jogging and then we ran slowly at comfortable speed for about fifteen minutes. We were passing an uphill grassy knoll. She held my hand and pulled me towards the hill and pulled me down and lightly fell on top of me. She hugged me and started laughing. She kissed me lightly and then fiercely. "You are too romantic. Let's go home." And we left.

Lynda had a management training course for one week at the bank's headquarters and then she had to submit a paper in the following week. She told me that she would be studying and working on her paper during the weekend. Saturday morning, she called me to find out if I was doing anything. I told her that I was thinking of going to see Greta Garbo's *Two-Faced Woman*. They had an old film festival in Cleveland. She said, "Oh, no, Said, please, come here to keep me company, while I am studying."

"I might disturb you."

"No, please, honey darling. I would get bored alone studying. I don't even want to go out. We will order Chinese food in the evening. You can play music and watch a ballgame on TV. Please, I will be happy just to see you here. And I promise to make you happy. I can spare that much time for you."

So finally, I went there. She talked to me for a while. Then I listened to music, made tea for myself and coffee for her a few times, cooked lamb chops for lunch. Then I watched some tennis and a baseball game on TV. I didn't get bored because she entertained me in between by talking to me and she made me happy as she had promised. At night we went to the Chinese restaurant instead of ordering food at home. She made me sleep at her place. Most of the Sunday I stayed at her apartment.

"Good morning, Said speaking."

"It is me, Said. Do you know what happened to my friend Sue yesterday?"

"No. I don't. What happened? Did she have a baby?"

"Oh, come on, Said, she is not married yet."

"Who says one has to get married to have babies. You know that."

"Don't act smart. Sue is upset. Her date took her out for the third time yesterday and he was unromantic with her. He did not make love to her yet. On their first date he was shy. I just talked to her. She is very upset."

"I am glad."

"I what?" She raised her voice.

"No. I said, I am glad I am not her boyfriend."

"It is not something funny. Aren't you sorry for Sue?" she rapped me.

"Oh, yes, sure I am sorry for Sue."

Oh boy, oh boy, I did not know myself what someone was supposed to do on his first date, second date, and so on. I felt real non-American. I was not interested to know what Susan's boyfriend didn't do to her. I never saw her. Now I felt like meeting her.

Lynda had called me to remind me about their office party. Their bank arranged a couple of sales promotion parties every year. They were real nice parties, according to Lynda. Lynda had invited me to attend this one.

"You better shave again this evening and blow your hair nicely and wear that three-piece suit. You got to look sharp. After all, you are my guest. Please, don't be late, pick me at six sharp. Got it?"

By the time I knocked at her door to pick her up, it was ten past six. She was impatiently waiting for me.

"Aren't you late, Mr. Ahemed?"

"Yes, indeed. I am sorry."

"Good!"

The party was at the Hilton. I must say that it was a fabulous party. Some typical sale's promotion lectures by the bank's biggies. 'Bullshit', that was Lynda's description. And then the things of real interest for everyone – booze, buzz, food and dance, and of course music and the 'Bullshit'.

I knew almost all the staff from Lynda's branch. Her boss, whatever his name was, introduced Lynda to someone named Scott something. I did not remember his last name; it was simply not possible to remember all these names. This Scott was a young and smart guy in his early thirties.

"I am delighted to meet you in the flesh, Miss Lynda Smith, the person who talked to me on the phone so many times. World apart from what I had pictured you! I thought you as meticulous, in your forties, who is never ready to talk about anything other than the work. You are really a charming young lady."

"Thanks for your compliments and for your understanding of me. I have yet to learn how to talk other than business over the bank telephone. Maybe you can teach me."

"Oh, sure, I will."

"This is my friend, Said Ahemed."

"Glad to meet you, Said, I am Scott." We shook hands.

"Said is an engineer at Ross & Bros. He came from Egypt. He was in New York before. And Scott is an officer in our head office." Lynda made my position respectable.

Scott told me that he had been to New York to attend a one-week course in financing in 1972. He stayed at the New York Hilton on Seventh Avenue. He had heard so many crime stories about New York City that he chickened out and did not go out of his hotel room at night. I was not a bit surprised because I had heard similar stories before.

Everyone was enjoying the food and the booze. I was no exception. I danced with Lynda and a few other girls from the bank. By the time we left, lots of people were drunk.

I was going to drop Lynda at her apartment and then go home to take shelter in my bed. I also started feeling the glitch of booze in my stomach. She insisted on my having a cup of coffee with her. When I went into her apartment, she was in a different mood. She was romantic and sexy. She wouldn't let me go home. She asked me to stay with her and not go home. We made love twice. There was fulfillment and enjoyment in her eyes. I had my reward of her satisfaction and her appreciation.

There was challenge in Lynda's every move. She was full of life and ambitions. She was certainly enjoying every bit of life. I liked her and started falling in love with her and positively thinking that we could make a life together.

The next morning during breakfast, she told me that Scott was a widower. He had a son, three years old, and his wife had died of cancer a year ago.

Rajani Patel had planned a party in October to celebrate the Indian festival of lights (Diwali) with Indian friends. He had invited me. "We are strictly vegetarian. Please, don't expect any non-vegetarian food and only soft drinks. You will have a feast of Indian hot food", he had told me. What finally I concluded with input from Rajani and his friends was that it was a festival equivalent to Christmas that runs for four days with different religious significance for each day. Rajani explained me the importance of each day.

Rajani himself introduced me to all his guests. Everyone tried to speak to me after they learned that I was Egyptian. A few elder ones spoke high praise for Egyptian ex-president Nasser. And a few of them showed interest in opening some kind of Indian business in Egypt and its prospects. In short, I was constantly talking.

I was fascinated by the ladies' dresses. I had seen Indian women in Queens in their native dresses. But I never paid much attention. The ladies were wearing two different types of dresses. One type was a thin and fine fabric, mostly silks. It was worn around the waist hanging down to the feet and then over a shoulder and ending on the chest. Rajani's wife, Sonali, was wearing the other kind. Those tight pants were made of silk. The top was a silk midi-length gown with full sleeves and only top buttons on the back side. I liked that dress. And you know that dress was similar to the Arabic women's dress except Indian designs were more stylish and beautifully woven in gold threads.

Reasonably loud music was playing on the stereo system. I recognized that music as I had heard it before. I told Rajani, "You know, I had heard this music in the restaurants in Cairo." He was surprised and told me that those were the songs from Indian movies.

The food was delicious, oily, hot and spicy. Egyptian are used to eating hot food. But this was something different. I told one of them, "You people must have an extra stomach lining to cope with this kind of spicy food." I was enjoying the food, at the same time, it was burning my stomach. His wife, Sonali, had prepared an Indian version of Baba Ganoush. I told her this dish was identical to Baba Ganoush. She was surprised to know. I enjoyed different kinds of sweets. One kind of sweets was Halawah, similar to Egyptian Halawah.

At the end of the party, Rajani asked me whether I liked the Indian food. I told him, "It was delicious and I ate with great interest.

Now my stomach is on fire." He talked to his wife in his language and in a few minutes his wife gave me a glass full of sweetened buttermilk flavored with rose essence. This would help my stomach, she told me. And it really soothed my burning.

The next day was Sunday and I spent a quite a bit of time running to the bathroom and I had to buy Pepto-Bismol to take care of my condition.

With this company I had to travel frequently. We were working on a proposal to build a new coal handling facility for the Republic Steel Company, in Chicago. I and my boss went there for a meeting with the company people. My boss went back to Cleveland in the evening after the meeting and I stayed behind for the next day to work out some site details. I was staying at the Holiday Inn in Homestead, which is in the southeast corner of Chicago. In the evening I was so bored and tired that I wanted to enjoy a good dinner. So, I asked the receptionist at the hotel for a good restaurant. She told me the best restaurant she knew was in another state.

"No, I don't want to know the best restaurant you know from New York. I am talking about a restaurant around here for this evening."

"No problem, it is still in the other state. You can drive there in fifteen minutes. The name of the restaurant is 'Surf and Turf.' It is my favorite. But it is in Gary, Indiana, about ten miles." She gave me the directions.

The restaurant was so crowded that I had to wait thirty minutes before I got a table. They had a big waiting room and in there they had about an eight-foot-tall stuffed white bear standing on its hind legs in a ready position to attack. It was spectacular and scary. The restaurant was big and was famous for steaks. I had one drink at the bar before I went to the table.

I ordered Wild Turkey and filet mignon. My favorite salad dress-ing in those days was blue cheese. I finished half of my drink and half of my salad, and then I went to the restroom. The restroom was really small for that size restaurant. When I returned to my table in ten minutes, would you believe my table was not only cleaned, but a couple was sitting there and going through the menu? To avoid embarrassment, the manager came running and apologized to me. I had to wait a few minutes before I was seated again. I was mad and already tired. Before I finished my dinner and dessert, I had two more drinks at the dining table when normally I would have only one more. When I saw my check, I found that the manager had put my drinks on the house for my inconvenience. I thanked him.

Two weeks after the bank party, Lynda called me at the office.
"Guess what, Saidy?"
"What?"
"You guess."
"You got a promotion?"
"No, my dear. Scott called me today. He is taking me out for dinner, at 'Crystal' this Saturday. I am looking forward to it. Do you know what?"
"No, I don't know? What?"
"Scott is a big guy in the bank. If he becomes my friend, I will get my next promotion soon."
"That would be great. Have a nice time on Saturday."

And as the days passed, Lynda and Scott became bosom friends. Lynda called me a few times, mostly the topic was Scott and his charisma. They started playing dating games.
And that was the end of our relationship. So, that was the story

of 'Us.' 'We' had a short life. 'We' became 'She' and 'I.' It was sad that it ended. I was a hurt. As Lynda had said, 'Gone with the wind.' It was not easy for me anyway. I guess we were not made for each other.

After our break-up, whenever I went to the bank for any reason, Lynda would take care of me immediately as before. She never made me wait in the line and always talked to me casually, and sometimes told me her progress with her new boyfriend and asked me once if I found any other girlfriend. I answered her that I was not looking for one right now and would take it easy. On that she said, "Don't worry. You will find someone of interest."

Lynda stopped calling me in the office and Betsy realized that I did not receive a call from her. It was true you could not hide these kinds of telephone calls from your secretary. Betsy knew about Lynda and me. When I stopped receiving her calls, she asked me about her.

"My friend Lynda! Well, well, we could not stay the same way as before. It was her choice."

"Were you serious about her? Do you feel hurt?"

Sometimes Betsy used to shower me with a kind of motherly love.

"I was Involved. I had feelings for her. I am hurt."

"I am sorry for you. You will find someone better."

"You answered her phone calls many times. How did you like her?"

"That is not up to me. You know her better."

Betsy used to take messages whenever I was not at my desk. When I insisted, Betsy told me that Lynda never sounded friendly. She was cold.

CHAPTER SEVEN

O ur secretary Betsy introduced me to Nancy. Betsy knew that I had seriously finished with Lynda. She took me to Nancy's desk.

"This is Nancy, Said." And she left.

"Hi, how are you? My name is Nancy Laker." We shook hands. Her hand was soft.

"I had seen you in the office, had no chance of talking to you. `This boy is called Said Ahemed.'" And she laughed. She was shy, simple, and good-looking, with black hair and black eyes.

Nancy was a secretary for one of the projects. There was a big bulletin board on the wall next to her desk. A few memos were tacked on it. Besides the memos I saw a few signs neatly tacked in different locations of the board.

'THE GOD IS GREATER THAN ANY PROBLEM I HAVE.
THE LORD IS LIGHT UNTO MY PATH.'

The other one read,

'WHAT YOU ARE IS GOD'S GIFT TO YOU, WHAT YOU MAKE OF YOURSELF IS YOUR OWN GIFT TO YOURSELF.'

"How long have you been with the company?" I asked.

"About eight years."

"That long?" I was really surprised.

"This is my first full-time job right out of school. And then I went to evening college and got my bachelor's degree in social sciences last year." She had to tell me her credentials to impress me. I knew she must be good to be a project secretary.

"Where were you before?" It was her turn to ask me.

I told her I worked in New York before, told her the name of my previous company and told her that I was Egyptian. She said Betsy had mentioned to her that I was Egyptian.

"How long have you been in this country? You speak good English!"

"Still I have a strong accent."

"That's OK. I can understand you well." I had realized that my accent had improved with Lynda.

"That is good. Me too!"

"What?"

"I mean I understand you well too."

"It's so beautiful here in the summer," I added.

"Gee, I love the summer."

"Do you go skiing?"

"No. How about you?"

"I did a few times here in Cleveland."

"That's great. How did you like it?"

"It was a lot of fun and a great sport but I quit skiing as the snow disappeared from the slopes."

"You mean you quit for the season. You are very witty, Said."

Almost every day we talked for the rest of the week. We both were interested in developing a friendship. At least I was. Two weeks later I asked her for an evening dinner. She was almost waiting for it. With a sort of dramatic hesitation, she accepted my invitation. Her face glowed with a smile and her well sized breasts expanded an inch from that smile. I literally saw it.

"What would you like to drink? Wine, cocktail, or hard liquor?"

"Excuse me. I don't drink. I will just have a coke."

"That's OK. You won't mind me drinking bourbon."

"Not at all, sir."

I was about to say "Gee," but I did not. I remembered Karim's younger son used to go crazy for coke since he was just one and a half years old. Gee, that's right. Almost everybody loved coke, me too!

I cheered my Wild Turkey with her Coke, "To our friendship." She said, "Cheers!"

"Do you like lobster?"

"Gee, I love lobster."

Lynda loved lobster and with her I learned to enjoy lobster tails; I had never tried lobster before and never ventured to try a whole lobster. The price was high for a lobster as usual and Nancy was hesitating. I insisted. So, she had a lobster and I had 'King steak with lobster tails'.

Half of the time we were talking about the office. And the other half of the time we talked general things about our families and our lives. She asked me about Egypt.

"Are the marketplaces like the one they had shown in the movie *The Man Who Knew Too Much*? Are the houses the same as I had seen in that movie?"

"Yes, very much so."

She had been to New York during her high school senior trip. She told me how she enjoyed it and they stayed out late at night visiting different bars and she enjoyed all the fun of her schoolmates because she was not drinking. Then she asked me how I came to the states. I told her I came here as an astronaut. When I explained to her the meaning of 'Astronaut,' she broke into big laughter that the people around us started looking at us. Then after that she kept laughing a little loudly at my witty talks. I felt like I was drinking whisky and it was affecting her.

I enjoyed her company. We had a nice time. I dropped her at her home and I kissed her good night. She knew it was going to happen; she was not surprised. Her lips were soft and cool. I held the kiss a little longer. For the same reason, I kissed her again. She liked my kissing her twice, well that was my imagination.

After a week I wanted to ask Nancy if she would like to accompany me to a movie. I went to see her and from a distance I heard her talking on the telephone in a flat and loud voice, "Oh, No. I am not surprised at all and won't be surprised even if you tell me something different about her." I realized it was not going to end soon. So, I went back.

When I came back after a while, she had six bottles arranged on her desk and she was taking one pill from each bottle.

"Are you so sick to take all these pills?"

"Oh, no, these are different vitamin pills."

"Oh, boy, you are sure going to be strong to lift and throw someone like me. I better be careful."

"Gee, I liked your joke. These are vitamin pills pills. Somebody suggested taking one multi-vitamin pill instead of so many of these.

But I am used to these."

"Are you busy this evening?"

"No, not really."

"I was thinking of going for a movie. Would you like to keep me company?"

"I guess it would be fine with me. When do you want to see a movie?"

"This evening, after work."

"I will call my mother and tell her."

"Do you have any particular movie in mind?"

"I would like to see *Benji*."

"That is kid's movie, rated G."

I had *Once Is Not Enough* in my mind. The movie was based on Jacqueline Susann's novel, rated R, and was supposed to be a good movie. And here she had started with *Benji*. So, finally, we compromised on *Love and Death* starring Woody Allen and Diane Keaton. Nancy was a bit scared and suspicious about the movie from its title. She said it could be a drama and tragedy. Well, she was right about that part that we were going to enjoy the movie and not to cry. I definitely knew that it was not a sad movie but a comedy. She was not ready to believe me. So, I told her, "How could you go wrong with Woody Allen? Believe me, Nancy, he is going to be a king of comedy in the future." Anyway, finally she agreed upon it.

Before we entered the theatre, Nancy ran for popcorn. I had never eaten popcorn while watching a movie. I always thought it was kids' stuff. I was absolutely wrong. That was my first experience and honestly, I enjoyed it.

"Oh, my goodness. What have you done to your hair?"

"This is what you had suggested the other day. I thought at least you would like it. Isn't it terrible? No one had liked it."

And she broke into tears in my office.

"Well, it does not look that bad." It was a little lie. Under the circumstances, that was the best I could do. "Yes, I had mentioned a few days ago that a boy-cut would look nice on your face. I am very sorry for my suggestion. Believe me, it is not that bad." I was trying to console her. I made her sit. It was certainly not a cheering hair-style for her perfectly round face. It was certainly not terrible look-ing. Well, if you see it from a friend's point of view, then it was bad, but was acceptable if it was according to your own stupid suggestion. If you were Nancy's rival for competing for a boyfriend, you would feel happy for this kind of situation. She was still crying.

"I am very sorry, Nancy, you should have consulted hair dresser. It looks like I don't know anything about women's hairstyles. I am really sorry for my wrong suggestion. You will be all right soon."

A silence, more tears, I was worried, rather scared. What if some-one watched this scene? I tried to comfort her. I was not skilled in that art, either. And never did it before in English. That was well known to me as 'The language barrier' and I was facing that barrier in an extremely awkward situation.

"Oh, please, don't cry." I was more uncomfortable than her. I doubted how my words sounded.

"It will grow soon and then you can have a beautiful hairstyle from a specialist."

"It will take months to grow out."

"Naturally." Of course, I did not say "Naturally" to her. I was try-ing to calm her. "Don't worry. As soon as it grows a little bit, you will look beautiful again. Basically, you are a beautiful girl, aren't you?"

She did not answer. At least she was listening to me carefully.

"Don't you believe me? Aren't you a beautiful girl?"

"Do you think so?"

"Absolutely yes." I was not lying. She was good looking. She just had to wear the right kind of hairstyle and the right kind of make-up.

And finally, she stopped crying. I took her to Friendly's restaurant for ice cream.

Sometimes I used to feel like calling her, "Hey, Nancy pansy, how the hell are you?" And she would be surprised to hear that and after her first shock, she would say, "Gee, that sounds nice. I like the flowers of pansy. We have them in our backyard." But I never said so. Maybe she knew the meaning of the word 'Pansy,' the one I knew, and then she would be extremely upset. I felt she was not the type of girl who would appreciate my saying to her, "How the hell are you?"

You know something, sometimes among my friends we used to ask, "How the hell are you?" and the right answer to that is "I am hale and hearty."

One day I had asked Nancy in the office if she would like to go for a ride with me that evening, and then we would go to the beach on the lake. I told her it was a full moon night. She was thrilled, I thought, when I asked her.

"Gee, I am not doing anything in particular this evening. I guess I will be more than glad to say yes." I liked it. I mean the way she said it, I really liked it.

After the office, that evening we drove through the traffic. The driving on Lake Shore Drive was pleasant, especially when a beautiful girl like Nancy was sitting next to me.

"I am going to enjoy ice cream, double scoop on a cone. I am hungry. What about you?"

"I am hungry too. I think I will go for a milkshake. Oh, no, maybe I will have ice cream too! One scoop of vanilla and one scoop of chocolate." She had asked for sprinkles on her ice cream.

We walked on the beach holding hands and settled down in the sand. The beach was still crowded. A lot of people passing by were purposely watching us, mainly because I was different, I thought. A gusty breeze was blowing and her clothes were hugging her, especially on her chest. Her large bosom was showing a beautiful contour. She looked sexy and would have looked sexier with her otherwise long hair. Now she had that boy-cut hairstyle. I laughed to myself. I felt like kissing her. And unknowingly, I kissed her fleshy cheek. She turned around and I kissed her lips.

"Do you like to go out like this with me? Did you notice people are watching us because I look different?"

"Oh, sure, I noticed it, and I don't care what they think."

"Nancy, may I ask you a serious question? Do you know I am Muslim?"

"I know that."

"And you are Christian. I am saying, I am not very religious myself. I even don't follow the rules of my religion. But I trust my religion and our god. I would never mind if you are Christian and follow your religion strictly. It would not hurt my feelings. Do you have any hard feelings for me being Muslim?"

"I am glad you asked me. I have my own views about religion. I am religious to some extent. I go to church every Sunday with my parents. Somehow my parents don't understand; they do not like me going out with a Muslim boy like you. I do not care for their views.

"I always thought why people are putting this big wall between them and killing each other over religion. If all the people live happily with their own faith and don't bother people of other faiths, the world will be a paradise. I personally have no hard feelings for your religion or any other religion. Human comes first before the religion. That is how I always felt."

I didn't know where she learned this philosophy. I liked her views. One of the most difficult to follow for mankind, I thought. I did not know if she was going to digest it in actuality. I realized that because of her liberal views, Betsy had introduced Nancy to me, after telling her my religion. And Nancy had agreed to meet me. It was not that she was desperate to get a boyfriend. I was just a good candidate for her and I was looking forward to meeting someone.

After that conversation, I seriously thought over my relationship with Nancy. She could be good for me as a life partner. She was reasonably beautiful, educated, and simple. She had accepted my religion. Her philosophy on religions was good. I must say it could be the best philosophy for mankind. She was ready to accept me. I could go ahead in developing a relationship. I didn't know why, I had no positive feeling for her; I mean I had no heartfelt affection for her. She could not ignite a spark of love in my heart. She was cold. Nancy was too nice, too naïve, and too innocent. She was not my cup of tea. I did not want to hurt her feelings. I was sure she would have made love to me and we would have enjoyed it. I did not want to raise her hopes for me and then disappoint her. She was a baby in her family and preferred to stay that way and acted likewise. I decided to keep a good friendship with her and not to develop any further relationship. Lynda was smart, full of life and ambitious. I liked her. But it did not work. Nancy was a 'Gee' girl. She should seek a 'Golly' boy.

In November, Rajani took three weeks' vacation and the whole family went to India. Rajani came back alone after three weeks. His wife and children stayed in India for a total of four months. He told me that they go to India once every year during the same time and his wife and children stay in India with her parents through the winter. Rajani had a five-year-old son and his daughter was three, with those Allah-blessed names. I liked his logic for this kind of family vacation. One was his family did not have to face harsh winters and secondly, they saved on heating and food bills.

Rajani gave me a silk tie from India and a carved elephant of sandalwood as a gift after he came back. Sandalwood is supposed to smell forever, Rajani told me. He showed me a few silk shirts he had brought from India. The silk was smooth. The floral design on the shirts was colorful. I liked the shirts and asked him a favor if his wife could buy one shirt for me. I also asked if his wife could buy a ladies' dress for me. I would pay the price.

"Is it for your girlfriend, Lynda?" Rajani asked me.

I had already told him about my affair with Lynda.

"No, not for Lynda nor for anyone in particular. I want to buy it for my future girl, whomever I meet someday."

After I decided not to get involved with Nancy, I stopped looking for friendship with any girl for the time being. We (I and Nancy) sat at the same table at our office Christmas party and we danced a few times. We remained friends. Rajani became my close friend during that time. We used to visit each other on Sundays after he came back from his vacation in December without his family.

Rajani's family was vegetarian. He would eat eggs and chicken on occasions. He generally did not drink and did not keep any alcoholic drinks at home. He would drink at office parties.

We talked mostly about our countries, our customs, American politics, and our school days. Sometimes we spoke about our office things and office people. Whenever he came to my apartment, I cooked Arabic food, and when I went to his place, he cooked Indian hot and spicy food. Then we would spend quite some time discussing our cooking. Whenever I went to his house, I took a bottle of wine with me. We enjoyed sipping the wine. He played Indian instrumental music. I became fond of particularly sitar and Shehnai music. I already had one LP of this string instrument, sitar, played by music maestro Ravi Shankar. I had it when I was in New York. Frequently I used to listen to it, especially at night. That used to be so relaxing and soothing. Shehnai, as he showed me on the album, was like a flute. When I listened to it, the tunes were different from flute. They were high pitched, deep and touching the heart. Rajani told me that they play this music live during wedding ceremonies in India. While listening to Shehnai, I always remembered my mother. Those tunes were heavenly holy. Imagine what holy atmosphere it must be creating at the time of wedding?

I went to an Indian shop in Cleveland with Rajani and bought one record of Shehnai music and one record of sitar music.

I stopped going to Rajani after his wife came back from India. I missed our meetings and heartfelt conversations.

Lynda had invited me for the Christmas party as a favorite customer of the bank. She mailed me the invitation and also talked to me in person when I went to the bank to deposit my pay check. The whole thing reminded me of the year before. I told Lynda that I had already planned to take a vacation during that time and would visit my friends in New York. I would be back next year. In reality I went to New York after the party and came back one year later – I mean next year. I stayed there only a week.

I did not forget to call Lynda before I left for New York to wish her merry Christmas and happy New Year. I also wished that Santa would smother her with gifts. Before leaving for vacation, I went to the bank and gave her a bottle of Madera as a Christmas present. And I gave 'Charlie' to Nancy and said to her, "This 'Charlie' is good enough to smother you." She opened my gift immediately. She laughed and said, "You are funny, Said. Enjoy your vacation." She kissed me.

Once I was flying from Houston to Cleveland back home from a business trip. It was three-hour flight. As soon as I had my first chance, I ordered a drink, my favorite bourbon. It was my time to relax after a whole day discussion with a supplier. After a few sips of the drink, I fell into a train of thoughts. Mostly I was thinking of my life in the United States. And I started dipping deep into my thoughts and started enjoying it.

I saw a big lonely bird
flying amid the white clouds.
Far away was the big bird.
I could feel his loneliness.

Flying with many souls and hearts.
Just like me, full of thoughts.
Some surrounded by family love.
A few scorched in loneliness too.

In a moment the big bird was lost,
speeding away in the emptiness vast
constantly humming the song of roars.
The big bird had no heart to feel.

That's right; the big bird I saw was a plane carrying so many hearts and souls of different kinds of personalities.

I felt so lonely and all of a sudden, I remembered that girl so strongly. I could not get her out of my mind. I might not see her again in the whole of my life. Why the hell was I thinking of her? I tried to switch my thoughts over to something else.

I ordered a second drink. Then I took out a pen and started scribbling on the napkin I got with the drink.

I met a birdie in a flock of birds.
She made a dent; I can't forget her.
Sometimes, somewhere deep, in my heart I feel,
the wounds of love she made would never heal.
My heart cries deep in sleep ,
for my love for that girl.

I had a head-on collision with her. My head was spinning. My heart was bleeding. Could it be a love? It was not possible. 'The criminal does not know. She is innocent.' I mean, how could it be? I had nothing to do with her. I was in Cleveland and she was in New York. We had no contact. We were long lost.

I did not want to think of her. Thoughts of Milly being criminal and I being the victim of her love delighted me. I must sue her in the court of hearts for her grave crime of attacking my heart.

'Oh, come on, I just do not want to think of that moody girl. Allah only knows what kind of girl is she?' I wanted to get rid of her from my mind. So, I drank one more Wild Turkey. 'Shanti,' I meant 'Peace,' and I slept to the happiness of turkey wilderness.

I woke all messed up and scared. I had that dream in broad daylight. All that spirit I had in my stomach evaporated at once. It was the same dream, the one I had on the night when I met her very late riding the elevator with me. And she was very drunk that time. The dream had slowly developed in full details since I had it the first time. I did not bother much. I was drunk enough to fall asleep again. But I could not. I tried to shut my eyes but in vain. I read the lines I had written on the napkin again and again without making any sense out of those words. I didn't want to drink more. I tried to read an airline magazine; but I could not. I could do nothing. I shut my eyes and again she was in front of me. I didn't want to think of Milly. I was not doing anything other than that. I was really restless and upset over that dream.

Finally, I was a little relaxed when I let half of me know from the other half, that both those halves would call her after they got home.

I did not have her telephone number. I called the directory assistance and asked for her number in Queens. I was told there was nobody by that name in Queens. Milly might have moved out. Maybe she finally got married. There was no way of knowing. I decided to call her at her office the next day.

That was one of those few nights when I really felt how long the night was.

Next day I was going to call Milly at her office. I did not have that number. But I remembered the name of her firm just because it was an interesting name—'Accounts on Us.' I obtained the number from directory assistance and called her office and got her extension. I recognized her voice. At least she was in the same office and safe. I had nothing to talk to her about. I just hung up the phone.

The nightmarish dream, that I saw again in broad daylight, had been like this:

I was traveling on a subway at around midnight. Something happened in the next car. I saw a cop and people running towards the commotion. I joined them. A small crowd had already gathered around somebody lying on the floor. I pushed my way towards the center to get a closer look. Oh, my God. Some girl was lying motionless and face down in a pool of blood. The cops turned her over and I screamed and fainted when I saw her face.

I will never forget the horror of this nightmare. I always woke up at this point. For the first few times, I did not see her face. My God, when I did see the face, it was Milly. Dead!

And that night I had the nightmarish dream again. It tortured me. Where could she be right at this moment? Maybe she is traveling on the subway? Maybe, in bed with some stranger.

I was bored of Cleveland, a steel town, an industrial town as I looked at it. There was nothing there except a big lake that also did not have a nice beach. There was no activity for me. There was nothing like New York, Broadway plays, which I really missed. Just walking in the streets of New York was delightful. I heard a vicious joke about Cleveland on the radio. The joke goes like this: 'There was a competition and the prize for the third place was to spend a weekend in Cleveland. The second prize was to spend a weekend for the husband and wife. The first prize was a one-week vacation for the whole family in Cleveland.' Did you get the point? These prizes were nothing but punishments. I mean there was a lot of sense in that joke. Cleveland was a badly rundown city in those days, with absolutely no sightseeing places and no entertainment whatsoever. It was a steel town. And those wintery days looked dull.

I had no real friend there. Rajani was my friend. He was good. But he was going to be busy with his family as soon as they came back from India. With this thought, I started feeling lonelier. In New York I had my bloody buddy friends around. I used to talk to them on the phone from Cleveland. But that was not enough. I truly missed them.

I remember, once in the Big Apple, the CITY had planned '*Keep New York Clean Week*' and the garbage collectors, the employees of the City of New York timed their strike at the same time. It was interesting to watch the banners saying, '*IT IS YOUR CITY, KEEP IT CLEAN AND MAKE IT A HEAVEN*' and the sidewalks piled with garbage bags and the streets smelling with rotting smell. It was such fun to watch the girls walking on the sidewalks holding their noses.

Another thing I missed was the Hare Krishna people. The way they used to dance and chant in their melodious voices on Fifth Avenue, in such a trance. I used to love to watch them. I was sure at least their God would be pleased with their chanting and devotion and shower them with blessings.

And of course, I missed Racetracks. I had decided not to gamble and here in Cleveland at least I was winning the races by not playing them. Apart from gambling, one could enjoy the whole evening at the racetrack. And the worst I missed, the Jones Beach. I am just unable to tell you how much I enjoyed those lonely and lovely evenings there.

I wanted to go back to New York. I wanted to visit all those New York places. I wanted to visit Grand Central station and get lost in the mesmerizing picture Kodak used to display. I had an urge to roam those crowded streets of Manhattan and eat hot dogs from the street vendors.

The thoughts of Milly were constantly peeping in my mind. She might have changed. She might not be the same, the way I knew her. We could be good friends. We might find something of interest. We might like each other. Our friendship might grow deeper and deeper. And who knows what? And... and suppose I found her married to someone. Oh, no, I did not want that to happen. And maybe she got killed at one of those night places. Oh, God, I did not want to think of something like that, either. Those thoughts used to torture me. I had to go back to New York. What if Milly was the same 'Bad' girl? Then... then I might have to go looking for another girl. Maybe I would find somebody, to be my new friend. I was sure I could find my happiness in New York. That thought used to be a relief. I could not stay alone. I had enough of it. I needed companionship. I wanted to love someone and wanted to be loved.

CHAPTER EIGHT

And I came back to New York in search of happiness. That was the first week of April, 1976.

Before coming to New York, I had visited Egypt for one week. My mother was not keeping good health, as my brother had written to me from time to time. It was the first time in all these years she felt extremely sad when I left for the States. Every time she felt sad. This time I felt it was different. That bothered me. The whole day she was quietly weeping. It was also the first time she ever had a heart-to-heart talk with me. As a matter of fact, she advised me to get married and said that would make me happy and she would also be happy. She knew me so well, I thought. She was certainly right. She was sad and was crying for the last two days of my stay. I told her, I was looking for a girl and would marry soon.

I had no address in New York, I was a man of no place. I had a standing invitation from Karim and Mokhtar to stay with them after I came back to the Big Apple. I decided to stay with Mokhtar till I could find an apartment. My new company had agreed to pay me two week's expenses if I stayed in a hotel. Mokhtar and his wife, Mona, insisted on my staying with them and I myself did not like the idea of staying in a hotel. They were happy when I agreed to stay with them, and their little son, Khalid, was extremely excited with this news because Uncle Micky was going to stay with them. He was four that time. It was convenient as Mokhtar lived in Queens. It was also easy to search for an apartment as I had decided to rent my new apartment in Queens.

I always came back to the States on a Friday, so I could adjust a little bit of the jet lag and time cycle and get over homesickness. My first priority was to find an apartment, a furnished one and second interest was to call that girl Milley. I had called her once from Cleveland. I did not keep her telephone number. Again, I had to call telephone directory to get her office telephone number. I called her on Wednesday.

"Hi. This is Said. Do you remember me?"

"Sure. I recognized your voice. How have you been? Where are you calling from?"

"I am fine and in New York." From her voice I could tell she was in a good mood.

"Are you visiting on business or on vacation?"

"Both wrong. I am back for good."

"Oh, how nice. Welcome back to the Big Apple and lots of luck."

"Many thanks. I got a job with Moore Consultants in downtown Manhattan. How are you? Are you married?"

"Not yet, maybe someday." At least she sounded optimistic.

"How is your family? How are your father and mother?"

"They are all fine, thanks."

"That's good. I would like to meet you one of these days. Would it be alright with you?"

It was hard for me to ask her. I did not know how she would react. My heart was as cold as ice. It practically stopped for a moment. I felt it for sure.

"I don't know when. I am busy as usual. This evening I am going to see my mother. Friday, I am going to my brother's for the weekend. Tomorrow I am thinking of seeing Robert Redford's new release. It will be next week sometime. Anything in particular?"

"Well, I thought of .... well maybe, we could go for dinner someplace. I thought, oh, just to meet you, catch up on old times. It is a pretty long time since I last saw you and I missed you. So, I thought ... oh, I thought of meeting you after coming to New York." We decided the day and place to meet after work.

Now my heart was racing faster and faster like a train and missing beats along the way. I truly missed her but I did not want to say so. Unconsciously I said it, and that was my true feelings. At least, I would have never asked her to dinner if she was married.

Anyway, it was over.

So, finally she agreed to meet and have dinner with me next Wednesday. I started counting the time until five thirty on Wednesday. That was when I was going to meet her after such a long time. It was like a countdown for me.

And that was my memorable meeting with her, I had told you about that meeting right in the beginning.

To select apartment, my first choice was Forest Hills as I loved the area. On Saturday I went to the superintendent of my last apartment building. He was the same guy. He recognized me. He had nothing available in his building. He suggested I go to the other building down two blocks and, "He will show you the apartment only if he knows you. Tell him Jose two sent you. Tell him you lived in my building." And it worked, not without the gift – he asked for $200. The rent was $420 a month for a one-bedroom furnished apartment. The furniture was just one year old. The apartment was on the fifth floor facing the street and the other apartment building.

So, there was no privacy like I had before. The only problem was it was not ready for immediate occupancy. The present tenant was moving out after one week. It was going to take at least four to five days to fix and paint the apartment. Till then I had to stay with Mokhtar.

We (I and Mokhtar) had a ball every night talking about our college life in Egypt and our early bachelor's life in New York. We talked about those past memories till late at night. The funny thing about our talks was we had talked the same things over and over again; there was nothing new in our gossip. We never got tired of them. Mona could never enjoy our talks and never participated and did not complain about it.

From Egypt I had brought three replicas of the boy king, Tutankhamen's, head made of brass that were similar to the one I had sent to Milly. I had figured out that this particular piece of brass was a great gift from Egypt. As I was writing the addresses on the parcels, Mona was watching me.

Mona started asking me questions and teasing me about having three sweethearts and I could not decide whom to marry and that's why I ran away from Cleveland. She asked me when I was going to marry one of those sweethearts. I told her there was no such a thing as sweetheart. She was not ready to accept it. So, I said "OK, you can call them my ex-sweethearts, they are only friends not girlfriends." So, she started asking me if I was really interested in marrying a beautiful Egyptian girl.

Mona always had a great interest in me as a marriageable candidate. She had quite a few cousins who could have been a match for me, according to her. I did not say anything to her. To act dumb was my policy in this matter.

I wondered what the reactions of my friends would be when they received the heads. Probably Rajani would be glad that I remembered him, and the head would always remind him of me. Lynda would be glad and would not give much importance to the 'Head.' In her autobiography I would be one of her many 'Gone with the Wind' affairs. When I was writing Nancy's address, I could not remove her from my eyes. She might get tears in her eyes when she received my gift. She would feel sad that I left. She still might have soft feelings for me. Such a simple girl!

And on Wednesday evening I had a memorable meeting with Milly, which I had told you in the beginning. I met her and her new size, I mean her new version. I liked the new Milly. I was optimistic about our new friendship. I was still wondering what she meant by 'She had changed'.

I wanted to call her on Friday and ask her if she had any specific plans for the weekend. And if not, we would go to see a movie and drive around. On second thought, I wanted to go easy. So, I did not call her on Friday.

I called her on Monday and talked in general. I wanted to ask her for another date and all of sudden I did not know how to ask her. Finally, I gathered all my courage and asked her, "I am looking forward to seeing you again. I enjoyed your company. How about Wednesday, maybe we will go to see Dustin Hoffman's new movie, *Marathon Man?* We will eat some place and will go to see his movie." She agreed and she was anxious to see Dustin Hoffman on the silver screen. I had remembered that he was her favorite actor. On Wednesday, I called her to remind her and to meet at the same spot as last time, in front of Bowery Bank. The movie was going to start at seven o'clock and we did not have enough time to eat leisurely at any restaurant. So, we went to a Greek diner. She had a gyro sandwich on pita bread and I had Souvlaki (Shish Kebab) also on pita bread. And you know I had never before enjoyed Souvlaki as much as I enjoyed it in her company. She was smiling, laughing and was thrilled with the idea of seeing Dustin Hoffman's movie. She told me she liked Dustin Hoffman's acting; "My favorite actor", she had said. I told her that I rented a furnished apartment in Forest Hills. I had not moved in yet. I told her the exact location. She remembered that building.

It was getting late for the movie, we had to walk from 33rd Street to 41st Street on 7th Avenue. And this being a new release, we were expecting to stand in a line to get tickets.

She was engrossed in watching the movie. After the movie we had strawberry cheesecake and coffee in the nearby diner. That's the time she told me, "My life has changed a whole lot. I don't go out at night like I used to, you know what I mean."

Oh, God! I had such a relief to hear those words. It seemed like I was waiting for years for this kind of change in her life. It made me so happy that I kissed her and realized my eyes were wet. "I am happy for you, Milly."

I kissed her good night on her lips when her train came at the subway station. A short sweet kiss! I said "Mesa elkheir, Good night, Milly."

When I was staying with Mokhtar, I used to tell my own made-up stories to Khalid. One evening I was telling him a story about how I went to the moon. I told him that Big Bird was selected to go to the moon. At the last minute he got scared to go.

"No. No. He don't get scared. He must be sick. He was sick last week."

I realized my mistake. You can't say anything bad about any of these Sesame Street or Disney characters. They are heroes for small children.

"Yeah, yeah, now I remember. He was sick that time. Then the American President realized that if either Micky or Big Bird goes to the moon, there will be no show on TV till they come back from the moon. And all the children would feel sad. And they would cry. So, the president sent me to the moon because my name is Micky."

He was looking at me with great surprise and respect.

"How long is the moon?" What he meant was how far away was the moon.

"Oh, it is far far away."

"I know it is more than Egypt."

"Oh it is far, far, more than Egypt." I had a problem of explaining to him the distance. So, I said, "It took us one week to reach there."

"How long is one week?"

"Seven days."

"Seven full days." He could not imagine what a seven-day period was. He said, "I know it takes one day to go to Egypt. Uncle Micky, did you drive the rocket?"

"Oh yes I was the captain. We were three pilots. I was the chief. They called me Captain Micky."

Khalid asked me how long did we stay on the moon? Was I scared? Was there a monster on the moon? And I answered him to his imagination. He started feeling very proud of me.

"There was a big, very big, monster on the moon."

"You killed him?"

"Oh, yes. I had taken a big sword from Egypt. I killed that big monster with that big sword from Egypt."

Some company had put out a TV commercial that showed a man walking on the moon. I told him that was me. Thereafter, whenever that commercial was being played, he would yell, "That is Uncle Micky," and would call Mona to watch the commercial. And she had to come to watch the commercial. Mokhtar and Mona were amused to listen to my stories through Khalid.

Khalid asked me, "Do you like Halawah, Uncle Micky?"

"Yes, I like Halawah."

"How much?"

"Oh, a lot. Very much."

He spread both his arms and asked me, "This much?"

"Yes, that much. Do you like Halawah?"

"Yes. I like it this much too."

He spread his arms again. And then he went into the kitchen and told Mona, "Mommy, Mommy, Uncle Micky likes Halawah very much, this much. Will you make Halawah for Uncle Micky every day?"

And Khalid insisted on Halawah every day and ate it every day with great interest. I lost interest in eating it after a few days. Khalid would tell me to eat it every night during the supper. And I ate it every night happily. He was afraid if I did not eat it any day, his mom would stop making it. Anyway, I enjoyed it for him.

The following Sunday evening I moved to my new apartment. I didn't have to make two or three trips to get my things from the car as I had done when I moved to the Forest Hill apartment about three years ago, and this time I didn't meet any girl like Milly. I pictured distinctly the whole scene that happened when I first met Milly and her big size and that innocent smile on her moon-like face. And that memory pleased me like a feather moving over my face. I smiled to myself. The world had changed since then.

When I opened the door of my apartment with all my belongings and with Mokhtar, Mona, and Khalid, I thought of opening a door to my new life and the happiness I was searching for. I prayed to Allah to let these things come true. And my thoughts revolved around Milly.

It was not going to be a champagne apartment-warming party.

Mokhtar had quit drinking when Mona joined him.

The first thing I did was take the color TV I had bought last week from its box and connect the TV to the apartment antenna socket and put it on so Khalid could watch it and wouldn't feel bored. Mona inspected the kitchen cabinets and approved the whole apartment as a good one. She prepared three cups of tea (Mona had bought a box of tea bags and milk for me from home) and served 'Halawah,' which she had brought with her to celebrate my new apartment as a sort of good luck. We started chitchatting. Khalid, who had watched TV for a while, had started running around the apartment by this time. In a few minutes, we heard a thud on the floor. That was a warning from the apartment down below my apartment to stop the running. Khalid got scared and stopped running and started watching TV.

After they left, I was alone. I already had supper with Mokhtar at his place. I watched TV for a while and started feeling bored. I had decided not to go to the race track too often as before; at least I did not want to go there that day. I felt like drinking a beer, so, I went to the small delicatessen-cum-grocery store at the corner. I could not buy beer there because it was Sunday and beer sales were prohibited in New York State on Sundays.

I came back and started watching TV. But my mind was mostly thinking of her. When I went to bed, I was almost mesmerized by her thoughts, thinking of her in a bright yellow satin dress, my favorite color. She looked sexy. And I realized that in a small corner of my heart I had started loving her. I wished I had sweet dreams of Milly that night and every night. The next morning, I realized I didn't dream of Milly. Oh, poor Said!

The next Monday I called her at home in the evening to ask for a dinner and Broadway show on Wednesday. She agreed and sounded thrilled on the telephone.

"How was your weekend, Milly?"

She told me that she did her laundry and grocery shopping on Saturday morning. In the evening she went to see Julie. Both of them went to Coney Island and enjoyed rides including the big cyclone. Julie's husband went to bar with his friends.

"I was all alone on Sunday. I went down to Sheepshead Bay and bought two pounds of mussels for just fifty cents. I baked them and ate them all by myself. There was nobody with me to share. I was all alone."

"Oh, you could have called me."

"Do you like mussels?"

"I never ate them before. I am sure I would have liked them."

"How do you know for sure?"

"Well, if I would have not, I would have enjoyed watching you enjoy them."

"Cute."

I thought of reserving tickets for *My Fair Lady.* I called for the reservations. The show for Wednesday was almost sold out except the last few rows in the mezzanine, and I certainly did not want to see the play from the last row. Other plays on Broadway were Neil Simon's *California Suite, Debbie, Godspell, Guys and Dolls, Pirates of Penzance, Oh! Calcutta,* etc., most of them were musical and all of them were hits. So, there would be the same story of getting the tickets. The only chance to get tickets for almost any play would be to go to the 'Tickets' on Broadway around 43rd Street, where they sold canceled and unsold tickets on the day of the play and that too at half price. I would have to take off from the office for one hour and would have to take the subway to go to midtown.

I called her on Wednesday morning to tell her where to meet.

"What play are we going to enjoy?"

"Well, that is going to be a big surprise." In reality it was going to be one.

"So, you have surprises too."

"I guess so?"

On Wednesday, I drove my car to Manhattan in the morning to work. So, I could drop her in Brooklyn after the play. I had already told her about it.

In the evening, by the time I drove from downtown to midtown through stop-and-go traffic and found a parking lot in the Broadway district, it was close to six o'clock. We met near the Chemical Allied building in Times Square. She was waiting for me.

"What is the surprise?"

"Can't you keep it that way?"

"No, my dear."

"We will meet the lady."

"Oh, my my! That is the one I really wanted to see for a long time. I am absolutely thrilled. Thanks, dear." And she kissed my cheek and then wiped the lipstick from my cheek with her hand.

She knew some family-run Armenian restaurant on 47th between 8th and 9th Avenues. It was a small restaurant a few steps below the street level with about ten tables, old-style furniture, handmade embroidered napkins and table settings, and sterling silver cutlery.

"I love the cucumber soup they make. The food is authentic Armenian. It is good. You will enjoy it. One of my boyfriends brought me here."

We had a glass of pinot grigio. We ordered Armenian specialties. She was thrilled when she got the soup. After she ate some, she asked me to taste it. It was shredded cucumber with buttermilk with a few spices.

"Oh, God, you call it a soup. My mother used to make it almost every week as a salad and she used to put different spices and it was really tasty." Anyway, she enjoyed it.

"Hey, Said, I forgot to tell you good news. I learned the most thrilling thing of my life."

"What is it?"

"I learnt swimming last winter. I was damn scared of water before that. Me and my friend Julie took lessons at the Y."

"Where?" I interrupted.

"At the YMCA. Julie got married two months ago. I am very happy for her."

"That's good news."

"I forgot to tell you some bad news. Do you remember the old ladies in our building used to meet in the lobby for gossip? One of them died a few months after you left. The one who mostly used to wear red or pink clothes in summer and green in winter. Do you remember her?"

"No, I don't."

"One day while riding the elevator, she collapsed. She was rushed to Long Island Jewish Hospital. She had a heart attack. This happened on Saturday. I visited her on Tuesday. She was stable and scheduled for surgery on Saturday. She looked good and talked to me. She had motherly advice for me. She said, 'Milly, you are such a nice young girl. Put your life on track.' I told her, 'I am trying.' She said, 'God bless you.' She had a massive heart attack on Friday and she died. I went for her wake."

We had orchestra seats in the eighth row. I thought that nothing could have been better than this. We had a glass of pinot grigio during the interval from the theater bar.

The play finished at half past eleven. By the time I got my car from the parking lot and reached Brooklyn to Milly's apartment building, it was half past twelve. She invited me for a cup of coffee, which I was thinking of declining saying, 'It is already late. I will make it some other time.' The second thought, I realized, she would feel sad if I declined, so I accepted.

Her apartment was on third floor. The entrance was in the living room as usual. The living room had a dining area and the whole place was pretty large and was painted in mint color. There was an old couch and a love seat, and a coffee table, TV set and three-in-one compact stereo set were in one corner. The floor was carpeted except the dining area had linoleum. She had a small dinette set with four chairs. All the furniture was old. On the wall, in the front of the couch, was a beautiful picture of two horses that was eye-catchy. The picture must have been five feet by three feet. I went close to look at it. You won't believe it. That picture was extremely beautiful. It was hand embroidered. The horses were in a playful mood. One was full brown with a white spot on the head and all legs half white from knee down; the other one was white with all legs half black and black spots on his head and black ears. The white one was in front and hiding the brown one. The brown horse was running ahead and only half of him was hidden. The picture was very realistic. The grass was embroidered with long woolen threads like a short shag carpet. The blue sky and a few white-black clouds were done with non-shiny threads. A kind of shiny material was used for the horses. And different types of stitches were used for different parts of the horses. For example, the tails, the eyes, the mane, and the hoofs. Their eyes were extra shiny. Everything was done artistically and with great care. The whole combination was creating a wonderful effect and liveliness as if those horses were going to jump out of the picture.

"It's wonderful work of art. Must have cost you fortune to buy it?"

"I did it myself."

"I can't believe it. I mean I do believe you did it. It is unbelievably beautiful. Oh, Milly you are such a fantastic artist." And naturally I kissed her cheek.

"Well, I bought the picture already traced on the jute cloth. I selected different fibers than they had suggested and chose the different stitches. My brother and my friend Julie Anne gave me some money as a gift for my new apartment. I bought this picture from that money. It took me four months to complete it. My brother framed it for me."

"Milly, you are simply great."

On the wall right above the couch was a blown-up black-and-white picture of a sweet-smiling baby girl.

"Oh, how cute you look as a baby."

"How do you know that it's my picture?"

"Well, well, that ghost in that corner told me. Am I wrong?" And I blinked my right eye.

"No, smarty, how could you be wrong?"

I had a guided tour of the apartment. "This is my bedroom. That's the kitchen and there is the bathroom. I painted the whole apartment after I moved in."

The bedroom was light pink and the windows had white curtains with pink flower design.

"This is my buddy. I had him since childhood. He is never rude to me, never answers me back, and only listens to all kinds of my talks. He knows all my secrets and my feelings." She lifted him from the bed where he was sitting. She hugged him. "His name is Georgy. Isn't he cute?" And she kissed him. That was a cute teddy bear about two feet tall. There on the wall was a narrow, long, and horizontal Chinese painting painted on black silk cloth, mounted on a board but not framed. That was hung above the bed.

A few cosmetics were neatly arranged and a couple of photographs were placed on the dresser. "That is my brother, Bill, and his wife, Susan, when they got married. And that is his whole family a few years ago." In another frame a birthday card was framed. On half of the card a usual happy birthday wish was printed. On the other half, some prose was written. I read it.

'THE HAPPIEST MOMENT

It may not be as simple as it says.
At least you can try to smile,
When you first open your eyes in the morning.
Anything bad can happen in the day ahead.
And that is why it makes the happiest moment of a day,
When you first wake up.
Welcome to that moment with a smile.
----Amit'

"Amit, what kind of a strange name is that?"
"I don't know, I never thought of it. Is it Arabic?"
"No way, Miss MO."
"My father gave me that birthday card. It has really helped me through my life. I always tried to keep happy in the morning. Sometimes it simply does not work."

Afterward, when I went to the bathroom, I was literally shocked. It was painted with a shocking pink, sort of burnt-pink color. I thought one would not spend more time there than needed, at least because of that color. I mean it was shocking. As soon as I came out, she asked me, "Did you like that color?"

"I was not going to comment on that. It is dark pink, an unusual shade and rather shocking."

"I liked the sampling spot on the paint can and I had selected that for my bedroom and the bathroom. When I tried it on the bathroom, I was totally shocked. The sampling color really deceived me. At least thank God I didn't try it first in the bedroom. Doesn't it help you to get out of the place quickly?" I knew she had a good sense of colors.

She made an espresso coffee with foamed half and half. She did not have small cups for espresso. So, she served it in regular mugs.

"It tastes better with an Irish whisky." She brought a small, un-opened bottle of Irish whisky and gave it to me to open. I had never tasted espresso with whisky. I liked it. It was fantastic.

I felt happy that I did not decline her invitation for coffee. She must have planned for espresso and especially with whisky, and she had to buy a bottle especially for this. If I had declined, she would have felt sad.

Before departing, I kissed her, holding her in my arms. She also put her arms around me. It was a long kiss. "I love you, Milly." I could not believe myself. Those words just escaped from my lips. I did not want to say that so soon. But those were my true feelings.

Once Milly was telling me about her boyfriend. "I had a boy-friend; he would always order food for me when we went out in restaurants. He even would select my dress for me if he came to pick me up at my apartment. He would come early so that he would pick my dress for that evening. It pleased me in the beginning. Then I thought he was bit cuckoo.

"Anyway, next Saturday I will treat you to a German restaurant in our area. Their sauerbraten is scrumptious."

And it was really tasty food when I tasted it on the following Saturday. Many entrees on the menu were pork dishes. Muslims do not eat pork for hygienic reasons. I told her. Both of us selected sau-erbraten. We shared black forest bread pudding. She felt happy to pay the check.

After the dinner, we went to her apartment for ice cream, a

nightcap, and coffee. She played the old records she had and we talked a lot about our school days. She told me how they used to play 'Complete the square' game with red and blue pencil in the school and how one of them would cheat and they would fight, pulling each other's hair. I told her how I discovered Helen on the soccer field. She was thrilled and felt proud of me.

She played records from *The Sound of Music*. I had this record with me and my stereo system was better than hers. The songs I shared in her company that evening felt heavenly sweet. The songs were touching my heart.

"I will make some coffee for you."

"I would like to have 'Finjan chai,' if you don't mind."

"What is that?"

"A cup of tea."

"Oh, I am sorry. I forgot to buy tea."

I enjoyed the coffee she made. I kissed her and wished her sweet dreams before I left.

When I came home, I was in a dreamland with Helen, romancing in the past with the sweet moments we spent together on the bank of the Nile. Those tunes of flute floating on the breeze started ringing in my ears. I wished Helen was with me at this moment. I wished her happiness in life. At least I could do that much.

Milly invited me for dinner at her place. Her invitation was almost two weeks ahead of time. I had asked her, "Are you going to make cooking experiments on me?" and she said, "I don't have to do experiments now, Said, I had done enough of them when I was in Forest Hills." I told her about Lynda's cooking experiments. She reminded me about the dinner a few times, "In case if you forget and go to meet your friends. It never happened before. It might happen now."

She was happy to see me. I was not late. She was ready and waiting for me. She gave me one of her special big smiles. She had a beautiful satin dress, light blue color with little flowers of a darker blue shade. I said, "First thing first, may I kiss you hello!" and I kissed her.

"How sweet and romantic!" she said.

"I like your dress. It's beautiful."

"Isn't it? I picked it at Macy's last week. They had it on sale for just ten dollars. It is a steal for that price."

"I think it is fantastic. And it looks pretty on you."

"Thanks. And thank you, Said, for the flowers. Hey, I like your shirt." She touched it.

"What is it?"

"Silk, pure silk."

I was wearing the Indian silk shirt with colorful floral design on it, the one Rajani Patel's wife, Sonali, bought from India. It was beautiful as a casual shirt.

I gave her a gift-wrapped box.

"What is there in the box?"

"Well, I gave it to you. It is yours now. You are at liberty to open it now or not to open it for the next twenty years. Be careful whenever you open it."

"Shut up, you mean."

When it came to think of what I should take for her, I was involved in a debate with myself. My first thought was a bottle of white wine and a bouquet of flowers. It was a firm idea for a few days. The last few days I thought of the lady's Indian dress Sonali had brought for me.

She opened the box. The Indian dress was there. "This is the similar fabric as your shirt." She touched the silk and she liked the smoothness. She was excited to wear it. Within a few minutes, she was wearing it. It fitted her well. She looked cute. She kissed me thanks. And then we kept on kissing like that for some time, putting arms around each other. I did not remember how long we stood like that. The time had stopped for me. The next thing I remembered, we were in the bed, my lips were tasting the cherries of her lips and my hands were exploring and conquering valleys and peaks of her body. And I realized she had legs, oh, I meant beautiful legs, smooth, white like the stalk of a banana tree.

"'Gamila,' Beautiful, you are beautiful, Milly."

Her body was made of different roses, white, pink, peach, red, burgundy. Have you seen 'Midnight rose?' I had. That was also there.

"You are made of roses." She smiled sweetly, hugged me, kissed me. She liked my calling her roses.

I was moving my fingers through her straight, soft, silky light brown hair and yeah, her hair was like dried oak leaf. I enjoyed playing with her hair so as she, I thought.

I was enjoying the softness of her body kissing all over softly. I was caring for her feelings and her pleasures. It was a new feeling I had not experienced before. She was enjoying. I felt so.

We made love for the first time. Her only comment was, "I like the way you kiss," and she laughed.

Wasn't that late? I mean for love making? Maybe yes, according to Lynda, it was a disaster. Well, if I would have not done it with Lynda at the right time, she might have thought of something else and must have left after a few meetings. I myself did not know what the American standard was for this course of action. Things did not work well with Lynda and Nancy. We were not made for each other, I guess. Milly and I went out so many times. I mean I had so many opportunities of making love to her. I had never made any progress beyond kissing and petting. I wanted to make sure that the relationship could be developed between us and the love-making should come naturally. I just did not want to act like an animal, the kind of people she might have met in her life at those night places. I did not want her to think I was also like one of them. That's right, she had told me that she had changed and she had stopped going out at night, which was true.

I was happy that she enjoyed love making.

She offered me my favorite, Wild Turkey. Matter of fact, she had bought a new bottle for me. She had a Bloody Mary.

The first course was salad, made with different kinds of greens, pieces of different cheeses, and walnuts. The salad dressing was her mother's special recipe. She had cooked sweet-and-sour lamb chops in pineapple, delicious Spanish rice with spinach and fresh baked string beans. And she had baked fresh bread with split grains and mild spices in it. "This is a result of my cooking experiments when I was in Forest Hills." I still accept that it is an art to cook. Even to cook good rice needs a lot of skill. Every dish was fantastic. I must say she was a good cook.

"How do you like my cooking?"

"It is fantastic."

"Do you mean it's not good?"

"It is extremely good. I loved those lamb chops. They were out of this world."

She was happy to see me eating with so much interest. She kept looking at me eating, rather than eating herself. After a while she asked me, "Do you really like my cooking?"

"Oh, sure. Why? You are not ready to believe it."

We enjoyed every moment of that evening.

We made love again when she was making coffee. Poor coffee was never made.

I called Milly. She had come home by that time.

"Milly, it is me. I received a telegram my brother had sent. My mother died two days ago."

"Oh, my god. I am so sorry. I will come to see you."

She came in an hour. As soon as she came in, just looking at my sad face, she started crying. She hugged me.

"I am really sorry to hear about your mother." She walked me to a sofa and we sat down.

"She was not keeping good health lately. I did not expect something like this. She was crying for the last two days when I left Egypt in April as if she knew that it was our last meeting."

I started weeping and could not speak for a while. "She was the only person who really understood me. I remember when my year-older brother downed. It was a great loss for her. She understood that it was my big loss too. My brother and I were very close. We did all the things together and shared everything. When the news came of my brother drowning, she hugged me and both of us cried." Milly was holding me in her arms close to her chest.

"She was the only one who supported me after my divorce. She understood my circumstances. All others in my family and elderly close family friends considered me a crazy person. She would have loved you as her own daughter. When I left Egypt for good, she was sad but at the same time she was happy that it was a good decision and I would be happy in America."

Milly was holding me for a long time. After a while she got up and prepared a peanut-butter-and-jelly sandwich for both of us. She stayed the whole night with me.

The next time, I asked her for dinner. "This time I am going to cook myself, hot and spicy Egyptian food and treat you at my home. Would you mind trying my cooking? I am not really a bad cook and I am sure hot food won't kill you."

On that she made fun of my cooking and said, "I am not so sure and I am not looking forward to die. I might enjoy it. At least I will give a try with open mind." Finally, we agreed on Saturday for a dinner.

I had prepared all Egyptian dishes. For appetizer I had Hummus bi Tahini (chickpea dip) with pita bread, then Shourabit Adas (lentil soup). Salad was Salatet Lubi, which is green bean salad. Main dish was Laham Mah Khodra, which is lamb vegetable casserole. Vegetable was Bamyi (okra). Basically, all the preparations were spicy Arabic style. Milly was enjoying them.

"How do you like Egyptian food and my cooking?"

"Oh, it is scrumptious. I love it. It is really spicy and too hot for me." I gave her a glass of sweetened buttermilk, Sonali's quick remedy. I had already bought buttermilk in case she would need to soothe her stomach.

And I asked her exact meaning of 'Scrumptious' while she was still eating. She started explaining to me and she choked that brought tears to her eyes. I told her to look at the ceiling that comforted her a bit. She drank water. She was miserable for a while.

After dinner we were sitting very close hand in hand, talking on different issues and to my surprise she opened totally different topic. She took her hand from my hand. She moved away from me.

"Don't you want to know about my first marriage and divorce?"

"I remember you telling me you are a widow. I do not care to know but would be interested to know if you tell me."

"That is right, I am a widow. I had started divorce proceedings before he died. He was a dirty sex maniac, a weird and lazy man without any ambition. We did not have much sex before marriage. He had finished his military service in Vietnam. He had joined engineering college and was working a part-time job when we got married. Then he took the full-time clerical job and stopped going to college. He was totally weird. While love-making once, he wanted anal sex. I refused. Then he squeezed my breasts. I was in pain then he squeezed my neck so hard I was choking. He was a different person. He was saying 'All the c**ts are witches from the hell.' Somehow, I kicked him in the back. That made him release his hands. Then he started slapping me. I got away from him. Then he started crying. He did not realize what he had done. I was so confused and scared. The next day I told him to see a psychologist. He refused my suggestion. Then he behaved normal. After that he started going out with his friends at least twice a week after work and would come home late and drunk. He used to drink beer. It was clear to me that he loved his friends more than me to stay home in the evenings. One night he peed in the bed, he was so drunk he did not even wake up; he slept like a log. I had to clean the bed. A few months later it happened again, he squeezed my neck. I had kept a rolling pin under the bed. I could not get to it. I managed to punch him in his stomach hard. He was hurt. He fell from the bed. I got out of the bed and I hit him in the head with the rolling pin. Before he could get up, I collected my wallet, apartment keys, and my shoes. I ran out of the apartment and closed the door." She looked scared as if she was reliving the past scene. I was sitting next to her. I got closer to her and put my arm around her.

"I went to Julie to stay. Next day I came to my apartment with Julie in the afternoon, took my belongings, my saved money, and wrote a note that I was starting divorce proceedings. After that he called me in the office a few times begging me to come back. He never agreed to seek professional help. He always said that nothing was wrong with him. I told my mother and brother how Richie acted. It was difficult for me to convince my mother because she liked him. She always thought, most of the times I made mistakes. This time she believed me. Both supported my divorce. A few months later, while overtaking a bus in the daytime, he had a head-on collision with an oncoming car. He was drunk and speeding. He was in a coma, never woke up, and died after three days. His family blamed me for his death." Milly was furious.

"I am glad it was over quickly. Where did you meet this guy?"

"At Brooklyn College. I was taking accounting classes. I was looking at my final year results at the college bulletin board. I had passed with 3.6 grade average. I was happy. Somebody was standing behind me. He said 'Congratulations' to me. I looked behind at a well-built young man. He extended his hand to greet me. He asked, 'Where is your name on the board?' I showed him. He said my name, 'Milly O'Mara. You got a good score; congratulations again, Milly. My name is Richie Weber. I finished my military assignment recently. I was in Vietnam. I am thinking of joining the engineering school this summer. I know this is a good college. I am trying to get into Brooklyn Poly. I have a good chance because of my military service. I like you. Can we meet again? I shall call you.' We exchanged phone numbers. We started dating. He joined the Polytechnic. I was happy that he was going to be an engineer. My mother was impressed that he had joined engineering college. I liked him. He was a nice and happy guy. Everything just changed after our marriage beyond belief." She was mad and disgusted.

"After Richie's death, my mother, brother, and Julie were happy that I was out of my mess sooner than anyone expected. They all congratulated me and advised me to make my marriage a history and look forward to a new life.

"Going through the divorce affected my job. After my Associate's Degree, I was hired as a trainee accountant. I learned lots of new things in a short time. I was given a junior accountant's position within a year. They gave me good raises. After I was married to Richie, all my marriage trouble started soon and then I began divorce proceedings, and I could not concentrate on my job. My performance deteriorated. My boss warned me. I told him all my family troubles and divorce proceedings. He was sympathetic to me and instead of firing me, he offered me a secretarial job at a lower pay. He promised to give me back the accountant's job if I could get out of my situation. I didn't feel that it was possible for me to find another accounting job and hold it. So, I had to accept the job he offered me.

"My boss told my situation to my office people. They were sympathetic and helpful to me. My colleagues would advise me how to look attractive and how to look for a boyfriend. I used to stay away from those highly educated people. I only talked to people like clerks, messengers, departmental aides and not those highly educated class. I kept a distance from office secretaries. Most of them were married and they had different topics to gossip about." Now she was relaxed

I assured her, "Milly, I am with you now." I hugged and kissed her. She hugged me and put her head on my shoulder. We stayed like that for a few minutes. Then she released me and wiped tears from her eyes.

"Mil, can we make life together?"

"I am not ready, yet."

She felt good that she told me all these things. She was relaxed and happy. It was too late by the time we finished dessert and a nightcap. I drove her to Brooklyn.

The next Saturday we decided to go for a drive and spend the day in the Pocono Mountains. When I arrived at her apartment building, she was waiting for me. I was late. "When I stepped outside my apartment building, some rascal had spilled car oil on the pavement. I was stupid not to see it as my eyes were looking at the sky. The sky started getting cloudy. I slipped over and fell in the oil pool. My pants and shirt were spoiled and I had to change." I was not making false excuse for coming late.

"Are you, all right? Did you get hurt?"

"Nothing happened to me. I am strong like steel." I jumped on my toes, spreading my legs, and clapped my hands, holding them straight above my head. I did it a few times. She said, "Oh boy, steel is soft like Said."

In New Jersey, we stopped at a rest area for a coffee break.

"Milly, would you like to drive my car?"

"I wouldn't mind. Are you sleepy?"

"No. I thought maybe you would enjoy driving on such a beautiful highway."

"Oh, I would, I guess. I would enjoy driving your expensive machine. You even did not ask me if I knew how to drive."

"Well, I figured you must."

"Good guess. A lot of New Yorkers don't drive. Do you trust my driving?"

"Yes, miss, I do."

"I learned to drive after I was married. My ex insisted that I must know driving. He also wanted me to learn swimming. I was too scared. My brother always told me to learn to drive but my mother never allowed me. She said if I started driving, she would have a heart attack. That's it. Now sometimes I drive her car and she not only sleeps but snores. Isn't it interesting?"

I just nodded my head (typical of me) and handed her the key. She was fully concentrating on driving and was driving a few miles less than the posted speed limit. She was very cautious and careful. I liked her driving.

"Oh, look at that sick car. It needs a doctor."

"Oh, Milly, Milly, look at that son-in-law of Uncle Sam giving a ticket to a young blonde. I bet he must be a sadist enjoying ..."

"You shut up, Said. Please. Don't talk to me. I am not an expert driver. I need concentration."

"I am sorry, miss." I kept quiet after that.

After rejecting my persistent invitations, of course her excuses were legitimate. I neither challenged them nor argued about them.

Finally, she accepted this one, a simple invitation from a simple guy like me to my sweetheart.

I had asked her many times to come to my office, we would have a nice walk in Battery Park and for the walk she would have a special imaginary red-carpet treatment from me. Then we would have dinner at the 'Windows on the World' on the hundred and seventh floor of the World Trade Center overlooking the Hudson and the Statue of Liberty, and the New York skyline and seagulls and sailboats and sweet Milly. Of course, sweet Milly was going to be strictly my pleasure.

My secretary in those days was an ordinary-looking girl with a face that had no expression and no smile. One thing that was happy about her was that she had a boyfriend, so usually she never was in a cranky mood. She had a framed picture of both of them on her desk. Surprisingly this boy was really good looking, quite handsome. One of my colleagues mentioned to me that there was a different boy in the picture last year and that boy was much more compatible with her looks. Since I saw her for the first time, I prayed to Allah, 'Please, make her a little more charming.'

I did not expect Milly to arrive before five. At 4:30 our receptionist called me. "There is a sweet lady, and she wants to see you. Come at once." Our receptionist was a middle-aged, happily married lady. I was wondering who that could be. Milly? Then she was half an hour early.

And it was her. She was talking with our receptionist. Oh, my! She looked adorable dressed in a beautiful pink dress. She gave me a big smile.

"I did not know you were going to wear a pink dress. I would have put on a matching pink suit."

"I have never seen a pink suit. It must be from Egypt. Right?"

"No. I don't have one yet. I would have home dyed my beige colored suit."

I was sure she would have said 'Dumbbell.' By this time, we were right in front of my secretary, Michelle, who was busy with her makeup, time to go home.

I introduced Milly to Michelle. They had a little talk. Then she came in my office.

"Please, be my guest and sit down, Milly. Be comfortable. This is my desk. This is my chair and this is my office. And this is me and my body and a dumbbell brain in my head there. This is my telephone that listens to your every word and doesn't keep any secret between us."

"You said you like your secretary and she is beautiful, you said."

"Oh, yeah. I like her. She is good looking and charming. Isn't she? She talks nice. She is like a doll."

"Oh, I see that."

"Did you see that sheet of plastic under her chair? I always wish that should have been a mirror."

"I will kill you, Said."

"All right. It is OK with me." And I made a funny face. She pinched my cheek hard. Then she kissed my forehead and my cheek.

We strolled through Battery Park hand in hand. Then we took the Staten Island ferry, got down there and walked around and got into the next ferry back to Manhattan. The whole round-trip ferry cost us only ten cents each. She had never taken that ferry before. We were moving all over the ferry from one end to the other. Afterwards we absolutely enjoyed the dinner at the 'Windows on the World.' She was happy.

Once we were going to see a play. She was asking me what she should wear. We were talking on the telephone from the office. It was lunchtime. My office was deserted and I had all the freedom in the world to talk freely on the phone.

I said to her, "Nothing, absolutely nothing. You know in your birth-dress you look gorgeous, beautiful. You don't need to wear anything." She busted out in laughter at the other end.

"You, naughty boy!"

I started describing her:

"My words are mute to sing your song.
My thoughts are young and the feelings strong.
I see your eyes, sea deep and bright
that shoot arrows with delight,
that turns purple hearts white.
Your smile is like a sprite.

My words are mute and the thoughts are strong
But my words are not wrong.

Have you seen a stock of a banana tree?
Those are your legs when fabric free.
Cherries are your lips, and you are a fairy.
To my song will you be merry?"

"Hey, hey, Mr. Poet in Disguise. Oh, you, naughty boy." She was trying to stop me. And I was not stopping.

"My words are shy to sing your song,
and my young thoughts went agog.

What are you hiding in there at the top?
Two white doves with red beaks apop.
Or two snow-white balls with roses on top.
Anyone looking at them is going to hop."

Finally, she succeeded in tricking me by saying she heard some-one's footsteps through the telephone; it could be my boss. So, I had to stop. The lines I could not finish, were:

"The moon will sigh.
The flowers will be shy.
When they talk of beauty
They will choose you their deity.
My words are truly mute to sing your beauty."

Yes, she was beautiful and my heartthrob, the queen of my heart? Yes, for sure, she was, beautiful!

I was playing with her silky soft hair. That became my hobby. In a few moments I was tracing a contour of her head. Something made me look through her hair and for sure there was a scar about two inches long on the back of her head.

"What is it, Milly?" I was tracing it as I was looking at it.

"It is a scar."

"I mean how did you get it?"

"Oh, that is a slight bang from my school days. When we moved to Brooklyn." And she stopped; she did not want to tell me whatever the story was!

"And what happened?"

"Nothing."

"Oh, you mean somebody cursed you and you got a scar."

"I do not want to talk about it."

"All right!"

I did not press. The whole thing made her a little upset. I ran my fingers around her belly button and on the sides of her tummy. She was ticklish. Her upset mood just vanished in a moment. And then we continued our romance.

She told me the story of the scar on her head after a week without me asking her.

"I was born in New Jersey. We lived in Roselle at that time. My parents owned a house. We moved to Brooklyn when I was ten years old. My father had a hardware store in Elizabeth.

"I went to public school in Brooklyn. I was in the fourth grade at that time. We had a gym class. When I came back from gym, I opened my locker and a frog jumped on my face. With a scream I fell on my back and hit my head on a bench. I still remember the girls watching me broke into laughter. I passed out. This scar on my head is the memory of that horrible joke those girls played on me. The girls who did it to me got a big punishment. The girls in my class would giggle at me for quite some time after that. I never felt comfortable with my classmates. They would make fun of me at every chance in the beginning. Then after a while they became friendly."

She was all upset with those memories.

"I am sorry for you." She did not say anything. It was getting late, I did not want to leave her in that mood.

"Where did you learn that nice cooking, Milly?"

"I picked it up on my own. In the beginning, I went through cookbooks. I am glad you enjoyed it." She was treating me again at her place.

I made coffee for her and tea for me.

CHAPTER NINE

The last Saturday of July we had our picnic, our annual event. Would you believe me that all my friends used to wait for this awesome event right from the beginning of the winter? I mean during the winter every one of us used to talk about the summer and by remembering our picnic which used to help us forget the winter. Everyone was looking forward to the picnic. I was back in New York. Mokhtar had decided to move to Houston soon and he had started seriously looking for a job there. So, he might not be here next year. Of course, I did not miss last year's picnic as I had flown from Cleveland just for the picnic. No one ever talked about changing the place other than Jones Beach after our one picnic in New Jersey. Well, we had a lot of fun as usual. Ladies were always aggressive in teasing me and as usual all enjoyed making fun of me for staying single and suggesting me various eligible friends and relatives. And they even brought their photos and showed me every time I met them. This time it was not different. After they enjoyed teasing me, I told them that I may not stay single for a long time. So, they started picking my brain for my secrets. Rehana took the major share of asking me questions and teasing me. "See how he enjoyed our teasing and now he is telling that he found a girl." Their tone indicated that they were disappointed to learn that she was a white American Christian and not from an Arab country and not a Muslim. Now they all wanted to meet her.

After the picnic I went to New Jersey with Karim and Nafisa to spend the remainder of the weekend.

And Milly? She was going to spend the weekend with Julie. Her husband was travelling. She told me that they would go to the beach both the days and she would match the color of my skin.

On Monday morning I called her "Good morning, Milly dear."

"Oh hi, Said, how was your weekend?"

"Terrific we had a really terrific picnic and after the picnic I went to Karim's as I had told you. How was your weekend? Did you get a nice tan? Can you beat me?"

"You have to see me first and then you tell me. My weekend was also terrific. We had tons of fun at the beach. We ate raw clams at Coney Island and baked mussels at home."

"Oh raw clams, that's yucky."

"Oh, no! Said they are just yummy."

"Well, well, I wouldn't dare to eat them. Anyway, are you doing anything special during lunch?"

"No, I will have a bite if I feel hungry or just walk around in the heat. Why?"

"I have something for you. I would like to see you during lunchtime. I think we shall have a quick lunch together. How about that?"

"Oh, no."

"Why? Why not?"

"Ha ha. Just no real reason. I will be late for work."

"Oh, I know, you want a special invitation, I see that. OK, here is my special invitation for you, Oh, my darling, honey bunch, dear darling Milly, oh, my Lily, would you do a favor to a poor boy named Said?"

"Oh, my dear poor boy, 'Mr. did say,' that's enough of your invitation. I accept it. Where would you like to go?"

"Some good restaurant in your area?"

"You will be late for work."

"Oh, come on; don't worry about it. I think we shall go to 'Funoochie's.' Is that all right with you?" She agreed.

We met at the restaurant. "Oh, you got such a terrific tan. You sure beat me."

We compared our skin colors by touching our hands. Her skin color was brown mixed with red. Mine was just brown. And I spotted a white circular spot on her right hand. It was a pencil size. I touched the spot with my figure. I looked at her face with a question mark on my face. "It is incense burn, a childhood punishment. I was four then. It shows when I get tan." She became serious for a few seconds. I kissed the spot.

I gave her a bunch of roses I had brought from Karim's garden, along with a handwritten 'Love you' card. She tore the wrapping paper I had put around it.

'The flowers I brought you
may not have fragrance you like,
nor nice colors and shapes.
They may not be beautiful as you wanted.

They may not be your favorite ones,
Nor they bring sweet memories.
They are delicate and beautiful, I think.
But will fade, if you don't care for them.

I wish you accept them the way they are.
Just because I picked them,
Thinking of you all the time,
With my heart filled with love for you.

From the hurting heart.

"Your song is wonderful and these flowers are beautiful. I liked them. Thank you very much." And she kissed the flowers and then me.

"You are always welcome. These are from Karim's garden."

I was watching her face and looking into her eyes. She was trying to avoid meeting my eyes. Her face grew serious and a little tense for a moment. Something I said she didn't like or maybe she recalled some old memories. Within a few seconds, she recovered and a smile appeared on her face. She met my eyes.

"It's nice of you Said. Thank you so much. I still remember you giving me roses from your friend's garden when we were staying in Forest Hills. I love roses."

"And you will have your own rose garden, right?"

"I don't know that."

"Somebody just like a flower gives me pleasure, just by being there."

"What did you say?"

I repeated.

"Are you talking about me?" Milly asked.

"No, no, not at all. I was talking about a ghost that is sitting on this table right in between Milly and Said."

"Anyway, thanks a lot."

And, where was I?

I was lost in watching Milly's face, so innocent like a flower and happy like the moon.

"Are you a poet?"

"No. I am not. A poet Said died a long time ago. I am just his ghost. Now you need an escort to carry these flowers to the office. I mean just open like this in your hand. You know I have a good suggestion, you carry these flowers in your hand and I will carry a sign saying, 'NUKE KILLS FLOWERS. NO NUKE.' And I am sure by the time we reach your office we will have a procession of ten people with us."

"It is sure a funny idea. But people are not that stupid."

"Who knows? Maybe or maybe not."

"You know one of my friends from the engineering college was an expert in spreading rumors. He would start by saying something like, 'This is a top secret. Don't tell anyone. You promise? Our professor of mechanics is going to marry a secretary from the science college and she would be his third wife. I learned it from a very confidential source. I am just telling you because you are my buddy. Please, don't tell it to anyone.' And for sure the rumor would spread the fastest way you could imagine. It was a lot of fun to kill the dull life of the engineering college."

"I am enjoying your stories. I am late. Please, let me go back to the office. Thanks for the flowers and the lunch, and special thanks for your idea of 'The no nuke rose parade.' But I can't accept it."

She called me in the evening. "I am mad at you, Said."

"Why? What did I do wrong?"

"I am mad at you, that's it."

"But why?"

"Because you did not do something."

"Oh, dear, I am sorry. What is it?"

"You should have invited me to the picnic with your friends. Am

I not your friend? I have heard so much about your picnic."

"Well, I am sorry about it. I apologize for not inviting you. I was thinking of asking you. Then I changed my mind."

"Why? What happened?"

"Well, it's nothing much. There is nothing bad, I thought of something. Please, don't misunderstand me. I love you. If I tell you my reason you may get upset."

"Oh, then it is more of a reason to know what you were thinking."

"Please don't misunderstand. All my friends are conservative Egyptian Muslims. They would not like me seeing an American and that too a Christian girl. They had after me to meet an Egyptian Muslim girl. My friends' wives know a few eligible girls in relations. I had not told them about you until yesterday. I told them about you during our picnic. Their faces showed that they did not like me to have a Christian girlfriend. Anyway, now they want to meet you. I am very sorry; I was wrong. I should have taken you with me. Please don't misunderstand me. I love you, Milly."

"OK. I fully understand your concern. I am not mad at you anymore, Mr. did say."

During the week we talked casually. When I called her on Thursday, I asked her, "Do you have any specific plans for the weekend?"

"I have planned to watch the movie *A Star Is Born* that is playing at the Erasmus theater near my home on Saturday with my darling friend. Then we are going to have a nice dinner at a family-run restaurant nearby. Then I will have a cup of coffee with Irish whisky with my darling friend."

"Oh, I see that you have a new darling friend."

"I got my overtime paid today so I am going to treat him."

"OK, then enjoy your Saturday."

"There is a slight problem. I have not asked him yet."

"Oh sure, it is a problem. Isn't it too late to ask him, and if he goes out with his other girlfriend?"

"He doesn't have another girlfriend. He is a mean guy. No one would be his girlfriend. The movie starts at four sharp. And you cannot come late. Take a subway. So, traffic jam is not your excuse. See, I asked the mean guy and he said yes."

She reminded me Friday and said again to take a subway. "I shall meet you at the theater. You find out where the theater is. I already purchased the tickets for the movie."

On Saturday I reached the theater twenty minutes before four. She came ten minutes after me. After the movie she took me to a local restaurant that was Dutch and old style with low ambiance. The food was scrumptious, in her words.

As planned, we walked to her place. After the coffee and usual conversation, she said she wanted to tell me something serious about her. She was sitting close to me on sofa. She got up and sat on love seat away from me.

"After my divorce, my whole outlook changed. My boss gave me my previous job and old salary. I rented my own apartment in Forest Hills. I was happy and started making friends with office people. They noticed the change and one of the ladies introduced a guy from the neighborhood office. His name was Steve. He was a graduate and had a good administrative job. We started dating. He used to come to my office to pick me. My office colleagues liked him. 'Made-for-each-other couple.' We were going steady. He was a nice guy. It looked promising. I invited him for a dinner when my brother was visiting my place. After a few months of our courtship, his old businessman uncle in Toronto died and left his properties to him and another of his cousin. The uncle owned gas stations and rental properties. Steve went to Canada to take care of the business and promised to keep the relationship. He never called me. I enquired in his office. No one knew anything about him. He never called his office and did not care to resign his job. He just vanished in thin air.

"I was seriously looking for a relationship. I met another Steve, Steve number two at my college annual get-together. He used to take classes with me. He was looking for a girlfriend and we got together. We were dating for about six months. Again, things looked bright and promising for me. One Friday evening he arranged a dinner at a restaurant in downtown Brooklyn about two miles from my home. When I got there, he was already at a table with another girl drinking wine. He introduced her to me and told me she was his previous girlfriend and she came back to him and they were going to marry. I was furious I flung wine at him and at her. I walked out of there. He played a cruel game with me by calling me there. He simply should have told me on the phone; he did not have to make mockery like that. I was furious, disgusted, another unexpected failure with such an insult. I didn't know how I walked home instead of taking a subway. I hit a bar in our area." She was furious.

"Depressed, disgusted, girl with nice figure at a bar is always assumed as a target for mischief and sex for men ready to satisfy their lust. I became a prey. That started my filthy nightlife filled with sex with strangers."

I got up, sat next to her and tried to take her hand in my hand. But she did not hold my hand and moved away from me.

"Julie Anne was the only person who knew all about my activities and would convince me that these things would never bring me happiness. If my mother had known about my night life, she would have killed me. Julie was right. But I could not do much about it. For a while it would help me and I would stop going out to those night places. But I never stopped. She suggested that I enroll in college, get a degree in teaching and become a teacher, my favorite occupation. I had no mind to go for study.

"I used to meet all kind of weirdos at the night places. Can you imagine what kind of sadistic mischief somebody once played on me? I received an anonymous parcel last Valentine's Day along with a funny greeting card. When I opened it, I found a beautifully wrapped, scented package. Inside was something sealed in a thick plastic bag. Its color and appearance repulsed me. I did not bother to open it and immediately threw it in the incinerator. Can you believe, it was human excrement, pure shit! What kind of a person would waste his time and money on such a cruel joke? I laughed to myself. It was his agony, not mine. A year earlier I might have completely pissed off and would have gone berserk. Now I have changed. At least someone cared to remember me on Valentine's day. Thanks a lot." A joyful laughter broke on her face.

"I did not want to date with my office people. I had liked you. I was afraid, something would go wrong and you would hate me. It was a real pleasure to chat with you in those days." She got up to drink water.

"Friday used to be a big night at the single's bar. One Friday some vicious, crazy guy made a mischief on me and insulted me badly. He said a person like me would rot in hell. I was badly hurt and pissed off at myself.

"I was so mad at myself that I came home late at night and saw my baby picture that was mocking at me. I hurled a pillow at the picture. The pillow landed on the floor; the picture did not fall from the wall. I threw another pillow with all my strength. The frame fell, the glass broke. I threw all my things around the apartment. I was so mad I did not out of my apartment during the weekend. At night I went out daily for the next week to enjoy the fun and sex. I did not clear the mess. After a week I calmed down. That little girl did not do anything wrong. I got the glass fixed.

"I was going out with a boyfriend for a few months. I thought it would work out and he would propose me. That time I told him a little bit of my nightlife and he got furious. He cursed me. 'You bitch. Don't ever call me again,' and he walked out on me.

"I remember meeting you once when I was coming home from my adventurous night. I saw extreme pity in your eyes for me. I did not want anybody's sympathy, especially when I had good time. After that night I always watched for you on my way home. A few times I saw you coming and used to hide behind the staircase door. I did not want to face you.

"I tried to avoid going out at night to have a filthy life of sex and booze. Sometimes I would stick to booze. I tried to force myself to stay home at night by making myself tired by taking long walks and jogging, stuffing myself with food and taking sleeping pills so I could fall asleep. It did not work all the time except I gained a lot of weight. I also drank booze until I collapsed or went out to a late movie in an area away from bars. Nothing ever worked permanently. Sometimes I stayed away from those places for two to three weeks. I was taking revenge on my strict mother, my bad luck and my ex maniac.

"Whenever I had a boyfriend, I did not go out alone at night. Something would happen and I would lose my boyfriend. I used to have headaches for days and days. You can't imagine what I went through. You don't understand a woman's feelings."

"Well, that is right. But I can understand human feelings."

"That is not my point. At one stage in my life, I hated the whole world, the whole human race, I was that frustrated.

"There is a specialized single's bar called 'Taboo' on 108th Street near the subway entrance that was one of my favorites, just a walking distance from our apartments. They have private rooms upstairs.

"At 'Taboo', I used to meet this truck driver named John. We enjoyed sex. One day he was very drunk, slow and boring. So, I teased him. He got wild. After he finished, he stood up and lit a cigarette. I smelled a danger and began to leave the room. And suddenly, he grabbed me and tried to burn my breast with cigarette through my dress. I just happened to put my left hand in between and got a burn on my left hand. This angered him and, in a rage, he began cursing and hitting me. He reached for his jacket and a big knife fell from his jacket. He wanted to kill me.

"I fled from the place barefoot and ran for my life up the street and around the corner. It was hard to run fast barefoot. I looked behind and spotted him chasing me. I was panting as I fumbled to open the front door to my building. I didn't know how I got there. Every second I lost moved me closer to death. He must have been right behind me because as I was waiting for the elevator, I heard him rattling the front door.

"I was scared to death and was trembling. By now I was safe in the elevator. My heart was racing. I fell on the floor and bruised my knee. I did not want to die at the hands of some maniac. I would stop going out and lead a normal life rather than getting killed.

"I lied down on the bed and it was impossible to sleep. I couldn't even shut the lights off." She was trembling and was out of breath. Her words were coming at a slow pace. I got up and sat next to her and put my arm around her. "I am with you now. You don't have to worry." She took my hand from her shoulder and sat on sofa. She did not look at me.

"He must have seen what apartment I lived in from the light in my windows and someday soon he was going to kill me. The following afternoon I talked to Julie on the phone and she came that evening to comfort me.

"She suggested that I should leave that building. That was the one in Forest Hills where you had lived before. I moved here in Brooklyn. It happened about a year ago.

"That incident changed me completely. I stopped going out at night. I was scared of that kind of dreadful thing happening again and I may not be lucky the next time to escape. I dieted seriously and reduced my weight down to my present size. I also learned to swim at the YWCA."

While telling me her story, she did not look at me. Sometimes her eyes were focused at the floor, sometimes at the window. She was not looking at anything in particular. She never looked at me. Her eyes were nowhere. Now she looked at me.

"That is my story, Said. That is my luck and that was my life-style; independent, full of freedom to its extremity. That kind of life-style is not acceptable to any man or any society. At least I am lucky to be alive and out of that hell. I have changed and I am living my new normal life. I feel ashamed of my past."

"I am really sorry for whatever happened to you in your life."

"I am glad that I was able to tell you all about me. Please! Forget me. I am not worthy of you. Men do not marry girls like me."

"Milly, to err is nature and correct it is human. And you did it. I admire your courage to come out of that terrible situation. I love you the same way as I did before you told me your story. I am proud that you are not that Milly anymore, the one I met in Forest Hills. I am glad that you trusted me to open your heart."

Milly became serious rather than being relaxed after telling me her story. I told her I would stay with her tonight to give her comfort.

"I am not in a mood for any romance."

"No, no romance. I will stay here so you feel comfortable that you are not alone; I am with you now."

"No, Said, you go home. I will be all right. Now I feel good. Said, there is a lot to take into consideration. I would not mind if you want to call it quits. Said, please, leave me alone now. Please, go away from me. I can't bear to hear you saying good things about me. Please, Said, leave me alone."

I had no choice! I left.

As soon as I reached home, I called her. "Hi, you sweetie, aren't you sleeping? I knew you wouldn't be. I just got home."

"I am not sleepy. I feel reborn."

"Relax, Milly, please, believe me, I love you and would like to marry you. There is no second thought in my mind."

"Said, please, think it over. Take your time. I don't want you to make a hasty decision. It is a question of your life. You can say no to me."

"Mil, I am not lying. I love you from the bottom of my heart. Please, relax and get some sleep."

"I don't know."

"I will see you tomorrow. Be a good girl and sleep. Good night and have sweet dreams. By the way, I had a little nap on the subway and I had a dream.

"I saw you in my dream.

"You are in my dreams all the time,
When I walk, you walk with me in my dream
Hand in hand we walk, you lean on me
And you smile and you kiss me.

When I ride a subway, you sit next to me
You keep talking. I say something and
You pinch my cheek.
When I sleep, you are next to me. You hug me.
And I don't sleep in my dream."

She waited till I stopped. She did not say anything, just hung up the receiver.

I could not sleep for some time. "How can I make that girl understand me?"

On her birthday! The 22nd of September! I invited her for a dinner at "Fujiyama," a Japanese restaurant in Levittown, Long Island. I had gone there alone for dinner twice. Their specialty was a smorgasbord. A Japanese chef would cook a variety of dishes on a portable hot plate in front of you and while cooking would play a lot of hand tricks. It was great fun to watch.

As decided earlier, I picked up Milly at her apartment after work and we drove practically in silence. I asked her, "How was your day, Milly?"

"It was OK. Nothing special." She paused. "And how about yours?"

"Great. I had interesting day in the office." My enthusiastic reply startled her. Otherwise there was not much talk between us. I was mostly busy with my driving in heavy traffic in Long Island. She mentioned that she was twenty-eight today.

We were interrupted by a chant-like greeting at Fujiyama, "How are you this evening?" from a broad-faced, short, Japanese receptionist with a broad smile from New York to Tokyo.

"Fine, 'Damo ari gato.'" She looked at me and repeated the broad smile and said, "Do itashimashite." And I surrendered to her. I did not understand what exactly she said. My vast knowledge of the Japanese language had only one phrase, 'Damo ari gato,' and I was finished with it. I was sure she had said something nice like, 'You are welcome.' I did not ask her.

"And happy birthday to you Milly, right?"

"Right. Thanks."

"Ban-zai," the receptionist said.

She shook hands with Milly and kissed both her cheeks, ignoring me completely. I envied Milly and that cute little Japanese girl for two different reasons.

"What is the meaning of 'Ban-zai?'" I asked the receptionist.

"One thousand years old means you live a thousand years."

"Live one thousand years with each year of ten thousand days," I added and looked at Milly. She neither disliked it nor appreciated it.

They had a big list of exotic cocktails. Some of the names, if I still remember them correctly, were 'Formula for long life,' 'Sips of nectar,' 'Intoxicated drink of love,' 'Enjoy life,' 'Meditation mood.'

"Would you like to try these nectars from heaven?" She was also going through the list. She said no to me.

So, I ordered champagne. I toasted Milly with "Happy birthday, my dear deer, many, many, more happy returns like this," and kissed her with deep love in my heart. She acted cool.

We ordered smorgasbord. She sat looking at her champagne glass while she was rotating it and sometimes sipping from it. I thought she was engrossed in her own thoughts. A few seconds passed. I was watching her face and trying to catch her eyes. They were downcast. Her face was blank, without any expression. I held the hand that was playing with the wineglass. "Milly."

"Yes, Said." As if she woke up from a dream.

"How is your brother, by the way?" Well, I had to start somewhere. Maybe I thought that would elate her mood.

"Oh, he is all right." There was no change in her mood.

"When did you last visit him?"

"Oh…I don't exactly remember when. He was busy during the summer. I visited him a few times, though. We had a barbecue once and the other time we went fishing with his friends."

"I think I remember you going to your brother's place and you mentioning to me about your fishing trip. How did you like the fishing? Did you get a good catch?"

"It was fun. We had a lot of fish that day."

The conversation stopped again.

Meanwhile a chef dressed in a long white gown and a tall red chef's hat had brought a portable hot plate in front of our table and started cooking our food using hand tricks. He was saying, "Add some Japanese garlic, grown in California. Now put some Long Island spinach because Japanese spinach tastes the same," and things of that nature. He was constantly playing with his cooking tools, throwing them in the air and catching them with funny actions. Milly was watching him with great interest. He served the food and we started eating. I fed her a shrimp from my dish. She was delighted.

"Let me see your wrist. Something is stuck on it." She showed it to me and I put a wristwatch on it. "Happy birthday."

She continued watching it with surprise. It was a Bulova quartz wristwatch.

"It is so beautiful. Thank you very much. I liked it. There was no need for a gift."

She was gazing at it. She kissed me, "Thank you for a wonderful gift. You did not have to buy such an expensive gift. "

"You are welcome and here is for many more like this." I raised my glass.

She grew a little concerned over my remark.

"Hey, Milly do you remember your earliest memory?" I asked her. She nodded.

"How old were you?"

"Three years"

"What is your earliest memory, Milly?" I thought it was a brilliant idea to start some conversation.

"It is so strong in my mind that I don't have to think about it, the earliest memory in my life."

"Oh, good, I would like to listen."

She looked at my face.

"It is not a happy one."

"I am sorry about that. Can you tell me?" She paused.

"I was like a doll."

"I can imagine."

"Why. Don't you believe? I will show you my pictures."

"Oh, I believe you even without you telling me that you were cute as a doll and cuddly and even now you are squeezable and cuddly. Of course, I would love to see your pictures. Okay, tell me what happened!"

She hesitated, then started talking, "My mother was watching one of those soap operas on TV. It was noontime and time for my milkshake. Mommy used to prepare it and keep it on the kitchen table. As a rule, I was not allowed to drink or eat anywhere other than the kitchen.

"One day, I was drinking my milkshake and I heard something exciting on TV. I ran with the glass in my hand to the family room to watch the TV. I don't remember how it happened, in a moment, I was flat on the floor with the milkshake on my dress and on the floor. I don't remember whether the floor was carpeted or not at that time.

"The next thing I remember was my mother hitting me on my palm with a foot ruler; she had one solely for the purpose of beating me. She slapped me on my face too and then locked me in the laundry room for being a bad girl. Since then I remember the words 'Bad girl' very well.

"I was scared to death thinking that there was a mouse there. My little heart was racing and thumping like a train. The next thing I remember, my brother Bill opened the door and hugged and kissed me and took me out. He put on my shoes and took me to the candy store around the corner, carrying me in his arms. He bought me all sorts of candies and my favorite 'Pelican' chocolates. I will never forget that incident. Bill loved me so much."

"Oh, Milly, I am sorry that you have such an unpleasant childhood memory."

"What can you do?"

"That is true."

I felt sorry for her. It was my fault. I should have never started this topic. I thought, she might have some sweet childhood memory just like me. Now my sweet memory had a sad edge to it recently.

We were in a pensive mood. She was the first to break the silence.

"After that incident, I used to have nightmares that I was closed in darkness and rats are attacking me. They grew larger every second. And then I used to scream in my sleep. Bill and I were sharing a room. He would take me in his arms."

She was not looking anywhere. She was reliving those nightmares. I felt guilty for starting this. For a moment I thought she was going to say that all her life was full of such memories. She did not say anything. Her sullen face showed me how she felt.

After some time, she asked me what my earliest memory in life was.

"Well, mine is a sweet memory about my mother. I must have been three years old. Believe me, I was a dumb kid." I stopped and smiled and started looking into her eyes.

"I believe you when you said were a dumb kid." She was cold.

"I was crazy for my mother. Being the youngest baby in the family, I usually never left her alone in those days.

"The earliest incident I remember was my mother watering our flower garden. She used to love the flowers and had a nice flower garden in front of our house. Every evening she would work in the garden and water the plants. Then there was a drought and she could not water the garden. My mother prayed to Allah for rain every day. There was no rain. One by one all the plants died. I was seven years old then." I stopped, smiled and started looking into her eyes.

"Now I truly believe that you were a dumb kid to have had the first memory at the age of seven." She started laughing.

"Listen, that is not my first memory, smarty. I was talking about what happened to our garden when I was seven."

"Okay, okay. Tell me what happened when you were a dumb kid of three?" She was behaving herself. I mean she was taking an interest in my story.

"My mother used to water our garden and I used to play nearby in the dirt and mud. She used to yell at me for spoiling my clothes and dirtying myself. Sometimes she would slap me lightly. I would never cry. I was not a crying baby anyway. After hitting me, my mother would hug me and shower all her love on me.

"I distinctly remember those white lily plants in our garden and my mother watering them while I stood next to her. I still remember that mild fragrance of lilies mixed with the cool smell of mud that sprang from the hot ground when water was sprinkled. I will never forget that smell. I wish I could have stayed in that place watching my mother and filling my heart with that fragrance for the rest of my life. The name Lily reminds me of my mother. That name has holiness of my mother and her love. Those are a few of the happiest moments I don't ever want to lose. So, that is my first memory of my life. The sweet, delicate holy flower of lily filled with love for my mother!

"My mother loved the garden the same way she loved her family. She loved everything in life and finally the God loved her. I am sure she is resting in peace. We are the sufferers in her memory."

Milly did not say anything. She felt sad too. I said "Well, that's God's wishes."

I started playing with the water goblet and she started watching me. I started feeling the silence. This was not the right topic to talk on her birthday. How could I possibly imagine she had a sad memory like that.

"Milly, did you have a nice garden around your house in New Jersey like most of the houses?"

"Yes, we had. In front we had evergreen plants and a pink climber rose at the corner. It would bloom in June and had over eighty flowers. I used to count them. In the backyards we had some flower-ing plants. My father's shop was closed on Sundays. After church services on Sunday he would work in the garden. I would help him, rather I would be playing in the backyard. In spring we would plant flowering plants. He would ask me to put the plant in the ground. Those were happy days."

It was time for dessert. The waitress told us that Milly was go-ing to get a birthday dessert on the house. I asked for a coffee. She served the coffee immediately and kept us waiting for the surprise.

Within a few minutes, a procession of waiters, waitresses, and a couple of chefs headed towards our table. The chef leading the pro-cession had one lighted candle on something. He put it on our table in front of Milly. It was half a honeydew filled with cream and fresh strawberries. The lighted candle was placed on the honeydew. They all gathered around our table and sang a Japanese song, clapping all the time. Someone was ringing a small brass bell and the other was playing tambourine. The song was joyful and had lots of 'Ho-hoes'. Milly was bashful. I was sure she never had such an experience be-fore. She blew the candle out and all of them wished a happy birth-day to her "Ban-zai Ho, ho, ho."

Finally, it was time to go. She thanked me for the great evening and the beautiful gift. "Can you imagine I am twenty-eight years old today?"

"Well, you look like a sweet-sixteen-year-old cute doll."

Then she asked me about my birthday.

"Well, my birthday is a special day, invented by some genius. I am a special guy anyway. Right?"

"Is that February twenty-ninth."

"Yes, you are right smarty. This body is thirty-two years old."

On the way back to her apartment there was not much conver-sation. She was quiet and sleepy. I could not forget the following conversation.

"Can you imagine I am twenty-eight years old today?" She was repeating it, but was saying it as if she was saying it for the first time. "Maybe it could prove to be a milestone in your life. Who knows?"

"Oh, no, I don't think so. Maybe you are right. Who knows? At least I know that I am twenty-eight and all my life has been a mess so far."

"I am sorry if you feel that way."

"I feel that way? No, I don't feel that way. I know it for a fact." She was sounding mad.

I did not want to ask her any more about it. I knew it would upset her more and I did not want my plans for the night with her to go down the drain. The plans I had made for the past few days.

As we were approaching her place, she started saying nice things like she liked the gift I gave her, she enjoyed the dinner, the place was gorgeous. And she thanked me again for all this and so on. In short, she was preparing to say good-bye to me as soon as we got in front of her apartment building. She was not sounding good either. I knew for sure as soon as she closed her apartment door, she would cry her heart out. I parked my car and got out. She said "Good night!" She did not want me to come with her. She even told me to go home, that it was too late and she did not mind my dropping her off like that.

I said, "I have to give you something."

I bet she must have panicked when she heard that because she was in no mood for anything romantic. In the elevator she just stood looking dumb and staring at the floor.

As soon as we entered the apartment, I felt like hugging her and asking her, 'What was the matter, Milly? Why are you so upset? Could you please let me know?' I thought if I did that she might burst into tears and I didn't want that either.

So, as soon as we were inside the apartment, I pulled an envelope from my inner pocket and gave it to her. She was surprised.

"I know the language of my heart, and my heart knows the

language of your heart. Do you know these stupid hearts love each other? Am I wrong, Milly?"

She was not ready to answer.

"I don't know, Said. What is it?"

"Open it. It is for you."

She opened the envelope and found a greeting card. One pink and one blue rose were drawn on that card. She opened it still wondering what it was all about. She found something written in my handwriting and in seconds she was engrossed in reading it. It simply said:

"September 22, 1976.
My darling Milly (and a happy face next to it)

I am the king, the king of my life. I am the king of my kingdom (that doesn't exist).
Would you like to be the queen of my kingdom?
Would you like to be the queen of my life, Milly?

Milly, you are my Lily. You are lily of my life.
Would you like to share my life?
Would you like to enjoy the bloom and
the gloom of life with me?
The winter and the spring on the way?
Would you like to share the hope the sunrise brings?
And the peace of the sunset with me, Milly?
Would you like to enjoy the lush and drought of life?

Would you sing with me when I sing with the birds?
Would you smile with me when I smile with the flowers?
Would you give your voice to my songs?
Would you like to mix the colors in my life?"

And I had signed my name "Said Ahmed."

It looked like my note did not make sense to her. She looked confused. I went down on my knees. Before she could realize it, she was more confused for a moment like nothing made any sense to her. So, I said, "Milly, will you marry me?" Then she said, "Yes, yes, yes, Said. I shall marry you. I love you. I love you." I slipped a diamond ring on her finger. She helped me to get up. She hugged me and started crying. She held me for a long time. "Yes. Said, I shall marry you. I can't believe it is happening."

This was the first time she had said she loved me. She did not let me go home. I stayed with her. The whole night she just held me in her arms.

CHAPTER TEN

The next day she called me in the office. She invited me to her birthday party on Saturday at her mother's place (I mean her father's place too! When I told her so, she said, "You are right, smarty, they are still married and live together"). Her parents and her brother used to celebrate her birthday every year to cheer her. This year they were having her birthday party at her parents' place and she was inviting me to attend it. "You will meet all my folks and you have to pick me up from my apartment and we shall go together in your car. My brother would fancy your car. Julie Anne, my best friend, always participates in my birthdays. She is very anxious to meet you. Her husband will also attend the party. He is in town, otherwise he goes on business trips and sometimes stays away during the weekends". She sounded very excited. I asked her if we could go to a movie this evening after work. She said, "Excuse me! I am booked for this evening. I am going to see Julie at her place. We are just going to talk and talk till we can't speak anymore. Sorry darling, I don't want your company."

And she laughed. "I pray the God that this doll will speak to me by tomorrow at least."

"Nope!"

I went to her apartment to pick her to go to Brooklyn for the second celebration of her birthday. As soon as the apartment door was closed, I said, "First thing first, let me kiss you hello!" She kissed me, putting her arms around my neck. "Oh, my dear blue handsome smarty, you are late, my darling. I was so worried." "I am sorry for being late. I did not mean to be. I was getting ready to leave and my boss called me. He was working in the office today and he had a question for me on my project. We were talking for fifteen minutes."

"It's okay, dear VIP. I was just worried."

Suddenly I recalled what Nancy had said when I was late once. I had said to her at that time, "Oh, I am sorry, Nancy. I was busy the whole day. I did not even realize when it was five o'clock." And she had said, "It's all right. It happens sometimes."

Milly was wearing a powder blue skirt with a white, silky, long-sleeve blouse and a navy-blue jacket. It perfectly matched what I was wearing. She was setting her hair. I said, "Let me kiss your hello for the second time today." And I kissed her and stood behind her and put my arms around her. Soon I started kissing her silky hair and started scattering it with my mouth. She was enjoying my touch in the beginning. Then she realized that her hair was a mess. She shouted, "Hey, hey, naughty boy, you spoiled my hair." Before she could say any further, my lips were clamped on hers and we started enjoying the softness of each other's lips. I can't say how long we were like that. She got away.

"Said, please, we are late. They must be waiting for us."

"'Ahebbek gidden!' I love you, Milly."

On our way to her parents' house, she was in a great mood, telling me about her family.

"People say I look like my mother and my brother is like my father."

"I think so."

"What?"

"I agree with the people."

"How come? You never saw them."

"All right, I don't have to see them to know this."

"I don't understand."

"Milly, didn't you tell me the universal truth? Anybody will agree to the fact. I mean if your brother was not like your father, but like your mother, then he would have been your sister. Right?"

"Gotcha, smarty!" and then she added, "You did not make any new invention. It is a PJ. My father was such a wonderful person, jolly and loving. His whole life changed completely after he lost his business. Sometimes I think he is barely alive. I feel sorry for him."

Milly's mother opened the door. "Mamale, this is Said Ahemed, my fiancé," Milly burst out.

"Milly?" That sounded a little loud. "But you did not tell me?"

"Ma, believe me, it is true. Look at my engagement ring. It just happened days ago on my birthday." And she showed the ring to her mother. Now her mother turned to me and said, "Hello, Mr. Ahemed. How are you? Nice to meet you." She shook hands with me.

"Pleased to meet you." I was stunned to see her eyes.

"Oh, your eyes. You got Milly's eyes. Her eyes are exactly like yours."

"No, she got my eyes." Of course, she was right. I tried to smile. Well, I did not expect a warm welcome like, "I am very pleased to meet you, Mr. Ahemed, or may I call you Said?" I thought that was because I was brown and different in my looks.

Milly ran inside and brought her father to meet me. He offered his congratulations and wished that God would bless us. A man in his whatever age looked worn out as if he had lost all interest in life. Maybe I felt so because Milly had told me about him.

After going through the formalities, he kept looking at me with his mouth gaping. Then Milly's mother reminded him that he had not finished yet and had to get ready. So, he went inside.

Millay's mother was constantly looking at me, which made me feel uneasy. She had not yet questioned me about my origin, religion, or my profession. She was clearly upset, because of my accent and complexion. Milly must have noticed it. She told her mother, "Ma, Said is a mechanical engineer and he is Egyptian." I was sure she did not like my being Egyptian. At least my profession impressed her. She didn't show any emotions.

"Let me show you the house." That was Milly.

And she showed me every corner of the house where she had lived most of her life. Lastly, she showed me her room with great pride. Milly's blown-up picture, when she was three years old, was hanging on the wall. It was identical to the one she had in her apartment.

"My father had shot that picture and he enlarged it himself. Photography was his hobby."

In the closet all her dolls were neatly arranged. "Now, this is our guest room. If you need to stay here tonight, you will have to sleep here alone. And that cat in the corner will bite a bad boy like you." There was a wooden carved cat on the corner table. It was a beautiful piece of art. The cat had arched her back with her tail standing and she was mewing. It had a natural wood color. "My brother gave that cat to my father on one of his birthdays. My mother does not like cats. So, she gave it to me."

When we came back to the living room, Milly's mother was in the kitchen looking after the food. We sat on the sofa. Milly hugged and kissed me. Then she ran to help her mother.

A bell rang and Milly's mother came to open the door. Milly

went after her. "That must be Billy!" she said.

"Oh, Billy, do you know Milly got engaged?" she questioned as soon as she opened the door. There was a note of complaint in her voice rather than joy.

Bill shouted, "Congratulations, Mil." He ran to her and embraced her. Happiness encircled both of them as their eyes filled with tears. I had already come to meet Bill. Bill's daughter and son were left wondering and Milly's mother started talking to her daughter-in-law.

Milly almost pulled her brother towards me.

"This is my fiancé, Said Ahemed, and this is Bill." We shook hands. He had such a warm handshake. Milly was thrilled to introduce her family to me. "This is Susan, Stuart, twelve years old, and Stacy, nine. Right, Stess?"

Milly showed her engagement ring to Bill and Susan and said, "This happened on my birthday. And this is my birthday present." And she showed her wristwatch.

"What a nice thing to happen. See, Mil, you kept everything a great secret and it worked this time. I am glad. God bless you both." This was Bill.

After a while, Julie Ann and her husband, John, came. They would have come earlier as Julie was anxious to meet me. She had to wait for John who was coming from his business trip. Julie and Milly embraced each other and could not hold their tears.

Julie and John were recently married last March, John was one of the many sales managers for one of the tire companies. I don't remember exactly which one. It was one of those big names like Firestone, Goodyear, or Dunlop. Half the month he traveled, sometimes at a stretch of two weeks, Milly had told me. And he was in New York this time. One more 'Watchdog' to watch me?

He gave me a standing offer, anytime I wanted to buy a set of tires he would give them at cost price.

"You must be using your company's tires a lot?" I asked him. He used to drive his own car to nearby locations.

"No, that is not right, my dear friend. I use the tires of competitors. So that I can find out how bad they are and that adds to my selling point. I have full faith in our product whatever they claim. I know what kind of testing is done on our tires. It is a continuous process. We spend a lot of money on research and testing."

Bill was an accountant and was working with a government agency. They lived in Hicksville, Long Island. I told him that I was fascinated by Jones Beach.

"Then you must come to our place next weekend. I hope it is convenient for you. We still can do the boardwalk. The weather is still nice. Mil, you must bring Said to Hicksville next weekend."

Meanwhile Milly's father had joined us. He started telling how beautiful it was in Brooklyn when he was a schoolboy. The Coney Island beach was such a beautiful sight. They did not have all those rides and these hawkers in those days. There was just a beach and people would go there for swimming and sunbathing.

It was a Presidential election year. Everyone was talking about the election campaign and how it was getting dirtier day by day. They wanted Mr. Carter to win and he would be a better president than Mr. Ford and how Mr. McCarthy is spitting the votes. Milly's father had no interest in politics. He was talking to me about Egypt. What town I grew up in. How big and how far the town was from Cairo. Where did I go for college? How did I like to stay in America? Everyone had a drink. No one was keen on drinking.

Her father had blond hair once upon a time as streaks of brownish-blond hair were showing between his mostly gray hair. Her mother had dyed hers brown. Milly's mother hardly smiled. Milly had mixed features of her mother's and father's. Her brother had her father's looks.

We were at the dining table. Everyone was filling her or his dish with food, but mostly Milly's mother was serving everybody. One particular dish looked like a reddish-brown cake. It did look a bit odd. I asked Milly's mother what it was.

"That is a blood pudding, Mil's favorite."

"Would you please excuse me?"

"Don't you like it? Did *you* ever taste it?" Milly asked me.

"No."

"Try it. I am sure you will like it," Milly said. Her mother was waiting for my "Yes."

"I am sure, Milly, but I don't feel like eating it."

Milly also declined. Her mother kept on insisting.

"You love it, Mil."

"I don't want it today."

"But why don't you want it?"

"I just don't feel like eating it."

"Mom, don't force her." Bill came to her rescue.

Eating blood is against the Muslim religion. I did not tell them anything about it.

"Do you remember, Milly, when you were two years old, we had a big birthday party at my brother Bill's house in Brooklyn. We had a big cake good for forty people. I had paid only four dollars for it." Milly's father started talking.

Milly's mother interrupted, "She was just two years old. How can she remember it?"

"That's right. She won't. Billy must be aware of the big cake we had for four dollars. The same size cake I used to buy for a dollar before the war."

John and I were listening to him with great interest. From the faces of all others I realized that it was her father's favorite topic and must have been repeated every year. Later Milly told me so. Honestly, I did not exactly feel like the center of attention, but I was. I was generally under surveillance from all the eyes including Milly's.

On our way back, Milly told me, "Julie liked you, my darling."

"How do you know?"

"She told me. She was very happy about it."

"I see."

"I have one question for you, Milly."

"What is it, Said?"

"Do you call your mother by her first name?"

"No, why?"

"Well, when we met, that was right when we entered your house, you called her 'Mamale.' I thought that is her first name?"

"Oh, no, 'Mamale' means dear mother. I call her Mamale when I am extremely happy. Her name is Rosa, short for Rosetta."

"That's interesting."

"I hate my mother. I called her Mamale to tease her that I was happy. I knew she would not approve you being non-Christen and from Egypt. You should have watched her face when I introduced you. She showed such a disinterest. Would you mind, Said, if I tell you something?"

"Oh, no, say anything you want."

"Do you know that you are supposed to give a kiss on the cheek when you meet some lady, for example my mother or Julie or Susan, and also kiss them again while leaving. They kissed you when we left."

"Oh, I am sorry. I did not know this American custom. You know, they don't do such thing in Egypt. Imagine me kissing somebody's wife like that in my old country. People would beat me and put me in a rent-free room. In Egypt it is called 'sijn,' the one in America is called jail. Hey, you know what I am thinking for a punishment, of my wrongdoing?"

"What?" Milly asked me.

"I will kiss you all over tonight, all right?"

"Cute I knew you would come up with something like that. Naughty boy."

"That means I have full permission. Good. Thanks."

When we arrived at her apartment building, she said, "Walk me over to my door, plea...se, Said."

I went with her and then, "Please, Said, plea...se, stay with me tonight. I am so happy. Will you, plea...se?" I stayed there. Not that I did not want to.

The next thing we had to do was to register for marriage and decide the wedding date at New Yok City Hall. Both of us had to sign the application in the presence of the city clerk. We became anxious to go to the City Hall. We decided to go to the City Hall on Tuesday, September 28 for that auspicious task, thinking that Monday would be too crowded for overzealous couples who decided to marry during the weekend.

Both of us met at the City Hall at 9:00 AM sharp, which was the time to open the New York City Hall for daily business. We followed signs for the marriage bureau and made three right turns and found the marriage registration hall and the wedding chapel. The registration hall was a big waiting room and a partitioned room with a glass counter with sliding window. Behind the window a pleasant-looking middle-aged lady with smiley face was distributing marriage forms. Some anxious couples were ahead of us. We signed the log book and wrote our addresses. The lady explained how to fill in the form and told us she would witness our signatures.

This room was no better than a railroad waiting room except the chairs had beige-colored vinyl upholstery. There were two signs,

'NO SMOKING PLEASE' and 'NO GRAFFITI PLEASE.' I was surprised to see some graffiti on the chairs and man-made leather covered benches. There was more graffiti with artwork on the walls. The chairs were pretty old and there was evidence of trying to remove the graffiti but some of it was permanently there. The lighting, I would say, was poor. The walls were painted probably a decade ago, and the false ceiling had one row open for repairs. The piping above the false ceiling was showing its useful but unpleasant existence in the room.

After completing the forms, I started to read the graffiti: 'Arty and Patricia became one heart on September 23, 1970', 'bleeding heart and flowery Debbie went to paradise on June 21', next to that was a bleeding heart with an arrow and an angel at the end of the arrow. 'Dennis and Liz started their menace on December 29, 1974'. I told Milly, "I feel like writing 'Milly and Said were welded on October 21 and became one piece of steel.'" "How unromantic! Don't act silly."

At the time of signing the forms, the lady at the counter explained that the city would provide a priest for Christian weddings and a rabbi for Jewish weddings. We had a choice to bring our own person to perform the wedding ceremony. Milly selected the priest provided by the City.

We already had selected Thursday 21, October for our 'Memorial wedding day' and the clerk granted it.

During Milly's birthday party at her parents' house Bill had invited us and told Milly to bring me to his house. Milly was so excited that she immediately accepted and told him that we would visit him next weekend. During the week she decided on Saturday early morning and insisted we go there her way, which was taking the Long Island Railroad and not in my car. I agreed.

When we reached Hicksville, I looked at my watch and for no particular reason checked the timetable in my hand. Of course, the train was late. I remembered someone in our office saying that Long Island Rail Road (L.I.R.R.) printed timetables for the great convenience of the passengers just to find out how much the train was late. This was a joke in the mid-seventies.

"Do you know, Milly, the train is late."

"Oh, don't be surprised. It is nothing new."

I told her that joke of the timetable. She enjoyed it and said she had heard it before.

I followed her to the booking office. I mean I was two feet behind her all the time. She was a bit nervous and running ahead of me. She was looking for her brother and he was not there. "He is never late. He is always waiting for me at this spot and today he is not here. Either he is caught in traffic or maybe the train came earlier than he expected." She had no patience. She called Bill's home from the public phone and learned that he had left twenty minutes ago. Bill came within the next ten minutes. He was stuck in traffic on that gorgeous, bright and warm, summerlike day.

I had a warm welcome and I was treated with a lot of respect, pride, and love by all of them during that weekend.

"How come I never noticed it?"

"Because my dear deer, you close your deer-like eyes while making love."

"You are right, my darling. I am so happy in your arms."

She was talking about a scar on my back and I told the story. She lightly traced the scar line with her fingers for some time. Finally, she stopped, hugged my back, and rested her head on my back. A few moments passed. I thought of hugging her and I slowly turned to face her. I saw tears in her eyes. I held her in my arms and felt hot tears rolling on my chest. Mutely she was telling me how much she loved me.

The story of the stripe on my back goes like this. "I used to go to my father's grocery shop when I was a kid. My father would give me 'Pelican' toffees, which were imported from England.

"During the summer holidays, I would go to the shop in the afternoons so that my father could take a nap and I could look after the customers. He would lie on his back, resting his head on a high pillow, and fold his hands behind his head and his legs folded and crossed one on top of the other. He used to slide his tall fez over his eyes, resting on his nose. Most of the time he would be half asleep. Sometimes he would tell me to take two toffees from the jar. Once I took three instead of two. I never realized but he found out as soon as I started chewing the third one. He woke up and became extremely furious. He said that it was a theft, no matter how small, punishment in the Koran for a theft was cutting off the hands.

"My father had a whip with a leather cord. He used to use it for his buggy. He asked me to strip off all my clothes. He hit me with all his strength across my back. I fainted in great pain. My back was slashed and started bleeding. Then he took me to the doctor who had to stitch my back. That left a scar on my back. I was twelve that time."

Before the wedding I decided to tell her more about my personal life and about my family and about my first marriage. She had told me so many secrets and delicate moments of her life. She was never inquisitive about my past. Maybe that's the way she was. But for mutual trust and love, I thought she must know me more than what she knew. After all, we had to develop our own happiness and love through the mutual trust and friendship.

We had come to her apartment after doing our shopping. I

opened the subject, she said, "I would learn it from you in due course. I would be interested in listening to you."

I told her about my family background about my father, mother, brothers and sister. "I am the baby in the family. A brother one year older than me drowned when I was ten. We were in the same class. I had four sisters, now I have only three. All the sisters are older than me and all are married. All of them have a common business between them and their husbands."

"That's interesting, isn't it? Your whole family is enterprising. Your sisters must have big business among three families."

"Oh, yeah, it is on a large scale."

"What do they do?"

"Well, between them and their husbands, they have a production business."

"It's interesting. What do they manufacture?"

"Well, I mean, the product is babies. Those three couples, they produce babies. Among them they must have more than twelve babies so far.

"Every year somebody gets a new arrival. My mother used to inform me promptly. They have big competition. One of my sisters died delivering her fourth baby just before I came to the states. Otherwise she would have been in the competition too."

" Said. Don't you have any seriousness in you? You find fun in every thing."

"My eldest brother wanted me to go to college and become a doctor or lawyer. I was not interested in either of them. And just because of him I am an engineer and in front of you, my dear."

I looked in her eyes and she gave me a flying kiss.

"After getting a degree, the natural course of life was to get a job for bread and butter and marry so that a wife can cook the bread and breed a family. How could such an obedient and dumb boy like me be an exception to it? I got trapped in marriage that I did not want so soon. And that changed my whole life."

I explained our Islamic wedding customs. "Hold your breath and please don't laugh. It is different world in Egypt or any Islamic country. The groom has no choice of his own in our wedding system. Boy's family proposes to girl's family. Boy's and girl's parents decide marriage for their children based on factors like family standing in the society, boy's education, family financial status, boy's earning power and things like that. Girl does not participate in the wedding ceremony. *Alkahn* that is Muslim priest recites verses from Koran in presence of only males from both sides of families and friends. The marriage contract that is *meher, is signed during nikah ceremony. Meher is a contract the* amount the groom would give the bride if separated that is divorced. Music, singing and feast follows. The ladies and the bride celebrate their own singing, dancing and feast in different rooms. Men and women celebrate separately."

Her surprise and interest were clearly marked on her face. She did not comment nor did she laugh as I had thought she would do. She was listening with interest.

"The groom meets the bride on the wedding night at the bed-time for the first time."

"Was your wife beautiful?"

"Well she was ordinary looking, average height and a shade darker that me. When I heard about American dating game and selecting their choice of girl. I envied all of you who enjoyed the thrills of dating.

"She was my mother's cousin's daughter. Her name was Nadia. Her father was a cloth merchant. Along with his sons he had expanded his business and was a very rich man when we were married.

"After my engineering degree, I took a job in a textile mill at El-Mahallah El-Kobra; El-Kobra means the great, the great city of Mahallah, a city of textile mills about ten miles from my hometown. I used to live at home; I mean my parents' home and would commute ten miles every day by bus. After my marriage I rented an apartment in El-Mahallah El-Kobra. My family did not like the idea of my separating from them. I thought it would be the best for our happiness to start our own life independently.

"My father-in-law suggested to my wife that I should start some kind of engineering business or some kind of industry or at least a workshop. My father-in-law was ready to invest all the money I needed.

"I was not an enterprising man. I loved to write stories and po-ems. My stories used to get published once in a while and that used to bring me extra income. That was not big money, I never dreamed of becoming a rich man and my wife never stopped dreaming of rolling on a pile of money and becoming a wife of an industrialist. I could have written a novel someday and would have earned more money in the future. That would have been very little in comparison with an industrialist. And that was where we started our disputes. Nadia would be extremely pursuant after her mother or father vis-ited us. She never tried to understand me. She even forgot how once upon a time her poor father in his young age used to sell cloth, car-rying it on the back of a mule and going from door to door, from village to village in the hot burning sun. She just wanted to become rich. That was the only dream in her life.

"In due course we had a daughter. I named her Elham. Elham means 'Inspiration'. She was such a cute doll! She was love in our house. I used to call her Boss! She would laugh at that, not knowing the meaning. She was the foundation of our happiness. Our family love revolved around her. I used to forget all disputes and crankiness of my wife because of her. She used to wait for me at the door to come home from work. She would cling to me. I would lift her in my arms. She would give me many kisses. My shirt used to get spoiled from her dirty hands. My wife used to get irritated, I never cared. I really loved those moments.

"She died when she was two years old. She ran a high fever for a few days and that was it. Allah loved our child more than us."

I stopped. The thoughts of Elham were clouding in my mind. "That is a very sad thing to happen. I am sorry, Said." Milly came close to me, put her arm around my neck and pulled my head to her shoulder. Her eyes were wet.

"After she was gone, it was just a matter of time. We were divorced. It's very easy to divorce in Egypt. People don't do it and it is condemned by the society. People from my family did not like my divorce. They denounced me and considered me a crazy guy."

"I agree with you. I think you did the right thing to divorce her." I was glad she agreed with me.

"Only my mother could understand my feelings. She always thought that I did not do anything wrong. She just loved me, her baby boy. To get out of the frustration, I came to the States. That is how life goes."

Milly was still feeling sad.

We had to collect lots of things before we got married. For example, neither of us had a good dinner or cutlery set. Milly had a melamine dinner set. Some of those dishes were burnt from cooking accidents. And I was still using the remains from our foursome bachelors' kitchen. Different pieces from two different sets, one melamine and the other an inexpensive china set. The remains of the china set were just for namesake. Most of the pieces were already broken, and the remaining each had at least one chip. A part of our combined assets were various spoons of various origins in different sizes. The glasses were different shapes. Each of us was happy with his or her own kitchen assets. I was holding them because they had memories of my friends and my past life in New York with them. I thought Milly did not much care to buy any decent kitchen sets because she did not want to spend money and there was no real need for her. And there was never any need for improvement in our belongings, when we decided to become 'US' and start a new life together, there was an instant need for complete renovation.

"I am not going to eat off those plastic dishes. I want a china set or at least ironstone. And maybe we will have one ironstone and one china. If we get bored with one set, we would use the other one. And we got to have placemats. We shall eat like royalty. How about that, Said?

"We need new bed covers and pillow covers for a newly married couple and my blanket is worn out. We must buy a new one. They have a sale on blankets at Alexander's. Shall we buy an electric one?"

At least I was able to reject the idea of buying an electric blanket. Of course, I was scared of electric shocks and accidents. She awarded me 'Scared Cow' and I accepted it. And Milly herself agreed on only one dinner set and taking a 'rain check' for herself to buy another one at Macy's warehouse sale.

I never had my own furniture. That was my apartment policy, not to rent an apartment without furniture. Milly had one sofa, one chair and a coffee table, all bought from Queen's Salvation Army, a few years ago when she started her own single's life. "That is not worth living, but worth leaving," I commented on her furniture. And she accepted my verdict. "We can't buy it at regular price under any circumstances. We've got to wait for a bargain sale." That verdict I had to accept, the way she declared it, I did not have an alternative for me. Finally, we were able to buy a good Herculean sofa set during 'The Manager's White Sale!' at Sears. And it just happened that the sofa set was delivered on Saturday before the election and my dear fair lady, I mean my dear beautiful lady, enjoyed watching the election projections sitting on the new sofa, kissing the coffee mug on and off. Poor Said? She had no time to kiss him. She was busy watching the election results.

So, we were busy shopping and buying things we wanted, needed and a few not needed, useful and not so useful, wanted by only half of 'Us'. I did not hesitate to buy because I was going to spend my money. She hesitated to spend my money or buy expensive stuff. I guess that was the kind of economics she had learnt all her life. She badly wanted to contribute to this matrimonial shopping. I felt sorry because she hardly had any savings. I allowed her to spend some of it, a minimal amount. I did not want to hurt her feelings. After all, it was 'Our' shared new life we were going to establish.

This is what happened on one of our shopping sprees. We were coming back from shopping. She was extremely happy as usual after buying things. I knew why! She was dreaming about the things we just bought. She must be thinking how to decorate the apartment with those things. She must be dreaming how to decorate her new life again, again for the second time. She was going to begin a fresh life. A dawn to her nightmares!

So, we were on our way back from shopping. We had decided to live in her apartment because her apartment was much better than mine.

"Do you know John, Julie's husband?" She woke up from her dream.

"Nope, I don't. I don't know that creep at all."

"What? Creep. Oh, you know him. You met him at my birthday party. You are lying. And you said 'Creep'; I am going to kill you."

"Oh, sure, for John! Go ahead. But remember Julie will kill you. She won't let him go like that." And my God, I laughed.

"I am not talking to you. You are making fun of me. Aren't you?"

"You're not talking to me? OK."

And I turned the car on the cross street and double parked it wherever I found a spot. And before she could understand what was happening, my arms were around her and I was kissing the girl who was mad at me.

"Hunh, hu…Sa…"

She was testing all her strength in pushing me away. I backed. I had enough fun.

"Behave yourself, Said, we are in the street."

"Yeah, yeah, we are in the street, but we are not naked. Remember, Milly, you are not talking to me."

"You are a nut."

"A peanut!"

By the time we got home, it was 10 o'clock. She did not talk to me in the car, and even when we were in her apartment. She opened all the items we bought that day without a single word. She looked cute in her frozen mood. I really wanted to kiss her a million times. It would have been real fun! I tried to talk to her.

"Oh, my doll dearest. If you don't talk to me, I shall have to talk to the stars and the moon. Oh, the moon, tell me when this doll will talk again. All the stars, please kiss my doll for me. And oh, my darling God, keep this sweet doll mad at me, doesn't she look cute this way!"

She was giggling not openly and tried to hide it. She made coffee for both of us. And even gave me a kiss before we started sipping it. I tried again to talk to her. She was enjoying her silence.

"OK. Good night, my apartment is waiting for me."

"Oh, Said, honey, please don't go, stay over here."

"Yeah, yeah. I shall wear your frock to the office tomorrow."

Anyway, I stayed there.

And during my stay that night, she told me that Julie's husband, John, was inviting both of us for a dinner at 'Lundies', a seafood restaurant in Sheep's Head Bay in Brooklyn to celebrate our engagement. "Can you make it, honey?"

"Oh, sure thing. I heard they have giant lobsters at Lundies that they have to lish them."

"What did you say? Lish? I don't get you."

"Oh, lish, I mean the one they put around a dog's neck."

"Oh, you mean leash."

"That's right, leash on lobsters."

Anyway, I had this kind of language problem from time to time and all the fun of my PJ (poor joke) would be lost.

One evening I was watching TV and preparing my meal when the telephone rang.

"Hi, Said, it's me."

"Oh, hi me, how are you?" I answered in a cold voice.

"I am fine. What you doing there? Are you drinking, Said? Why do you sound so cold?"

"Who me? Oh, my mouth is eating grapes with seeds. I mean the grapes I bought are not seedless. My hands are busy in cooking and my dumb brain is dreaming of a wonder girl by the name of Milly.

"You are so excited so I was trying to stay cool. I am cooking nice and spicy meatballs. Can you smell? Want some? I will send them through the wire. What's up?"

"Now you sound yourself. Listen, I am calling you from Macy's at King's Plaza. I am here with mom. I found a beautiful bone china dinner set just for two placings. It has a beautiful design. It has a small kettle, a milk pot, and a sugar bowl. Just for two of us. It's a good buy. It's on sale just for ten dollars. You won't get something like that for this price. The salesman was also telling me. It's a fantastic bargain, believe me. I want to buy it for us. We will use it occasionally just for two of us. I liked it very much. Shall I put a deposit on it and you can have a look at it before we purchase it. Or shall I buy it right away? I am sure you will love it. What shall I do, dear?" She was so excited. Finally, she stopped; she must be out of breath by this time.

"Purchase it if you like it. I am sure I will love it."

"I hate you, Said."

"Why?"

"You should have been with me right this minute." She said it as if she was crying.

"Oh, I see. But I love you."

"Me too, Said."

And she blew a kiss in the phone. I did the same; it was a really beautiful set of china. We enjoyed using it. I would have loved it till today because Milly loved it. I did not imagine that the end of that set was going to be a disaster in my life.

CHAPTER ELEVEN

I haven't told you much about Vassily. I am sure you are interested to know more about him.

He was a good friend, kind and honest. I liked him. I did not like his fucking language. I did not go out of my way to look for someone like Vassily. Vassily respected me as a smart person. He appreciated my judgement, never really criticized me. Even my bosom buddies were always criticizing me for my lifestyle, for my gambling and going to the bars. They wanted me to get married and settle in life. I preferred to stay single and enjoyed it. My friends were not wrong. They knew I was a family loving person. Vassily really played an important role as my friend. He never called me by my name. Though he remembered my name, he always called me "Doc" or "Boss."

About three months after I met Vassily for the first time, he asked me, "Boss, are you gay?"

"Yes, I am a gay, happy man. My name itself is Said, which means 'happy man' in Arabic."

A week later he invited me for a dinner party at his place. It was Saturday evening. Vassily lived in Astoria. His apartment was in one of those high-rise buildings on the twelfth floor. When I reached Vassily's apartment, two of his friends were sitting on the sofa. They already had their drinks. Vassily introduced us. One of them as John and I forgot the other guy's name. They noticed I was an immigrant. "This is Said, a smart engineer from pyramid country Egypt." Vassily introduced me with great respect. They shook hands brother style.

John was wearing a stud in his right ear and the other guy had a ring in his right ear. And I noticed Vassily also wore a stud in his right ear.

Vassily gave me a tour of his apartment. His spacious bedroom was located facing west like my apartment and open to the sky. He had good-quality furniture; some nice curios were placed on night tables and two glass vases with artificial flower arrangements on his dresser. The furniture and all the furnishings were expensive. I knew Vassily had rich tastes. "My apartment gets all the shitty light and air in the world." There was a life-size seminude picture of a guy in his bedroom above the headboard. At least he had a well-built nice body. What the hell was this guy doing in his bedroom?

"This is Jack Wrangler, the movie star," he said as if he was his buddy.

That Jack or whosoever he was, I felt as if he was coming out of the wall. The quality of the picture was excellent. I checked my movie directory in my mind and that name was not familiar. My ignorance, I thought.

There was a small framed picture of nude Archimedes in a bathtub. "I love this smart guy," Vassily said.

When we came out of his bedroom, I saw the two guys were holding each other's hands and kissing each other. They stopped as soon as we entered. Two other guys had already come. Both of them had earrings in their right ears. Two more were supposed to come late. Vassily introduced me to the newcomers.

"No girls?" I asked Vassily.

"No fucking girls, just us."

Now I realized that it was a stag party of different kind.

Vassily served deep-fried thick slices of cheese with drinks. 'It is Saganaki,' he told me. He served seven-star Metaxa as a main drink. John was drinking beer. It was a hot summer day. The air conditioner was turned on full blast. And it was making a big comfort compared to the outside. I preferred beer. He gave me 'Dominican Ale.' "This is my brand," Vassily told me. One of them was watching me with a funny look. I was getting uneasy.

"It feels so good here. Out there it feels like you are on fire." My way of starting conversation. I was seriously thinking of a good reason for getting out of this place. We chitchatted for a few minutes.

"Oh, my God, now I remember that my friend's son is sick in New Jersey and they were going to admit him to the hospital. Can I call him from here, Vassily?"

I dialed Karim's number in New Jersey. I knew that Karim's family was visiting Mokhtar in Queens. So, no one was at home.

"Nobody at home. They must have gone to the hospital. Let me call my other friend in Queens."

I dialed Mokhtar's number and talked to him in Arabic. I did not tell him about the real situation here. I just told him that I was at my friend's as I had already told him. I asked him how was Karim's travel from New Jersey in that heat and New York traffic. I was trying to fool Vassily and his friends by keeping my face serious.

"Oh, my God. They had to put him in intensive care. They don't know what is happening to him. My other friend's wife was crying. They are starting for New Jersey. You don't know how close we are. I am sorry. I hate to quit a party like this. But I must be with my friend. Excuse me." I was lying. I didn't like to and I didn't want to. But I had to. I escaped from there.

The next few times when I met Vassily, first thing he asked me was, "How is your friend's son?"

"Oh, he is much better now. It was mini meningitis, they said." A big lie!

"That shit is scary sometimes." Vassily was a born opinion doctor.

A month later, Vassily asked me, "We are having a picnic in Cherry Grove Long Island. It is a heck of a beautiful island. That is a beach for 'Pansy' people like us. There is a lot of fun. Want to join us?"

"I don't like that lifestyle and I am not one of you." The way I said it, he did not dare to say anything. I just walked away.

Then, after that, we always met at the races as before. He never asked me about any party or any picnic. That topic was totally closed, our friendship remained open. Islam condemns homosexuality. I love my religion, Islam.

Before I left for Ohio, Vassily gave me a big farewell dinner at his place and called only his two sisters and their families. When I reached his apartment, both the sisters and their families had come. The sisters were in the kitchen. Their kids were busy playing the games they had brought from home.

Vassily called them and introduced me as, "This is my friend, Said, from great pyramid country of Egypt." The elder sister's name was Dimitra and younger was Olga. Their husbands' names were Alec and Stelios. Later in our conversation I learned all of their parents came from Greece. "We met our husbands in our Greek community programs in Queens," Dimitra told me. I was impressed that they had kept their ethnic identity.

The sisters had a glass of red wine and all the men had Metaxa. I preferred Metaxa. Vassily served stuffed grape leaves with yogurt dip and spinach pie with cheese for appetizer. We had another drink before we ate dinner.

The sisters and their husbands showed great interest to know life in Egypt. Both the sisters never met an Egyptian before. They had very little knowledge of Egypt.

Vassily's behavior was remarkable from the way I knew him. He used very polished language. He did not say 'F' word or bad language, except when something went wrong in the kitchen. Then he shouted, "What the fuck." The sister older than him said something in a language I did not understand. It must be Greek. Vassily replied, "Don't you worry. It is not serious." The elder sister, Dimitra, said, "He is not going to change."

Vassily was telling me the names of all the dishes he had made with its main ingredients and a short recipe. The meat was lamb. The food was spicy and delicious.

I enjoyed the evening. Vassily and his family were very friendly and hospitable. Then I realized that Egyptians are also friendly and hospitable to their guests.

After coming back to New York, I started going to racetracks at a lesser frequency than before. Between my presence at the tracks and Vassily's 'No show', my meetings with Vassily were not as frequent as before. When I saw him, I realized he had not changed a bit. I showed him my Porsche. I took him for a ride. He carefully looked at the gadgets. He was fascinated. I asked him if he wanted to drive my car. He said, "If you don't mind, I would love to." He drove my car with a big thrill. "Now I can tell my fucking friends, I drove a Porsche." He felt honored and proud. He was still working towards buying his dream car, a 'Classic Toronado'. He has saved enough money and he would buy it soon.

Vassily told me one day "Doc, when you had gone to Ohio, me and my friends had gone to Kentucky Derby. What a fucking fun."

One day I told Vassily that I am in love with a girl and I liked her.
"Is she American?"
"Yes."
"Is she white?"
"Yes."
"Is she beautiful?"
"Yes."
"Do you love her?"
"Yes."
"Does she love you?"
"Yes."
"If all yesses, what the fuck are you waiting for? Go and marry her."
"Soon."

I was telling Milly to come with me to the races. She agreed. But we would end up in doing something else rather than going to the races. Sometimes we would wander through Central Park after office hours. Sometimes we would attend free concerts in Central Park. She had not experienced the thrills of horse racing. So, she was reluctant to go. I had told her that I met Vassily at the races and he was my good friend and I would like her to meet Vassily.

Finally, one Friday she made it to Roosevelt racecourse with me. It was her first experience. She was thrilled to see the atmosphere and the happy and optimistic people there. I visited all the likely places to find Vassily but did not find him. That happened to be 'No Show' day for him. Milly asked how to bet and she put a bet on the third race for a win. I played exacta. When the race started, instead of watching the progress of the horses, I enjoyed watching her face. She won, I lost. It was true 'beginner's luck.' She was thrilled to win. I showed her around. We had a glass of wine in the pavilion. Later I told Vassily that my fair lady was with me and I wanted her to meet him. He felt sad that he missed us.

Next time we went to Roosevelt after three weeks. We met Vassily. I introduced him to Milly as my friend. "Said, I call him 'Boss,' told me about you. My pleasure to meet you. You are really beautiful." He shook her hand and kissed her hand. We were together in the stands. After a few races, Vassily insisted to treat us in a nice Italian restaurant in Woodbury. I told him he did not have to. He drove his newly purchased Grand Tornado. He showed me his car and asked if I like to drive. It was getting late so I said "Some other time." It was a beautiful car. I liked it. The restaurant was a good restaurant with tasty food. Milly liked Vassily. He was on his best behavior.

I decided to invite Vassily to my wedding.

The day had come, after it felt like a long waiting period. I could not really sleep that night. The whole night I was counting those yearlong seconds. I was imagining how Milly was going to look, what she would be thinking at the time of the wedding and what she might be doing right now. Thousands of times I thought of calling her. But I didn't want to disturb her. Whenever I fell asleep, I was floating on my imaginary dreams. I had Milly in my dream wearing the dress she was going to wear for the wedding though I had not seen her dress. Then I remembered the funny situation we went through with this wedding dress affair.

After our engagement, one day I asked her, "When are we going to buy a wedding dress for this girl?"

She was a bit surprised when I said "we" and started looking at my face. I got confused to see the expression on her face. So, I asked her "Why? Aren't we going to buy you a new dress for your wedding?" She said "No."

I asked her again, "Why not? We are going to buy a new suit for the boy who is going to marry this girl. Aren't you buying a new dress for the wedding?" The surprise on her face confused me more and more.

"Yes, I am buying a new dress for the wedding."

"Good, good. So, when are we going to make a big plan to go shopping for your dress and my suit? Do we need to hold a couple of hot discussion meetings to decide on planning our wedding shopping and the day and the date? If so, then when can we hold the meetings to discuss the agenda for the meetings and the place and the date and so on?"

Now it was her turn to get confused. She looked at me as if I were the most stupid person on earth. Then she must have realized something. So, she said, "Yes, Said, I am buying a new dress, I am not taking you shopping and I am not coming with you to buy your wedding suit."

"Why not, my dear?"

"Oh, dear god, are you kidding, Said?"

"No, my dear deer, I am not. You should just call me dear instead of dear god."

"Oh, god! You are acting like a dumbbell, Said."

"Why? What is the matter, Milly?"

"Don't you know that the bride is not supposed to show the wedding dress to the groom before the wedding? It brings bad luck, and we are not supposed to see each other in the wedding dress before the wedding."

"Nope, I never heard of it before. It is not our custom in Egypt. Matter of fact, the groom does not see the bride till the wedding night."

"Oh, Jesus, what a confusion? Now you know it. So, please don't bug me. I am a bit superstitious at least in this matter."

"Can we marry tomorrow, Milly?"

"Nope."

Finally, I got up at five, still fresh and happy. I closed my eyes and said to myself, "Milly, I love you very much." I had a lot of time on my hands. So, I tried to slow down my chores taking extra time for each thing, doing it extremely carefully, and thinking that I was an artist in each chore, for example, bathing, shaving, etc. After that I prayed to Allah. I was so happy. I was going to marry that girl. Every so often I kept thinking what she, my bride, was doing. What color dress was she going to wear? She had mentioned that it was a satin dress. Would it be a blue to match with my blue suit, or a cream-color satin, or violet, or just simple white or some horrible shade of purple? I bit my lip because Milly would never select some purple color for sure.

I was ready by 6:30. Milly's brother, Bill, was going to pick me up with his whole family around 7:30. I put on the television and realized that it was the earliest ever I switched on TV. I didn't care to watch what was on TV. It was just on to give me live company.

The time was ticking very slowly, I started thinking, how I was counting each second of those anxious moments. The happy moments, hours, and days passed so quickly that I didn't realize that I myself experienced those events until I again hit the sad days and started counting the time. Did I really remember how I spent 32 years of my life? And now all of a sudden, I was that old, I mean young. I had a strange feeling. I tried to think about my past life. I could not think about anything other than my mother and then I imagined my mother hugging Milly and two drops rolled from my eyes.

I went in front of the building ten minutes before 7:30 so that if Bill came earlier, I would not delay him. And as expected, I had to wait almost half an hour before he came. Nothing was going right as far as the time was concerned. We had to be at the court by nine so that we could keep our schedule.

"I am sorry; I could not come in time. What a terrible traffic on the L.I.E. (Long Island Expressway)! I have absolutely no doubt why they call it the world's longest parking lot."

We faced another traffic jam on the B.Q.E (Brooklyn Queens Expressway). It took us another 45 minutes to reach the municipal building in Brooklyn. Bill dropped all of us at the entrance of the court and went looking for parking, another of New York City's problems.

Julie Anne was going to pick up the bride and Milly's father and mother. They had not arrived. Julie's husband had brought Miley's grandfather. He was wearing a classic black tuxedo, white shirt, and bright red bowtie. Karim and Nafisa came within minutes after we arrived. I introduced them to everybody. Imran and his wife, Rehana, were coming from Stanford, Connecticut. They had not come yet. Mokhtar had moved to Houston sometime in

July. He had planned on attending my wedding but his son became sick and he had to cancel his plans. And my special wedding guest Vassily had already come. He was in a three-piece bluish-gray suit with beautiful tie. I introduced him as my American friend. He felt proud that I had invited him. He kept himself busy talking with the people. I talked to Karim about his ride and our ride and traffic jams. But my mind was not there. We all were waiting for the VIP party of the ceremony.

Finally, they arrived. Oh boy, she looked so gorgeous in that peach satin dress with frills and a beautiful hairstyle. She looked like my dream girl, like a fairy. She wore a perfume of flower of Lily. It was chilly and she was wearing a white jacket. I tried to look into her eyes. She was trying to avoid me. For a moment she looked at me from tip to toe and smiled at me. I blinked my right eye and she blushed pink. I noticed Julie was watching us. She smiled. I was sure others also enjoyed watching us.

After our wedding party gathered, we followed a sign for "The chapel and waiting room." It was a big waiting room and we had enough chairs to sit together. There were two signs posted that proclaimed 'NO SMOKING, PLEASE.' That sign was certainly not for the typist, who was smoking and hiding her cigarette in a drawer of her table. She was typing the marriage certificates and witnessing the signatures. I kept thinking how I would like to fire her and bring someone with a smiling girl in her place. From the expression on her face, it looked like she was typing death certificates. I mean, just think, all these people had gathered here to celebrate one of the happiest and the most precious moments of their lives, and this girl looked as though she was attending a funeral. I said to myself, 'Oh, Allah give these people some brains, so they employ a smiling (and also a dancing) girl there.' The other sign said, 'NO GRAFFITI, PLEASE.' People obeyed this sign and surprisingly there was no graffiti on the walls like the room where we filled our marriage registration forms, that was full of graffiti. The room was painted in a beige color and all the walls were clean.

We filled out whatever forms we had to get welded, I mean wedded, and waited for half an hour before the clerk called our names. Milly said to me, "I like your suit. You look handsome. My hero!"

I told her, "You look cute in that dress. I prefer you without any. You look like my queen."

She laughed. And can you imagine what she did? She pinched my cheek in front of all those people. "You, naughty boy!"

I was trying to kill time but actually time was killing me. The bastard was not moving at all. Before we could get married, it would be at least half an hour. There were so many couples getting married that day. I wondered how many people get married every day throughout the world. I was not the only person feeling like that. I could not imagine what Milly was thinking. She was rather nervous.

"Julie stayed with me last night. She packed my suitcase and helped me with my hair and makeup this morning."

"How lucky! Me too! You know I had employed my own ghost to do that job." She laughed.

"Did you sleep well last night?" I asked her.

"Uh, not really, why?"

"I thought so, because I couldn't myself."

"I was thinking of today. Sometimes I got scared you might not show up."

"Oh, Milly." I held her hand and squeezed lightly. I wanted to kiss her for that but I didn't.

"Can you imagine, Milly, where we shall be tomorrow?" She didn't answer.

Then she kept busy talking to Susan and I gossiped with Karim and Imran. Nafisa and Rehana were busy whispering right from the time they met. Nafisa was old-fashioned. But on this occasion, she had worn a dress. Rehana had a good and quite expensive dress. She was graceful in it. Well, our waiting period was over. We were called in by the mourning-faced chimney. She gave us a marriage certificate to sign. The sign on the door read, 'DO NOT THROW RICE.' Our waiting luckily lasted a few more minutes till the couple before us was delivered as 'Newly married.' One more couple was born. Their dating game was over.

We went inside the chapel. On a step-high platform a judge was sitting at a table. We were sworn putting Milly's hand on a Bible and my hand on a Koran. I was waiting for those words "I do." I was constantly watching her face. It was so much fun. She was too overwhelmed. In a voice out of this world, she said, "I do!" "You may kiss the bride!" We kissed and put our arms around each other. That kiss made me forget everything around me, gave me a feeling of happiness floating through me as if an electric wave was passing through my body. To my surprise, her kiss was the warmest, I had ever experienced and was full of love. Maybe it was my imagination. And I saw mixed emotions; on her face a sort of happiness and confusion, as if she was not ready to believe whatever was happening to her. The tunes of the Indian instrument 'Shehnai' that is played at the wedding ceremony in India started playing in my ears.

My heart was literally dancing with joy. That girl was mine and I was hers. I wanted to jump all over the place. Finally, we got welded. Well, being a mechanical engineer, 'welded' was closer to my heart than 'wedded.'

I was watching everybody's faces. Milly's father looked happy and bewildered and was watching the events with his mouth gaping. Her mother had absolutely no expression of any importance. The grandfather had tears in his eyes. Susan, Milly's sister-in-law, was happy and watching everything with great interest. Karim, Imran, Nafisa, and Rehana were enjoying themselves as if they were in a circus tent. And Bill, his eyes were welling and he was clenching his teeth and trying hard not to let the tears roll down his face. His little sister was getting married.

Bill had arranged a celebrity lunch at a nearby restaurant. The name of the restaurant was 'Alphabets.' We had a glass of white champagne and white or red wine. I had red and she went for white. The grandfather had the honor of giving the toast. He stood up. "Today is one of the happiest days in my life. My favorite granddaughter is getting married. Her darling grandmother is showering blessing from heaven. I am sure she will be very happy with Said. I am so happy, so happy. I cannot speak. I give my blessing and grace to newlywed Milly and Said." He raised his glass and walked to Milly. He hugged her for a long time. He was crying happiness. Then he hugged me and wished me the best. "Make my angel happy."

The food was scrumptious. I don't remember what I ate. How do you expect me to remember? I was already high before drinking wine. After all, I was married to that girl. We had an American-style wedding lunch by kissing each other on demand of clinking glasses.

We had made our honeymoon plans in consultation with Julie Anne. She had her honeymoon recently at Annotto Bay, a small town in Jamaica. Julie liked the place and my Milly was thrilled by Julie's description of it. So, we simply finalized the same location and booked the hotel 'Honeymooners Too!' where Julie Anne had mooned with her honey.

We had an Air Jamaica flight at four p.m. from JFK that dropped us at seven thirty p.m. at Kingston. By the time we reached Annotto

Bay and to our hotel 'Honeymooners Too!' by forty-minute car ride from Kingston, it was almost ten o'clock.

At the motel they had a tradition of presenting a bottle of champagne to the honeymoon couple on the day of their arrival.

Both of us were too tired to enjoy it on the first night. Milly said to me, "Honey, don't you think it would be more enjoyable tomorrow rather than today? I am tired." I agreed and asked the hotel manager for a rain check for the next day.

I was all messed up the last night and scared. At the last minute she might refuse to marry me. I did not have a good sleep last night and I was really tired.

When I opened door of our honeymooner's suit. "Said, lift me and carry me over the threshold. That is American custom." As soon as I lifted her, she put her arms around my neck and started kissing me. She would not let me put her down. With difficulty I closed the door. I carried her to the bed and put her on the bed and softly landed on top of her.

"I love you. Behebak gidden."

"I love you too, darling. Beback giddian."

"Oh, my 'Gaza' (Poetry), oh, my 'Kamara' (The moon), at last you are mine and I am yours. We have become one, Lily. Oh, my sweetheart, love me forever."

The hotel room was very romantic. They had electric candle lights with dim bulbs on the tables and on the walls beside ceiling lights. When we entered, all the candle lights were on and were making dreamlike effect. There were three switches on the wall for the lights. One was for all the candle lights. The other lighted a lamp in the middle of the wall, which produced perfect moonlight.

The third switch lighted a regular ceiling light that was only for the people who I thought get smothered with heavenly moonlight and dreamy candlelight. I thanked Allah for giving such a fertilized brain to the person who designed such a brilliant romantic lighting system for this honeymooner's suite.

I said, "Rehana!"

"Isn't that Imran's wife's name? Why me?"

"You are Rehana, Mil. That is the name of a fragrant flower."

We did not speak then after. I kissed her, I kissed her whole body. She was made of roses, with silky smooth skin. It was like drinking wine; the more you drink, the more you enjoy.

"You are made of roses, my dear."

"I like that, you are romantic."

"Oh, the time, please, please, stop here for me. I want to live this moment forever"

Milly had closed her eyes. Keeping her eyes closed was her habit.

And I remembered that 'Babo' from my previous New York office, the one who used to drink a lot of coffee, must have been married by now and must be reading the *Kama Sutra* to his wife in a bed step by step. What a rotten thought on our honeymoon night! It was not even worth telling Milly. At least that thought brought a smile on my face.

"Jamila! Beautiful! You are so beautiful, my dear!"

We were heading for a breakfast the next morning. Milly saw a few vending machines in the foyer.

"Oh, these are the cookies I used to eat when I was a baby. You can't find them in America anymore."

She got a package of the cookies and she was busy opening it and I was busy watching her face. She was as happy as a baby. Her mouth was almost watering. She opened the package and all of a sudden smacked it on the floor.

"Oh, shit!"

"What happened, Milly?"

"Goddamn it. I can't believe it."

"You know something; you look really pretty when you are a little mad like this. What is the matter?"

"Look at that. There is a small worm inside that cookie."

I picked up the package and a few pieces that had scattered on the floor. I did not want to confirm what she had found. I just threw the whole thing in a garbage pail.

"You know they should charge you a little extra for those cookies. They have more protein than the others."

"Damn it, Said, you find something funny in every little thing."

She was really mad at me. I tried to talk to her. She did not want to listen and put hands on her ears. I said, "'Shanti,' Shanti means peace in Indian language." Well, I had learned a few Indian words through my friend Rajani Patel in Cleveland. He had told me it is also a name of a girl.

Anyway, I brought her two packs of those cookies and fed them with my hand and she fed me a few of them with her own hands.

After lunch we went to the beach privately owned by our hotel. The water was deep blue and calm. The sand on the beach was fine, smooth and rosy red. A cool breeze was blowing. Behind the sandy carpet of about a furlong coconut trees were dancing to the rhythm of the breeze.

I had already told her that I didn't need any suntan. I would accompany her to the beach and I would sit under an umbrella. She had bought a sunscreen lotion for me so I wouldn't get suntan. We got a beach umbrella from the hotel.

She was upset for a while because she remembered that she had forgotten to bring her camera with her. She said, "It is not a fantastic camera. My brother bought it for me. It is very old. It still works and I wanted to snap our pictures with it. Goddamnit!"

We swam together in the calm blue water. I was glad that she knew how to swim. There was quite a big crowd of honeymooners and vacationers. But my mind was thinking that everybody there was a honeymooner. They had facilities for water skiing. The only water game we could play was love making, which we enjoyed in the ocean water. The hotel owned a golf course and a few tennis courts right next to the beach. We did not know any of those sports and thus we were not interested in any of them. Milly spotted a huge obese woman lying on a beach chair. Her body was bulging out of the chair. Milly had a nice kick watching her.

The day was short, and right after the sun set, it became dark. We were lying on the beach. When it started getting dark, Milly got scared someone might come and attack us. My words of assurance for safety fell short of comforting her. So, we had to go back to the hotel.

When we returned to our room, the promised champagne was sitting on a table in an ice bucket. She was overwhelmed. I toasted,

"For our happiness together,
The life we shall share forever.
For the feelings we care.
For you, my love, for us.
For our love, for our health, cheers!"

I swallowed and she sipped as usual. We could not finish the champagne because she had a glass of pinot grigio during the dinner. And we were too excited because the electric moonlight that was too romantic and inviting. I started getting a good kick from the champagne. So, I was drinking and she was watching.

"I feel like singing, 'You are the moonlight of my life.'"

"Oh! No, please, don't sing. I am too tired to appreciate you, and it is not *The Moonlight*. It is *The Sunshine of My Life*."

"Oh! Well, I don't want to copy that smart guy."

Whatever I muttered that night, Milly wrote it down and gave it to me after we came back to earth; I mean back home to the US.

"Let flow the wine, let it overflow.
Let sparkle the rainbow of love from it.
The rainbow with the colors of life
Let me sing with you, you are my life.

Let me drink you through my eyes.
Let me fill you in my heart.
So, I won't lose you, you are my love.
I am so happy, you my love.

Let me dream of you, you are my dream.
Let us be the dream of one heart.
Let our dreams come true?
My life was humming happy tunes again.

The next day after breakfast we strolled through the town, which was about a mile from our hotel. The downtown area was nothing more than a shopping area with a few restaurants, basically a market place for the tourists. A lot of street peddlers were selling things like straw hats, bamboo fans, letter holders, paperweights made of large shells, pens with colorful feathers, hand-carved items, leather goods, various kinds of seashells and brass items. I mean they had every-thing to attract tourists and things you could find in those big shops. We were warned to bargain for anything we wanted to buy. Those shopkeepers and the peddlers would tell you the price in the range of three to four times the real selling price. There were a few boys selling items like straw hats and hand fans. Milly just wanted to look around and did not want to buy anything immediately. "We will buy the things on the day before we leave. I would like to buy souvenirs for Julie, won't you like to buy something for your friends?"

"Souvenir, I mean remembrance of my honeymoon? Oh, no, please, my friends will never spare me from making fun of me. They are all old country. You buy whatever you want."

Milly wanted to buy a colorful gown; actually, it was a sack rather than a gown, leather slippers for her and one pair for Julie. "Why don't you buy one for yourself, sweetheart?"

"Why not? But on the last day! Don't you think we should buy straw hats right now? It is getting too hot."

"You are right."

We selected, I mean my 'Bos', Miley selected, two hats, one for each of our heads. The street business boy told us twenty-five dollars for the two hats, not a penny less, and that too was a special price just because we were buying two, otherwise the regular price was fifteen dollars for one hat. I started the deal with, "We don't want to buy it anymore." Finally, we made a deal just for seven dollars for two hats half a mile away from the marketplace. where the actual bargaining had started. We also bought two hand fans. I felt sorry for the boy who was hardly ten years old and followed us all the way in the hot sun with bare feet. I gave him two dollars tip for his hardship. The boy became so happy that he told me to buy the things from him next time. He would give me a good price.

The next day we had a reliable assurance of security - I mean reliable for Milly - from the manager of the hotel. There was limitless time at hand and we did not care what time we came back to the hotel. 'Let the stars witness our love.' It was the first time ever we enjoyed the thrills of love-making on the beach. "None of my boyfriends were so romantic," she said to me.

And to our surprise, we were not the only couple at the beach that night.

When I came to my senses in the morning, I found myself on the bed, stomach down, facing away from my love, so-called, my darling life partner. My right hand went around her and told me she was front side up, I mean face up. I was anticipating her hand asking my hand 'To have me more', but there was no liveliness in that part of the world. We slept late last night, so she must be fast asleep and might be in Alice's wonderland. Now I was really awake and opened my eyes. I felt the sun was strong and it must be late.

"Hey hey little birdy, hey my baby,
would you please, come back to the earth.
To the world of liveliness.
Would you please wake up?
The sun is up and strong.
He is calling you to bake your white skin.
Wake up, my honey bunch."

And slowly I turned to her. She was awake and staring up at the ceiling. Something was bothering her. I cuddled her. I kissed her forehead, lips, ears, and nose. When I kissed her nose, she closed her eyes so I kissed her eyes one by one. When I did so, tears rolled down her face.

"What is it, Milly? Oh, come on, don't believe those dreams. They won't come true. Looks like you had a bad dream?" No sound.

"Are you, all right? Don't you feel good? Don't you want to talk to me? Come on, darling. Are you mad at me? Did I do something wrong last night? Maybe I said something you didn't like? Please, let me know. I apologize for it."

I kissed her, tried to tickle her but nothing could change the lost expression on her face. She was lost in the past. Finally, she said, "You didn't do anything wrong, Said. It is just me."

"What happened?"

She did not answer. I asked her again. "Is anything bothering you? Don't you want to share your feelings with me?"

She said slowly, "I was thinking of my first honeymoon."

"Really? How sweet!"

"That was not sweet."

"Oh, I am very sorry, Milly." I kissed her cheek. I put my left arm under her left shoulder, passing it under her neck, and put my right arm over her and tried to turn her on her side so she could face me. She turned to face me. I held her close to my chest. "Don't worry, Mil, I am with you. You don't have to be scared about anything in the world. What's bothering you? Won't you tell me?" She was so upset. She looked in my eyes. She started talking slowly word by word, without any emotions, in a flat and depressed tone.

"My first honeymoon was not happy, Said. It haunted me like a ghost. It started on the third day of our honeymoon. I was looking for happiness. Said, you would never understand what that day meant to me. All my dreams burnt to ashes. My heart burnt like charcoal.

"I was so happy to get rid of my mother. I hated her. Everyone loves their mother. Didn't you love your mother? I hated mine. What a shame. She destroyed my whole life." She was furious.

"Milly, it is not true; all people do not love their mothers."

"I was so thrilled to get married. I was in heaven for the first two days of our honeymoon. I had my sweet dreams of married life, just simple dreams of an ordinary girl. I didn't dream of becoming a happy princess. All I wanted was my own children, my own home, and my own husband, someone rightfully mine to love me.

"I wanted my family to welcome me home when I come home from work. My family for whom I wanted to cook on my own stove with my hands. I am a woman, after all. I used to dream of my own children in my childhood. I would be singing lullabies my grandmother had sung for me, to my sons and daughters. I did not dream of a rose garden of my life. I just had an ordinary dream to have someone to love me and I wanted to love my own man and my family."

I held her close to me. "It is alright now. We will make your and our dreams come true."

"The third day of our honeymoon was the beginning of the horror that shattered my happiness. That thing started right on the third day right in the morning." She paused, clenched her teeth. "The shame, down to the earth. He was a goddamn son of a bitch, a sex maniac, a pervert. God, rot his soul in hell. No one would take him as a maniac, a sweet, charming, innocent-looking face. People thought I was nuts to go for a divorce.

"The pervert tried anal intercourse with me and squeezed my breast so hard; I was in great pain. He spanked me and was getting vicious. It was dreadful. He squeezed my neck. I could not understand what to do and started to scream. That brought him to his senses. He stopped, became normal and pretended as if nothing ever happened. It was hard to believe whatever he did to me. I still hate him."

"Don't you trust me, Milly?"

"I don't know. I don't know anything. I don't trust anybody right now.

"There was my mother again. If she would have allowed me to go with him for weekend trips. He asked me a few times, but my strict and rigid mother never allowed me, as if she was going to get a prize for teaching discipline to her daughter. I hate her." She stopped for a few moments and calmed down a little bit. "That would have been a different story. He would have acted like a maniac sometime in those days. I would have ditched him. My life would have never been messed up like this."

She could not control herself. Tears were running. She started crying. She had her head on my chest. I was holding her with both my arms. I kissed her forehead and again she burst into tears. After a few moments she said, "Said!"

"Yes, darling!"

"Said, I love you." And again, she started crying.

"It's okay, darling, everything will be all right. We will be happy." I was moving my hand through her hair. She was sobbing. The dam had broken. There was nothing I could do to stop her from crying. So far, she had never shed tears. It was different now.

After lunch we went to the beach. All the time she was sullen. She was laughing at my jokes but she was certainly not herself. I was trying to cheer her up.

"You have to get a good tan to catch up with me."

"I am trying hard, dear."

"Do you know something?"

"Like what?"

"I was thinking of my first honeymoon too! We had been to Beirut for our honeymoon. Beirut was Paris of the east. Both of us were happy. We visited different historical places in the afternoon. In the mornings we used to go to one of those castles they had. There was a small park there on a hill. And right straight below the hill there was that beautiful Mediterranean Sea. We used to sit on a bench in the park overlooking the sea. We used to dream our future. They were really like fairy tales that would never come true. We enjoyed that way." Milly was quietly listening to me.

"You know! The water of that sea is so blue. It is unbelievable. Clean blue water and clean blue sky! My girlfriend Helen in my college days, I told you about her, she had deep blue eyes like the Mediterranean Sea. The sea has a different kind of blue and green shades. And at the shore those waves used to make milky white foam. The slow noise of those waves was the beautiful music of life that we were dreaming. After all that was our honeymoon. Right? Someday it used to be windy, and those waves would be large and they would jump high on the rocks at the shore. Those waves were trying to meet the sky. That was like the depth of love and the struggle of life. We need both, right? I was in such a fantastic mood. I wrote some 'Shayari' (poetry) that had really good meaning. Nadia liked it.

"Poetry-wise they did not turn out to be good. Can you imagine what happened to those poems?"

"No, what happened? Were they published?"

"Well, well I sent them to one of the editors who used to print my stories in his magazine. Almost a month later, I received them back. The editor said in his letter, 'Imagine if we print them in our magazine, our readers will stop reading your stories after reading your poems.' You know that nasty editor killed a naturally born poet in me. Well, I died as a poet at that time."

She was laughing. "Some other editor published my poems in his magazine. So, that was a good end."

When we went to the beach in the afternoon, the fat lady was strolling in front of us.

"Be careful, don't laugh, she will get mad at you and curse you and turn you into a pumpkin."

"You mean bigger than I was before?"

That lady was sort of our entertainment. Every day we passed her intentionally and watched what she was doing. She would put suntan lotion on her huge body and would sit on her chair; sometimes we saw her in water. Lying on the sand was impossible for her.

Our honeymoon was short, sweet and happy, and one of a kind.

CHAPTER TWELVE

The flight from Jamaica was on time. We were coming from a foreign country and thus we had to spend almost forty extra minutes with U.S. immigration and customs before we were cleared. Forty more minutes by cab and we were in our apartment. Our one-of-a-kind honeymoon was over. We were back down to earth to face the realities of life.

She opened the apartment door. I lifted her in my arms and entered the room with new hope, happiness, and eternal love forever.

"Milly, you know, we are married now. What a difference!"

"It's hard for me to believe. Isn't it?"

"Hum."

And the next moment we were hugging each other. And...

"Oh! I forgot to call my dear friend Julie. I was thinking of calling her as soon as we came home."

"We didn't waste our time since we came home. We just enjoyed the time."

"Huh. Be a good boy. I have to call Julie."

"Hey...Bully Julie Annie," and she paused for a second, breathed deep, and almost shouted, "And shitty Sharon, how are you?" A bubble of laughter escaped her.

"Oh, we just came back...Wonderful, yeah...Huh. Everything

was fantastic."

They had eternally long telephone discussions full of all kinds of humanly possible sounds.

I enjoyed listening to her. I had to do a lot of chores, unpack and wash at least one load of dirty clothes, iron at least one set of clothes, for me and her. I had to see if my car was still in the garage. So, I started getting busy in doing these things one by one.

"Hey, Saidy, listen, bully Julie wants us to come tomorrow evening. She can't come here; she is stuck at home with a backache. I got a lot of things to talk to her. I told her we could make it. Shouldn't we, darling?" Why should I deny?

When I came back from the laundry room, she was still talking to Julie. When she hung up the phone. As soon as she hung up, her brother Bill called her. They made about ten minutes revenue for the telephone company.

"Well, I have one question for you. I heard you calling Julie Shitty Sharon." I asked her after she finished talking to Bill.

"Oh, that thing. It is an interesting old story. I tease her sometimes. Long ago, when I was ten years old, my family moved to Brooklyn and I started going to the school, where I found this Julie Anne and another girl by the shitty name Sharon. Poor me started mixing up the names and called Julie as Sharon. Every time this happened, this tiny Julie got mad at me. Even now I tease her, 'Shitty Sharon,' and she says, 'I will kill you.'"

"Did she say it today?"

"Nope."

The telephone rang again, and of course it was for Milly. I had to go down to look after the laundry. But I was interested to know who was at the other end of the wire.

"Oh, hi, mom…" It was her mother.

"I missed my office."

I laughed loudly. "You mean you missed your office during our honeymoon?"

"Oh, no, not during our whole trip, Bobo. Now after coming back, I feel like I missed the office for a long time."

I was still laughing. She said, "Said, believe me, it is true. My office was the only sane world I was living in for the past few years."

And I stopped laughing.

Milly brought in the mail from our next-door neighbor, who had collected our mail from the mailbox on a daily basis. There were two greeting cards, one from Julie's parents and one from my buddy Husen from Egypt. Husen had sent an English greeting card, which meant he had to go to El-Mohalla El-Kobra just to buy a greeting card. In my village they didn't have these kinds of cards. Husen had written a short and sweet letter along with the greeting card. He was happy and wished happiness to both of us.

There was a letter from home. My number two brother Rehman had written it and mailed it to my old address. The post office had done an efficient job in promptly redirecting it to my new address. Husen had mailed to my new address. Well, I had written to him as soon as we decided to get married and our new living arrangements. I had told him to break the news to my family, which he had done.

The letter from my home was cold. Nobody from my family approved our marriage, just because I married a Christian girl. I never expected them to do otherwise.

My father had resented that this kind of thing ever happened in his family during his lifetime. My other brother also didn't like our marriage. Rehman, who wrote the letter, I was sure he was also one of them but he did not say so. My father had conveyed a message, 'Allah is great, and maybe he might forgive you and will bless both of you. By his mercy and blessing you will be happy and grow your family. Always keep a faith in Allah.' And finally, Rehman wrote the whole family was wishing us happiness. I was sure that was his own creation. My whole family was unhappy about our marriage.

Later at night I told Milly the exact text of the letter and the poor girl was upset. I wished I never told her or at least could have told her something else but I did not want to lie to her.

The next evening right from the office we went straight to Julie Anne's place. Her husband was traveling.

"Hi, Julie." Milly was excited. And the next second, they were embracing each other.

"Oh, I am so happy, Julie."

Both of them started crying. I felt so emotional and embarrassed watching them like that. I went to the living room, sat down on the sofa, and started going through the magazines lying on the table. After a while they came to the living room.

"I forgot about you. How are you, Said?"

"Well, it is ok to forget me. I am fine too. How are you?"

"I am alone for at least a few days. John will be back in two days." Then she said to me, "Oh, you got such a nice tan!"

"Look at him. The lucky chum didn't even try to get a tan. All he did was hide under an umbrella like a coward. And look at me, white as a ghost."

"Don't complain, Milly. You also got nice tan," Julie said.

Both of them left me alone and went to the bedroom more talk.

All I could hear from them were whispers, a few words, and lots of laughter. They did not want me to join them.

Being a presidential election, both of us had a holiday. Milly was thrilled. It was her second presidential election that she was going to vote. This time also she was going to vote for Democratic candidate Mr. Jimmy Carter. She was disappointed that Mr. Edward Kennedy was not the candidate. He was her favorite, for the main reasons that he was young and handsome. Her election strategy was interesting. In her first presidential election in year 1972 she had voted for Democratic candidate George McGovern only for one reason. Her late husband Richie hated President Johnson and the Democratic policy for their involvement in the Vietnam war. Richie himself and some of his friends were drafted and sent to Vietnam. And he in turn decided always to vote Republican. And Milly now for the reason of Richie had decided never to vote for Republicans in her life. She told me that she and her friends were charmed by John Kennedy's campaign and euphoria he had generated in young Americans. She was too young to vote for him. This time she was interested to see her choice winning the election.

She woke up early as usual and was one of the early voters. I went with her to the polling station to keep her high spirits. I was not a U.S. citizen that time. In the afternoon we cleaned the apartment and scotch-guarded the new sofa that was delivered last Saturday. Then we went to see double-feature movies in one-dollar movie theatre in Brooklyn. During the movie she was only thinking to the evening election projections.

In the evening she was glued to the television and completely engrossed in watching the election results. If you remember, that election was very close. I was watching with her after a while I lost my interest and Milly gained more interest. I tried to disturb her. "Milly, oh, my Lilly. I love you." "Hey, Milly, don't you know you look cute when you are mad at me?" She was not at all ready to be disturbed and she did not want to listen to anything. I kissed her, I hugged her. She just put my head on her lap and her hand on my face trying to put me to sleep. Only during the commercial breaks, she spoke to me like "It is anybody's election." "It is a close race; I hope he (meaning Jimmy Carter) wins California, Illinois, Ohio, and New York. That will certainly make him a winner."

Once she said she was hungry but she did not feel like getting up. So, I brought her some ice cream, which she could not get around to eat till the next commercial. Finally, I made coffee for her at about eleven o'clock and went to bed. She was not ready to quit.

At about three a.m. she woke me up. "Said, he won. He came out and accepted his victory and gave a short speech too." I knew who *he* was. "Congratulations Milly," I said, and she accepted as if she herself won the election. "Thank you dear," and she hugged me and gave me a long-lasting kiss, which I accepted and appreciated. I was half asleep and slept again in minutes. I was sure she did not for quite some time.

I felt sorry for American presidents the way they win or lose the elections because of voters like my dear Milly.

Karim wanted to invite all of us for dinner after our wedding. Mokhtar and family were going to visit New York during the Thanksgiving. So, Karim selected that Saturday for this occasion. Mokhtar, Mona, and Khalid arrived on Thursday morning. Mokhtar was so eager to meet Milly that Karim, who went to pick them up at JFK on Thanksgiving Day, had to stop at our place before they went to New Jersey. Mona also wanted to meet Milly and see our apartment. So, Karim's and Mokhtar's full families visited us. Mokhtar felt sad that he could not attend our wedding. They missed all of us and New York. He was happy to meet Milly. Milly and Khalid became good friends immediately though he wanted to listen to a Micky Mouse story from me.

Milly's grandfather always had Thanksgiving feast for all his family. On our way to the grandfather's house, Milly told me how she spent summers at her grandparents' house.

"I and my cousins always spent summer holidays at our grandparents' house. They have a huge house in Brooklyn. You will visit it now. My mother was working and she did not want me to be alone at home. It worked really fine with me. I had good riddance of my mother and had a good company of cousins to enjoy the whole summer. Sometimes numbers of us would go up in teens. My aunts would come and stay to help grandma. They would take turns. We would play indoor and outdoor games. The most popular indoor game was Monopoly. We had three sets of Monopoly. Then we would play outdoor games like red rovers, frozen tags, and red light/green light in the backyard. Sometimes we had verbal fights and then no talking between few cousins. Sometimes we got in physical fights between boys and girls and then punishments. Two of my cousins were strong; they used to beat boys. My aunts who came to help and granny herself had handful of work every day. We always helped with a number of chores. It was a lot of fun. Grandma would take us to a park to spend a day. We had to walk to the park carrying basket of sandwiches, fruits and delicious food granny had cooked. We played frisbee in the park.

"Grandpa used to be busy with his business and would go out of town for days on assignments. One evening a week a number of people would come and gather in his office. They would smoke like chimneys and drink bottles and bottles of vodka. I never knew what he did. Then one evening grandpa would treat us in the same restaurant every year. All the people at the restaurant would salute my grandpa. Keep quiet; we were not supposed to talk. It was time for granny and grandpa to have leisure time with wine and dine. Grandpa would smoke a cigar in the restaurant, not at home. My grandma's rule.

"Grandma died when I was fourteen. She was sick for a few days. My mother was worried and praying to god. She had some complications and then died of pneumonia. Grandpa insisted that all the grandchildren gather for summer as before and asked his daughters and daughters-in-laws to come and stay and take care of us. It is still going on with the next-generation kids. I and my cousins still go there one or two weekends every summer. I did not go for two years. I went there this year."

She was thrilled to go there with me and introduce her newly married hubby to every one of her relatives.

"I can't wait to show my lovely and romantic hubby to them."

"Unless they experience me, how can they recognize me as a romantic husband?"

She pinched my cheek and said, "They just have to believe me, Bo Bo. I am not giving anyone a chance to steal you from me." Then she told me that since she remembered the Thanksgiving was the happiest day of the year when grandma was alive. It was still a happy day. All her uncles, aunts, and all her cousins would never miss this day. Grandfather had a big house and always catered all the food and hired servants to serve. Granny never touched a thing that day. That was her rule."

Milly had so many cousins and other close relatives. Everyone was looking forward to meet me. All of them congratulated us. Milly introduced each one to me. From their expression, I felt most of them did not approve Milly's choice. All throughout the evening I was under people's gaze.

Milly's grandfather gave her a diamond ring as a wedding present and a beautiful, expensive dress. The diamond ring was beautiful with a big diamond in the center and ten small ones around it. It was Milly's grandmother's wedding ring. While putting it on her finger, her grandfather mentioned that Milly was the most favorite grandchild of his wife and she deserved this ring. Milly was literally thrilled. Her whole face glowed like a honeydew and tears rolled from her eyes. I got a brand-new platinum tie pin with a nice size diamond on it, a beautiful tie, and a two-hundred-dollar Sak's Fifth Avenue store gift certificate to buy a suit.

On Saturday Milly was wearing an Arabic dress that Rehana had presented to her on her wedding day, I mean our wedding day. She had practiced enough how to walk and how to sit comfortably in that dress on Friday. It was made of the finest Egyptian cotton.

When we reached Karim's house, they were all waiting for us. Imran and Rehana had already come there late Wednesday and looked like they all had a ball of fun. As soon as we entered, they all gathered around us. All the kids knew that Milly auntie was an American. When they saw her in Arabic dress, they were surprised and kept gazing at her as if she were a figure in an exhibition. Karim's daughter, Shakila, was seven years old, a boy, Abdul, five years old now, and then a little boy, Usman, about two. Milly shook hands with everyone. All the children were thrilled while shaking hands. Khalid had already become Milly's great friend on Thursday.

After their first curiosity was over, all the children grabbed me. Khalid was calling me Micky uncle and Karim's two-year-old, Usman, was calling me Uncle Donald Duck. Then they started arguing about my name that whatever name the other one was calling was not the right name. Usman was just a little boy of two and within a few minutes he started crying and everyone started looking at me. Milly was amused. I was in big trouble with my two names and was seriously thinking of how to satisfy both of them. I even asked my friends for help. They could not think of anything and told me that entertaining the kids was my department. Meanwhile, I was consoling Usman, whom I had put on my lap, and was telling him that I had two names and Khalid was saying how could I have two names.

Then I remembered and said to both of them, "My name is Donald like Donald Duck and also Micky like Micky Mouse. My name is Donald Micky. Donald is my first name and Micky is my last name. Everyone has a first and last name. Do you know your last name, Usman?" He nodded. He did not know anything about this last name. Khalid said, without asking him, "I know my last name. My last name is Tantawi, and my full name is Khalid Tantawi." Now Usman was more upset and tears started rolling down his cheeks. I wiped his face with my handkerchief and kissed and hugged him and told him, "Your last name is 'Wahed' like my last name is 'Micky.' So, your full name is Usman Wahed." That made him happy and I got a big relief. By this time Khalid had jumped on my other lap and he wanted to listen to a story from me. I was busy with these two boys all day. Karim's other two were there all along listening to me and were amused by the whole conversation. Then they started playing a game they had brought from home. I had hardly any time to talk to anybody else.

Milly was talking with all the ladies, asking them about the twenty-two-karat gold jewelry they were wearing. She was impressed by the almost pure yellow gold. Mona told Milly to ask me to get pure gold jewelry for her. I felt bad that I did not buy her anything like that yet. In America the stores only sold fourteen and eighteen karat gold jewelry. I knew I could buy the twenty-two-karat gold jewelry at Arabic stores on Atlantic Avenue.

Milly enjoyed the food and ate with great interest. After lunch she asked them how different dishes were made and wrote down some recipes.

Milly's mother and father are going to visit us that Sunday. She was busy making a cake, I mean she was preparing a cake mix from scratch.

"Hey, you know something?"

"What?"

"I have a fantastic idea."

"What is it, Said."

"You put two spoons of baking soda and it will be baking soda cake. A novelty! Right?"

"Stop it. It is not funny. I am concentrating here and you are making fun of me."

"Am I? I don't think so."

"Men don't belong in the kitchen. Get lost."

"May I see a face of a great philosopher, please. I remember my great friend Mr. Socrates saying the same thing to me."

"Hey, hey." She showed me her tongue and literally pushed me out of the kitchen.

Well, it turned out to be a fantastic fruit and nut cake when I tested it in the evening.

"Look at my great friend 'Georgie.' He looks so sad, poor guy. I have no time to talk to him." She picked him, hugged and kissed him and put him on her shoulder. After our marriage her dear 'Georgie' was dethroned from the bed and given a sitting position on the night table hugging the table lamp.

"Don't be jealous, honey. Now you are my 'Georgie' who listens to me all the time without complaints," she said as she pinched my cheek and kissed me.

During Christmas holidays, we took a few vacation days and went to Walt Disney World for four days. We stayed at Disney's Polynesian Resort, reached there in the afternoon of Christmas Eve, and enjoyed dinner at the resort's restaurant. We enjoyed the Christmas festivity till midnight. By the time we came to our room, it was past midnight.

"Don't you want to open your presents?"

"What presents?"

"The Christmas presents that I got for you."

"Sure!"

She gave me three, nicely wrapped packages. First, I opened the smallest one. My gift was a beautiful, black leather wallet made in Brazil.

"Oh boy, it's beautiful. I always thought that only Italians made such beautiful leather stuff."

"I had a reason not to buy one made in Italy."

"I got you."

Inside the second box was a 'PURE SILK' tie in a rich, blue design, made in India. The color combination created a three-dimensional effect. It was gorgeous.

What was in the third box, which was the largest one? I was thinking while opening the third box that I would find a few pairs of underwear—one hundred percent cotton (cotton grown in Egypt, woven in the Philippines, stitched in South Africa, sold in the United States and bought by M.A.—Milly Ahemed). T.S. (Thank Santa) I did not say so. In the third box I found two polyester shirts, made in the U.S.A. One was a plain, light blue, dress shirt. The other one was a jazzy, casual shirt.

"Thank you, Milly. I like all your presents. You have wonderful taste. I also thank Mr. Claus, I mean Santa Claus, who made this occasion possible."

Now I realized why Milly snapped at me when I was putting her suitcase aside. "Don't touch my suitcase."

"Oh, I won't."

"I mean don't open it."

"Oh no, I won't. I won't mind you opening my suitcase, though. I am not hiding any scorpions in it." I did not realize then that she was hiding presents.

Now, she was waiting for my turn. She was a little disappointed when I did not give her any present. I was sure that she must have thought that I was really a man from the jungles of Africa.

The next morning, I was awake before her and waiting for her to wake up with her usual big smile.

She woke up, smiled, hugged me and kissed me.

"Merry Christmas," I said.

"Same to you, honey." And then she touched something around her neck.

"What is it?"

"I don't know. Looks like some spider is hanging around your neck." And my god, she screamed and jumped in the bed. It was a real scene and I was laughing. She got mad at me.

"You did it," she said.

"The spider is gone now," I said. She touched in front of her neck and took it off and looked at it. It was a small gold pendant with a blue sapphire that hung delicately from a twenty-two-karat gold chain. And she laughed and laughed and laughed till tears came to her eyes.

"Thank you, smarty. I love it." And she kissed me again and again. "I love you, Said. I love you very much. Don't ever leave me, please. I am very happy."

Milly was so happy that she wanted to go a church and pray to god. She had found a church in our resort. She told me to stay in the hotel and watch TV, behave myself, no loud TV.

"I will accompany you."

"For what?"

"So, no one would kidnap you." She refused my protection for her.

"OK, if you don't need my protection. Then I just like to give you company. I am sure you would not mind. I will keep quite like a baby; I will keep watching you while you are praying."

"Oh, no. Please don't do that."

"O.K. I will sit next to you with my eyes closed."

"Oh, no, don't do that, either. Just sit there and behave yourself."

"You mean like a dumb monkey."

"Said, don't come with me, please. Just sleep in the hotel or do anything you want."

Finally, she allowed me to go with her. She warned me not to keep looking at her, not to touch her and behave myself, which I followed.

After we came to our room, I said, "I am also happy that I feel like praying to Allah." I started doing my 'Salad' (Muslim prayer). She watched me with interest. For sure she had never seen any Muslim praying; maybe she might have seen it in a movie.

"Oh boy, I never saw one like that before. It was like a workout."

After my prayer, we went to Disney World. Being an employee of an engineering firm, I got a discount pass from my office and got a twenty percent discount on the ticket price. Milly had made a wish list of what rides she wanted to visit. First on the list was 'It's a Small World.' She enjoyed this ride. Being Christmas holidays, Disney World was crowded to the full capacity. There were long lines for all the rides and food stalls. You had to be lucky to find seating at the food stalls. Lines for the rides were at least half an hour long. She was scared to go on the big wheel but was thrilled during the ride. She wanted to go to 'It's a Small World' again. The lines were so long that we cancelled that. We were coming again the next day. Right in the morning the next day we went to 'It's a Small World'. Both of us were in a dreamland for thoese two days. Fully enjoyed Disney World! Third day we went to 'Sea World' and forth day we visited 'Wiki Wachi' to talk to parrots. In the fourth evening we flew home, our sweet home.

January of 1977, we had plenty of snow and during that particular weekend we had four inches of fresh snow. So, we decided to go to the Prospect Park to make a snowman. I had never made a snowman. Milly was thrilled at the idea. While going to the park, she was lost in her thoughts. "Oh, shit, idiot. Why don't you go to die in front of someone else's car, not in front of my car?" My heart panicked as I slammed on the brake to stop my car. I was going slowly on the snowy road; otherwise my car would have skidded. A boy ran in front of my car to avoid a snowball from the other boy.

We selected a spot for a snowman and started throwing snowballs, ducking and trying to avoid each other. She was good in attacking me. One of her throws lobbed right in my face. It was cold and still snowing, sometimes big snow flowers, I mean flakes. We had a great time.

I started collecting snow with the shovel I had brought.

"What is this for?"

"To make a snow-woman."

"Oh, no. That is not how we make a snow-man."

And she showed me how to roll from a distance a small snowball into a big one. It was really a great idea and both of us rolled a big hump of snow. We made a big snowman. I dug out two dirtballs from the ground, shaped them, and those became the eyes. Milly found a dried piece of branch and stuck it in the place of a mouth to make a cigar out of it. She put her scarf around him; I put my hat on his head and put a shovel on his shoulder. Milly put her arm around him and kissed the snowman.

"I love him."

"Don't love him too much, please."

"Why? Are you jealous?"

I hugged both of them and kissed the snowman.

"Hun, a man does not kiss another man. It's a dirty act."

So, I kissed her through the lip opening of the ski cap she was wearing. We took our pictures with the snowman and sat on the ground holding each other's hands. After some time, her hands started getting cold. I was wearing warm ski gloves. Her regular gloves were not warm. So, she put her hands under my long woolen coat. After some time, her hands started playing with me. So, I said, "Let's go home."

In the car going home, she told me, "Bill and I played in the snow and used to make a snowman in New Jersey, in front of our house. Papa took our pictures every year. I forgot to show you my photo album. I will do that after we go home."

She was thrilled to show me her album. It started right 'On the tenth day'. So many pictures of baby Milly. What a cute baby she was! And then there was her picture in which she was crying at full blast. She must have been about two years old. "Oh, that one, I was crying over something and was not ready to stop. My father said if I did not stop crying, he would take my picture and that is the one. Bill always says 'I will show it to your boyfriend. So, he will know how cranky you were.'"

She looked cute in that picture. I told her so and kissed the picture, she got mad at me. Then there was a photo from which that blow-up was made. And then lots of growing-up Millys in different poses, birthday photos, photos with snowmen. All cute! I liked her photo in a red winter coat in front of a snowman in which she was posed for taking a photo with her toy camera. In another one she was playing a violin. I realized her father was a good photographer.

"Bill gave me a violin on my twelfth birthday. Then I used to play violin in the school orchestra."

"You never mentioned it to me. I would love to listen to you playing violin."

"I know. Richie had loved me playing violin. One night, that is after he died, I got furious, just because he liked my violin recital, I broke my violin. I should have never done that. It was a gift from Bill that had his love."

"I will buy you another violin someday."

In another album she had all the family pictures. There were no wedding pictures and no trace of her first husband.

She took a picture from an old envelope and showed it to me.

"This is strictly for you. I still get mad at Bill for snapping this picture. On his twelfth birthday, Papa gave him his camera to try, and this is what he did."

In that picture, Milly was standing in a tub all wet and nude.

"Look, you were not crying that time."

"I loved bathing."

Then she showed me an old instamatic Kodak camera.

"It is old. It still works. My brother bought it for me. I was eleven then. It has a sad and sweet story behind it.

"When I was in fifth grade, I participated in a fundraising scheme from the school. It was Christmas fundraising for a blind children's charity. We were supposed to sell raffle tickets and depending on the amount sold, one would get a gift. I took my tickets to Thanksgiving dinner at grandpa's house. I had a big sell. Grandpa, grandma, my aunts and uncles bought a big number of tickets. I had collected close to two hundred dollars. I selected an instamatic camera as a gift.

"The camera was delivered home. I opened the package and took the camera out. My mother was watching me. She said, "Milly, it is an expensive toy. Be careful. Don't drop it, it will break." I was startled and the camera fell to the floor. It broke. I started crying. "You dropped it. Now don't cry." Bill was home that time. He had a regular full-time job and he was attending evening college. He came and saw what happened. He took me to a camera shop and bought the same camera with case and a strap.

I paid for the films and developing from my baby-sitting money. Sometimes Bill paid for the films and developing till I was able to pay myself. Bill always used my father's camera in those days."

The next day, after the snowman day, Milly had a backache. Her whole body was in pain and she was feverish. She could not go to work. She drank the coffee I made, with a few Tylenols. I called her from time to time to find out how she was feeling. The whole day she practically did not eat anything.

When I came home early. She was awake.

"How do you feel, my sweetie? Didn't you enjoy watching afternoon soap operas?" When I had called her once in the afternoon, she was watching TV and I had told her to enjoy it.

"I feel a little better now. And yes, I enjoyed watching TV. My back is still in pain. I could not sleep. I was waiting for you to come home."

" I came home early."

" It is sweet of you. I shall be all right tomorrow."

I made some soup and literally forced her to eat it. She just ate a few spoonsful. She insisted that I cook a hamburger for myself.

I knew Milly loved hamburger but she was in no position to eat anything that day. Anyway, I had a couple of slices of bread with soup and I enjoyed it.

I put on Bengay and slowly massaged her back.

"Why are you so nice to me, Said?"

"I know that."

"What?"

"That I am nice to you. Do you know something?"

"What is it, Said?"

"Why am I so nice? I will tell you a story. Well, it is a true story. Allah had decided to create a mass production of nice men to put them on the earth. So, he engineered, designed, and fabricated a happy and lovable prototype of a nice man. Now he was ready for mass production. Then Allah thought for a while and was scared that if he puts so many nice men on the earth, then there would be very little crime and trouble on the earth. All the men would be happy. They would not need any help from him and they would not pray to him. This way he would lose all his importance. So, Allah decided not to put this sample of nice man on the production line. Oh, I forgot to mention to you, by the way, Allah named his proto-type man 'Said.' 'Said' means a happy man in Arabic. And that is the reason, there is only one happy Said in this whole world."

"Ah, you are a good storyteller. I am very happy to have you."

The month of January was extremely cold. That was one of the coldest Januarys recorded in North America. February started on a milder note and everybody felt a great relief. It was spring compared to January's weather. And I thought of going to Jones Beach for a boardwalk. Usually March or April weather permits that kind of activity.

Milly supported my idea and within an hour on that Sunday morning we landed on Jones Beach. It was much colder and windy compared to what we had in Brooklyn. I was not surprised to see so many people on the boardwalk. Though it was chilly, I am sure everybody was enjoying the boardwalk and the sight of the ocean. We visited my favorite Jones Beach restaurant. It was crowded and we had to wait to get a table.

On the first day of the spring
I bought little little daisies
I bought little daisies for my love.
For my love, for my sweetheart.

And she liked them. She smelled them. Daisies don't smell. I felt I should have bought roses. I knew she loved roses. Anyway, she was happy to see those snow-white delicate daisies. And she asked me how I could find daisies. "Those are summer flowers. You can't get them so early in the season." She kept wondering where these flowers came from. And I kept wondering about her knowledge of flowers.

Every evening, we would try to come home from office around same time. I or she would wait outside the subway station for the other to come. As soon as we met, we would kiss and then we would go home happily hand in hand. On our way we would chit chat. First thing after going home we would wash hands with soap that was lesson learnt from TV. We would sit on sofa and put on TV,

NBC evening news. She would lean on my shoulder. Our kissing petting would start. "Kill that TV. It is disturbing us." And then serious romantic act would follow.

One day I decided to tease her. As usual she sat on sofa waiting for me to sit next to her. I sat on the love sit and started watching TV she had turned on. Big eyes were watching me. I ignored her and started seriously watching TV news. She couldn't take it any longer. She got up and sat next to me held my hand. I played cool.

"Are you mad at me?"

Simple "No."

"Then why are you not sitting with me?"

"Just no reason, just for change."

"Oh, Said, please don't do this to me. I got scared that you are mad at me and you would leave me."

"I am not mad at you and I will never leave you. I shall not do it again." And hugged her.

Sometimes we used to have high-level intellectual disagreements and then some intellectual verbal talk (I mean verbal fight). And then she would not talk for a couple of days, at the most three days. I would call her in the office, she would not talk to me, and she would just listen to me and never hung up the telephone in those 'Special days. I would offer her Chinese dinner; one of her weaknesses. And that evening when I would go home after waiting for her at the subway for half an hour, I would find her at home waiting for me for dinner. And I would tell her that I was waiting for her at the subway station thinking that she was late. After the first time she had said, "How stupid. Can't I come home alone?" Some smart guy had said that this kind of ritual adds spice to life's happiness.

In those days, she would cook all the dishes of her choice, sometimes Chinese dishes too. Of course, I had no specific disliking for any particular dish. One thing she would not forget and she would never cook any dish with pork in it or anything I really disliked. I would try to talk to her at home and she would not answer me. She would not even tell me to stop talking because that was her hundred percent non-talking policy. I would try to make her laugh by my tootsie talk. I would tickle her. But she wouldn't laugh and would not stop me. If my tickling became unbearable, she would either push my hand or hit it or simply walk away from me. Of course, no kissing, no petting, even touching was prohibited in those days. 'Oh, poor Said! Oh, poor me!'

And the next day right from the morning she would start the day very normal as if nothing ever happened the day before. She would kiss me good morning. Sometimes I used to be lucky enough to get tea in bed and sometimes lucky to make love. I would tease her by asking, "Do you remember about the last few days, Milly?" She would play innocent and say, "What about it? Oh yeah, a day before we talked a lot. So, I thought of resting our voices. Wasn't that good?" I wanted to say, "Oh, I see that." Before I could say that, she would clamp her mouth on my lips.

I always enjoyed her act of getting mad at me. She would look so pretty and sexy when she was mad at me.

Usually on Friday evening we would either go to a restaurant or go to a movie or go to a play. Sometimes she would suggest we go to a Chinese restaurant. Occasionally we would go to an Arabic restaurant on Atlantic Avenue. She liked Middle Eastern food. Every time we went there, she would ask me the recipe of those dishes. If I did not know the preparation, I would call the chef and he would explain in detail how to prepare some particular dish in Arabic and

I would translate. Then next few days she would be preparing those dishes at home. She would keep me standing near her to see if she was doing it correctly. Sometimes we would go to a disco after going to a restaurant.

Sometime in the beginning of April, after we had dinner at a Greek diner a few blocks from our home, we drove to a disco near Coney Island. They had a live band. A lady was singing a song:

"Come and love me, oh, the stranger.
Kiss me, hug me and love me.
In the cool of the night,
love me and make me happy.

Give me the warmth of love,
in the heat of the night.
My heart is burning,
And I am thirsty for your love.

Come and love me, oh, the stranger.
Kiss me, hug me and love me."

We drank white wine and danced two numbers and then came back to our table to sip more wine. "You are improving, hon." A comment from Milly. In a few moments, a young guy approached us. He was constantly gazing at Milly.

"I was watching you dancing. You are wonderful. Would you please give me honor to dance with you? My name is John," he said to Milly and offered his hand.

"I am Milly and this is my husband, Said." He shook hands with both of us. Milly went with him to the dance floor before the next song began. After they danced one song, I went to watch them dancing. Milly was an excellent and swift dancer. I felt proud of her. The band stopped for a break and all of us came back to the table.

"You were excellent, darling," I said to Milly.

"You better believe it. She was the best among the whole lot there," this guy, John, said.

"You are exaggerating," Milly replied.

"I don't think so. Where do you live, Milly?"

"On Thirty-Eighth Street between Flatbush and Bedford."

"Those houses there are beautiful. Do you own a house?"

"No, we live in an apartment."

"What are you drinking? I will get drinks for you." He ordered drinks for us.

"Where do you live, John?" I asked him.

"On Coney Island Avenue about a mile from here. What country you come from, oh, I forgot your name."

I told him my name and told him where I came from.

When the music started, Milly and I went to the dance floor and danced. During the next song, I saw that John had found some girl to dance with him and he moved in the close vicinity of where we were dancing. I felt he was constantly watching Milly. After the song, we went back to our table. And John also returned. "I loved to dance with you. The other girl was not so good. May I get the favor of dancing with you again, dear Milly?" he asked Milly. "Only one song; I am tired now." And they danced one song and came back to the table.

"I loved dancing with you. You must be good in ballroom dancing also. I would like to dance with you some other time. We should arrange for it. I will give you my telephone number. Would you please do me a favor and call me? I will be too happy." He gave his card to her.

"Are you married, John?" I asked him.

"No, not yet! I am still looking for a pretty girl like your wife to marry."

He hardly moved his eyes from Milly most of the time we were there. I was getting irritated by his intimacy with Milly. It was well past midnight. We were tired. The place was showing the weariness of the people. We decided to leave.

"Nice meeting you, John," Milly said to John.

"Hope to meet you again." Anyway, John came up to the door with us as if we were his good friends.

In the car I was mad at this guy John. I did not say anything till we reached home.

"This guy John was showing disgusting intimacy with you."

"Did you expect me to ask your permission to dance with him?"

"No, absolutely not. I did not expect it. I don't think he had any business to give you his telephone number and ask you to call him. If he had asked you for our telephone number, I would have simply objected. He was behaving as if you were an unmarried girl. Very immature!"

"That would have been very rude of you."

"I am sure, dear, it would have been. But that is what any husband would have done."

"No, Said, I don't think so. You are forgetting that you are in America and not in your old country. You cannot think of Egyptian ways here." She had raised her voice.

"You are absolutely right, and I don't think I was thinking in an Egyptian way." I was fully mad by this time.

"I think you were jealous of me for getting that kind of attention."

"Whatever you want to say. I was not acting differently. Any husband would have acted the same. It is just natural."

"You are overreacting. You are a staunch, orthodox Egyptian at the bottom of your heart!"

"Oh, yeah. You put yourself in my place and then tell me how you feel, right?"

"Oh, yes."

We did not say any more after that. I hit the bed. She also did the same thing. I turned my back to her. I was furious and could not sleep for some time and I realized that she was also awake till I slept.

CHAPTER THIRTEEN

As soon as I woke up the next morning, she hugged me and started sobbing. "I am sorry for last night. I should have never said the things I said to you. You are right, Said. No one would have liked his behavior. I am sorry. Please, forgive me. I love you, Said."

I hugged her back and started comforting her. "It is all right! You have no idea how much I love you." She gave me a watery smile and kissed me deep.

That was really a cozy disco place with a live band. Milly was not willing to go there. I insisted and we went there again after two months. We did not find John there.

That was the last Friday of April. We came home as usual.

"Aren't we going out for dinner?"

"Oh, yeah!"

I prepared the coffee instead of her. That was not unusual. I put cheese and crackers and some cookies for us to eat. This was not usual. So, she asked me. "Why is this special treat? Are we going to the Japanese restaurant on Long Island?"

"Maybe!"

"Anyway, I don't want to take my pocketbook."

"Oh, no, you better take it with you."

"Why? Don't you have enough money on you?"

"Yes, I have."

"So?"

"Please, take it. In case I feel sleepy and you have to drive the car."

"Okay, hon."

When I started the car, she asked me, "Where are we going, Said?"

I didn't answer. "So, you are going to keep me in suspense. One of your favorites. All right, you win." She didn't mind.

She must have remembered that one January weekend, when the weather forecast was slightly warmer temperatures in the upper twenties compared to the teens and single digits. That Saturday morning, we decided to go to the Poconos for skiing. It was not preplanned. She had never skied before and was scared. She did not want to learn skiing. I told her how I learned skiing because of my girlfriend Lynda in Cleveland. As soon as we entered New Jersey, it started snowing. She started saying that we should go back. We again heard the forecast. It was calling for little snow. I told her that I liked to drive in snow. I asked her if she would like to drive in snow. "Oh, no way," she replied. Anyway, as soon as we reached there, we made reservation at the Quality Inn in Stroudsburg. The next day was sunny. We went to "Shawnee" for skiing. I convinced her to take ski lessons and she did. By noon she ventured to go on bunny slope with the trainer.

She knew wherever I was driving was not going to spoil her weekend. So, she kept quiet. When we crossed Staten Island and entered New Jersey, she asked me, "Are we going to Karim's house?"

"May be."

"Then tell me where?"

"We are going to a place." And just to tease her, I added, "Believe me, I am not kidnapping you."

"I wish you were." I looked at her puzzled face and laughed and said, "O.K. Then I am."

"Now it sounds real. But where?"

"Listen to this music. Do you remember, these are the tunes from *Dr. Zhivago*? A beautiful movie! Wasn't it? I saw the movie in Egypt the first time. Once more in Queens. And you?" She did not answer.

And then she slept. When she woke, she let me know with a big yawn. "I am getting mad at you, Said."

"Don't you worry about getting mad at me?" I pulled her close to me. She stiffened and pushed my hand away.

"No, mister, leave me alone. It is no more fun."

"Oh, darling, don't you want to sit close to me, and give me a good kiss. I love you."

She pinched my cheek. I screamed. So, she said, "Good, I am glad."

I turned the radio volume high and immediately she turned it low. When it became dark, I started feeling hungry. "Are you hungry, my dear Mil?"

"Thank God. At least you realize that."

Next exit I stopped and we ate two small hamburgers each and had milkshakes. We had to eat two hamburgers because they had not invented double and triple decker burgers that time.

I told her that we are going to see Chesapeake Bay Bridge tomorrow morning and we will reach our motel in one hour.

"What about my clothes? Won't I need clothes for the night?"

"No, dear, you won't need clothes for the night."

"Cute! But what about tomorrow?"

"Don't you worry about it? You got your pocketbook loaded with money."

"Forget it. I am not going to talk to you."

"In an hour we should reach our motel."

She did not say anything. I thought she did not hear me. So, I repeated what I had said. Still she didn't say anything.

We registered at the motel in Kiptopeke in Virginia. When she saw a suitcase in the trunk of the car, she asked me when I put it in.

"During my extra-long lunch hour."

"You are so funny, Said."

By the time we entered our room, it was midnight.

That whole night we were alone. I mean we were just two of us in the room and nobody else with us in our bed. Well, the haunted image of Milly's maniac ex-husband was between us twice so far, peeking into Milly's mind. "My ex was such a lunatic; you wouldn't believe what he did to me in bed," she had said.

I woke up around five and tried to wake up my dear deer. She was fast asleep. When she woke, she was mad at me.

"Uh…let me sleep. I am so tired…Didn't I sleep just now? Oh, Said, what time is it?"

I told her it was quarter past five.

"We just went to bed. What has happened to you, Said? Have you gone crazy?" She was absolutely mad.

"I want to see the sunrise from Chesapeake Bay Bridge. Won't you like to keep me company? Oh, well, if you prefer to sleep?"

Within half an hour we were at the bay bridge. There were two observation galleries on East side, one at each end of the bridge, for people to watch the ocean and the sunrise. There were already a few people standing and sitting on the floor. We wanted to sit down but the concrete floor was dirty enough not to be worth sitting on, and I did not bring anything to spread on the ground. So, we were standing by the railing that was recently painted for the new tourist season. The flowerbeds around the deck had new spring flowers in full bloom. We were waiting for the sun to rise. All the sides together woke up the darkness and he walked away. The eastern sky was crimson and slowly turning to orange-red as if the whole sky was on fire. And there was the sun, just starting to peep out from the ocean and slowly opening his eyes like a newborn baby. A cool breeze was blowing. The shrieking of the seagulls was sounding so pleasant with the low background music of the waves. The whole atmosphere was heavenly romantic. In a matter of minutes, the eastern sky turned into gold. A few yachts and boats started showing their existence in the brightening light.

'Oh, the sun! Oh, the life giver!' I was praying to the sun. I knew that some people in the world pray to the rising sun. I wondered what they might be praying. 'Oh, the sun, you are the one who gives life to all human beings, to all the living beings, the whole nature, the whole world. You are the one who gives happiness to all on the earth.' And naturally I said, 'Oh, the sun, give life and happiness to them who missed it, who don't have it. I got my life. I have all my happiness right here, right next to me. I thank you, the almighty Allah.' And I put my hand on her shoulder. I was sure she was also enjoying the same way as I was. She did not disturb my ecstasy.

"What are you thinking, my doll with your eyes half closed?"

"I was filling my heart with the beauty of this sunrise through my eyes." I told her what I was thinking.

"Oh, boy, you poets always get into trouble with things like this."

"I am not a poet." I kissed her.

"Yeah, yeah, I know that too. You are a poet in disguise."

In the golden sunlight her hair looked blond and danced to a gentle breeze. And in that brightness her eyes looked more green than usual. They were looking into mine. In a split second I saw the same thing in those eyes that I never missed to see. Before I could realize anything, I was in her arms and my head resting on her shoulder. She whispered in my ears, "I love you so much," and she kissed my ear. When I saw again in her eyes, they were shining bright and were dilated. Her whole face was glowing in the sunlight.

"Hi, Gloria, you look so glorious."

I captured many of her expression with my camera. She took my pictures, and the camera with its timing device took ours.

Then we visited historical Williamsburg and the colonial lifestyle. We walked and laughed and ate and she sang and I listened. At night we ate in a good restaurant and boozed a little bit and finally got so tired that we had to retire early for the night.

The next day we drove back to New York, stopping in Washington D.C. to witness the world-famous cherry blossoms. Thousands of cherry trees circled the Tidal Basin in a shimmering pink halo. It was a simply beautiful sight. I thought the one I had seen in Brooklyn was out of this world. The ecstasy I enjoyed that time was far more than this joy. Maybe that was the first time I ever had seen such natural beauty. We really enjoyed this sight of blooming cherry trees. It was one of her dreams, to visit DC to watch the blossoms, she told me.

That was the beginning of our fun-filled summer weekends.

Some bread company had introduced a new variety of rye bread in the market and that commercial was a hot one on TV. The commercial ended with, "You don't have to be Jewish to taste our rye bread." I had a bad memory linked with rye bread.

"You know, I remember my Jewish friend Moses when I watch

this commercial." And I told Moses's story to Milly.

"Well, this is what happened during the Arab-Israeli War of '67. I tried to forget it. I couldn't. I still want to know the whereabouts of my friend. I wish I could meet my buddy someday somewhere." I paused, but she was too anxious to listen to my story. "What happened to your friend?"

"Well, that is what I do not know. I mean he is certainly alive; I hope so. His family was living right across the street from us. We were buddies since I remember. We were in the same class. His father had the only bakery in our town. The bakery was actually a part of their home. Moses dropped out from school to help his father run the bakery. He was the only son in the family besides three daughters. Even I used to like one of his sisters like I had a crush on her. She was like a sister to me. When I used to come home from college during vacation, he would treat me to special pastries his mother would bake for the family. I was like his family.

"In 1967 when the war broke between Egypt and Israel, I was in the college in Cairo. Moses just vanished one day. The villagers started saying that he had joined the Israeli army. His family told the people that he went to help his uncle close his jewelry business that was in trouble because of the war. No one believed him. They boycotted his father's bakery. The people did not get their satisfaction yet. One night they set their house on fire. All the villagers gathered and watched the agony of the whole family. They were bent on burning them alive in the fire. I am proud of my father. He came forward and told the crowd loudly to stop this nonsense. It is against Islam. Islam does not teach you to kill innocent people. He along with my brothers saved their lives and sheltered them in our house. He hired two reliable gunmen to protect them. You have no idea how the whole atmosphere in Egypt was filled with poison and the people were viciously bent over killing Jewish people. Thank Allah they were saved. Moses's father wished to move to Israel. So, my brother made arrangements with some Jewish association. They were safely transferring Jewish families out of Egypt. Then they left the town in a few days. The whole family was crying and ladies from my family and my tough father cried when they departed. It was so sad that war broke many loving families of generations.

"My father and elder brother were anxiously waiting for a letter from the family. Almost three months had passed without any news from them. Finally, we got a letter from Moses's father that was written and posted fifteen days after they had left and we received after three months. All that big delay due to war time scrutiny. Moses's father had written that they safely reached Tel Aviv after ten days of journey. They stayed in a shelter for two weeks. Then the Israel government gave them one room and a kitchen with common bathroom facilities in Kibbutz on outskirt of Tel Aviv and some money for survival. The letter was overwhelming. He had thanked for saving their lives and sheltering them. The family would never be able to repay. They thanked us in long words. They missed us all. The exchanging of letters continued for some time. After sometime the father got a baker's job at a big bakery in Tel Aviv. It was difficult to send and receive letters because of strained political relations between two countries. In one of the letters, we received later, the father had written that Moses had joined them and soon they would be moving into two-bedroom Kibbutz with common bathrooms. Our correspondence lasted a few months. Then stopped due to both the country's political relations.

"I was in college. When I heard the news, I cried. I want to meet my friend Moses. Maybe someday I might find him right in New York. A miracle, right? It could happen. Maybe his uncle migrated to America and he sponsored Moses. Who knows what happened to him? He was my great friend."

She hugged me. She was sad. "I am sorry for your feelings for your friend and your loss."

Once she asked me, "Said, do you believe in ghosts?"

"Who…me…no. Why?"

"Nothing, I just asked you. Nothing in particular."

"Oh, I don't believe in ghosts. But I had written a funny story about a ghost when I was in Egypt. The title of the story was *And a Ghost Was Born*. People liked it very much.

I don't want to believe you unless you tell me your stories."

"Well those were stories based on different background. You may not like them."

"How can you say so? I am sure I would enjoy them."

"Then I will tell you my stories."

I told her a few of my stories. She was engrossed listening to me. At the end of some story, she kissed and hugged me. "You are a great storyteller. You are a wonderful person, Said." Once she said, "You are an angel" and gave me a deep kiss. The other day while listening to my story, she had said, "Said, you are a bullshit artist." "I gladly accept your title."

During the summer we used to go to Prospect Park in the evenings. We used to come home at six o'clock and there used to be ample time and lots of daylight till dark. And we used to have a bar-b-que there in the park. "Mil, we will have a bar-b-que at Prospect Park tomorrow." Sometimes she would say, "It's a long time since we've gone to Prospect Park." "We went there last Thursday and today is just Tuesday." "But we didn't have bar-b-que. Why don't we have it tomorrow?" Milly used to marinate steak and chicken in her own recipe since morning. And we used to enjoy it very much, just the two of us. Sometimes Julie would join us, and sometimes she and her hubby John, used to be there. Julie and John both liked my spicy chicken.

One evening we went to Prospect Park for a bar-b-que. It was a warm and clear day, not even a white cloud in the sky. Our dear weather forecasters from TV and radio stations had not expressed even a doubt of a shower. Well, sometimes those experts say a trace of precipitation and it rains like the sky is torn. We started bar-b-que and were eating salad and drinking fruit punch spiked with vodka, Milly's specialty. Of course, alcoholic beverages were not allowed in the park. But our fruit punch was made an exception to the rules by both of us. And all of a sudden it became dark and started pouring cats and dogs with dances of lightning and roaring thunder. The lightning was so severe that we were scared. She ran to stand under a big oak tree. I pulled her away from under the tree. She suggested running back to the car. The car was in the parking lot and to go there we had to walk a good distance under the trees. Our best choice in that lightning storm was to go in the open ground that was just in front of us.

I was enjoying every bit of standing in the downpour and under that rain of lightning and my panicking queen in my arms. Would you believe, I had an urge to make love to her under the open sky and in the rain. And she was terrified and hugging me like that was the end of the world and praying to God to end this evil.

Sometimes we went to row boats in Prospect Park. They had a small lake there for row boating. There were white lilies in the lake. Milly used to enjoy touching them. And I always realized that when she bent to touch them, there was an addition of three lilies in the water, one of them used to be her face. It was fun to watch.

Sometimes we used to throw flat pebbles in the water and watch them jumping a few times on the surface of the water. We would see who created the maximum number of jumps. We enjoyed the nature and our association with it through different activities. There was not much talking. Our mute silence was our romance.

Sometimes we would go to Jones Beach, eat at the restaurant

there at the beach, and sit down on the sand watching the waves, listening to their music and at night watching the stars. We would stay there till midnight. We realized it was great fun and a thrill to make love at the beach in the dark, well, sometimes it used to be a moonlit night. We were not the only couple enjoying this kind of thrill.

One evening Julie and her hubby, John, were visiting us, and Julie said, "Ah, John, don't you notice a big difference in Milly's home? This place has its own soul. There is a warm welcome and happiness in the house. We feel like visiting you more often."

I felt glad about the way they felt. Well, there was happiness in our home and our lives.

'Imagine a couple of baby Lilies and baby Saids were running around the whole house and were climbing all over the place and climbing over me and Milly, were fighting with each other, and Milly was getting mad at them and punishing them, and then feeling sorry for punishing them and cuddling them with love. Well, how about a dozen of them with a couple of twins? It would be a lot of fun. We would have a football team of our own. Oh, I mean soccer team. Mil would be busy all around the clock. Wouldn't she go crazy? Oh, I was just kidding. I thought either two or three babies would be enough. How about a baby Lily and a baby Said, that's it, only two? Maybe one boy and two baby Lilies. Oh, yes, twin Lilies, identical twins! And yeah, both of them should have Milly's eyes. Oh, boy, it would be such fun. It would be a paradise in our home.'

I was daydreaming and I had a sweet smile on my face. I said, "Milly, don't you think if we have babies, just two Lilies, identical twins, and one boy, the happiness would multiply?"

"Oh, yes, it is a wonderful idea and right time to start a family. Milly, take it seriously." That was Julie. Milly also liked the idea. She was shy, blushed pink, and smiled sweetly.

"Hun," she said. But after a few seconds, she said, "Said, I do not want any children. I won't be a good mother. Sorry, Said."

"OK, it's alright, we won't have any children. After Elham I was always skeptical about having children. I am still not ready to go through their sickness or more serious sadness. All right Mil, we do not want any children"

Once she told me, "I feel very happy the whole day when we make love in the morning."

"I love you Milly.
You are the dream girl.
Sweeter than the sweetest.
You are the dream of my life.

You are my lily.
The fragrant flower,
and delicate too!
And you are like a pearl too!

Pearl of water on the leaf of lotus.
That is prettier than a pearl.
That is shy and sensitive like you.
Why don't I call you Pearl?"

We had wheels on our feet. Every weekend we drove long distances for sight-seeing. We tried to come home at night because Milly was keen on expenses. If it was not possible, we just slept in a good motel, either waterbeds or no waterbeds. On long weekends we went extra-long distances. On Memorial Day weekend we went to Niagara Falls. Both of us had been there before. But the thrill of the enormous waterfall was the same as being there for the first time.

My nonexistent diary for 4th of July weekend would read as:

On Saturday, we four, Milly, her darling (myself), Julie Ann, and her honey (John) went to see a performance of the musical *Show Boat* at the Jones Beach Marine Theatre. It was an outdoor amphitheater. We did not have tickets in hand. So, we went to the theatre around noon time, bought the tickets. After buying the tickets, by the biggest demand of four of us, we went to the Jones Beach for the other three's competition to match my skin color. We were prepared for the beach. They had their bathing suits and suntan lotion. For me, my sweetheart had bought the highest number sunscreen lotion that I was going to test it under the beach umbrella we had rented. P.S. – I was in my swimsuit and I went in the water with all other three.

After their big ambition to beat my skin color was over in bitter failure, we went to 'Guy Lombardo's East Point House,' a famous seafood restaurant, for dinner. I refrained from any alcoholic drink as I was the designated driver.

We went to Jones Beach theater early, about seven o'clock, to enjoy Guy Lombardo's band in a tent near the theatre. People were drinking. Julie, Milly, and John had one drink of wine. I did not. Milly had her second drink of the day. She broke her policy for a special event of this fun day. The music was melodious and the atmosphere was spontaneously joyful.

We went inside the theater with rented blankets. By the end of the play, the weather was going to be chilly. At exactly eight o'clock, the stage that was in front of the front row started separating and went in to the ocean, making a canal of about fthirty feet. In a few minutes, Guy Lombardo himself brought all the actors and musicians in his motorboat. We, all the people, were thrilled to watch this kind of beginning of the show. The play was *Show Boat*. It felt excellent and romantic due to the outdoor theater on the water. The cool breeze was blowing, making the atmosphere more romantic. During half an hour intermission, a lot of people lined up in front of the bar for drinks. None of us took drinks. Instead we enjoyed others drinking. After the play, the band played for an hour in the tent. We roamed around and enjoyed the music. Julie and John had one more drink. Both of us did not. All the time Mil was holding my hand and whenever possible leaning on my shoulder. She did not miss any chance to kiss me. By the time we came home, it was past one in the morning.

Next day, Sunday, in the afternoon four of us went to Coney Island. Their competition to match my skin color continued. This time they all had better success than yesterday. They all became reddish brown to my brown. I also got suntan though I had put sunscreen and tried to avoid sun. In the evening we went on rides at Coney Island and reenjoyed our childhood. At night we eat at 'Lundies'. All three eat raw oysters and I enjoyed watching them.

On Monday, 4th of July, we had invited Julie and John for barbeque. The main dish was lamb chops marinated in spicy mint chutney. I made cucumber salad (Milly's cucumber soup). It was extremely hot day. So, we enjoyed beer with our food. In the evening we went to the central park to watch Macy's firework. In the dark both the couple enjoyed romancing rather than watching firework.

Next day evening as soon as we met outside subway station, she was so happy, she said "Hay Saidy, people from my office liked my tan."

"Wow! Congratulations, I am glad." I was happy because she was happy in her loss to compete with me.

"It is such a nice feeling to come home and have my love with me to gossip, to make jokes with me, to make fun of me and waiting to play romance with me. A great change in my life. I am so happy, Said."

"Me too! It is a big happiness in my life too. I am glad that you feel the same way."

"Would you promise me, Said, you will never leave me?"

She was now looking into my eyes again. A question in her eyes. That expression on her face amused me.

"Of course, of course."

"What?"

"Of course, I will." I paused. "Not. I mean I shall never leave you, my dear deer 'Maha.'"

She was relaxed. She hugged me and kissed me.

"Oh, Milly, I love you so much. Why do you have doubts?"

"I feel scared sometimes." That made me laugh. Then I became serious that those were her true feelings and she was scared sometimes.

"I love you so much; I will never leave you, Milly my life, darling." And I hugged her.

Our wedding anniversary was on the 21st of October, you knew it already. It was on Friday. Early in the morning we wished happy anniversary to each other.

"I am so happy, Mil. It is one full year. I forgot the whole world around me. The time just flew like a flash of lightning. Milly, oh, my Lily."

I hugged her, kissed her very tenderly and then fiercely and then she had tears of happiness and ecstasy in her eyes. I gave her a beautiful string of pearls. She gave me a bottle of cologne and yeah, tons of kisses and lots of 'Love you's' and a greeting card. I remembered that I had forgotten to buy a greeting card for her.

And that afternoon, as I came back from lunch, a bouquet of red roses was waiting for me on my desk. I was so bashful. I never expected something like that. Well, they don't do it like this in Egypt. And I did not imagine doing it. I felt so stupid of myself for not sending flowers to Milly. I called her immediately. "I thank you, Mil. I love you."

"Thanks for what?" She was playing cool.

"The flowers, the roses. They are beautiful."

"Oh, your loved one from Mars must have sent them to you, not me." And I laughed freely.

I walked out of my office and went to a florist and explained my situation and requested him to send flowers to Milly immediately. I selected the card and selected the flower arrangement. The flowers were delivered to Milly at four o'clock from a man from Egypt. After coming home, she said, "Now you have jumped from Mars to Egypt." I said, "No I jumped on you." I said sorry and explained to her the ignorance of a man from Mars. She accepted my explanation.

Our wedding anniversary was celebrated again and again, the first time by Bill and his whole family. They gave a dinner in a restaurant on Saturday before the anniversary. Milly's father and mother were also invited. At the last minute they could not make it as her father was not feeling well. I must say that Milly was glad that they were not there. That Friday Julie and John celebrated our anniversary at Lundies. It was their favorite place. I enjoyed that restaurant and their seafood though I was not a great seafood lover. We enjoyed all those anniversary celebrations.

I was, or maybe we were, disappointed that we had to wait till Saturday to celebrate our own anniversary. No one was going to be invited, just the two of us. Well, well, we had invited fairies from paradise just to watch us celebrate and romance.

We had a candlelit dinner. She was wearing a nice dress and the string of pearls, the one I had just given her. I laughed and asked her if I was supposed to wear a three-piece suite. "You have your own choice, my dear." Oh, yeah, I had my choice for me and for her, too. But I was too bashful to suggest what I had in mind? For starter, I was just in my casual dress. I dabbed the cologne she gave me. We had a bottle of white sparkling wine as both of us did not much care for champagne. Honestly, I don't remember what we ate that evening besides a steak. Don't envy me. For any further details of that evening, I would suggest you celebrate your first wedding anniversary dinner in candlelight without anything to wear and tell your wife, "The clothes are getting expensive. So, we have to spare them by not wearing any." You would be unlucky if she did not pinch your cheek. Now you can imagine what could have happened. That was one of the most romantic evenings of our lives.

In the first week of November we went on vacation for two weeks. We flew to San Francisco and rented a car and toured all over California. Milly wanted to drive in California. So, I enjoyed relaxing and watching the dust-filled bushes, the heat-dried fields and desert. It was not a pleasant sight and was not a pleasure driving through the desert. I asked her if she wanted me to drive. But she said she was enjoying driving. It was her dream to visit California.

Neither of us had been there before.

We saw the Golden Gate Bridge and saw so many sights worth seeing in San Francisco and enjoyed the same kind of feelings and same kind of emotions hundreds of you must have experienced. There was nothing unusual in our sightseeing and vacation except I gathered some precious moments worth remembering. Our love bond became stronger.

Almost everyone in New York who had been to San Diego had recommended us to visit the Zoo and Sea World in San Diego. These two were on our bucket list besides visiting a beach there. Milly did not say anything till we reached San Diego. Then she said to me, "Haven't you seen the Bronx Zoo?"

"Oh, yes, sure, I have seen it."

"I have seen the Bronx Zoo a few times and I am not interested in seeing those animals. We should skip the idea of visiting the zoo."

"Well, I thought you were interested in the zoo. We ourselves are animals enough. I think all the people go to the zoo and act like animals to entertain the animals there."

Anyway, we both were not interested in the zoo. We visited Sea World, which was supposed to be the biggest in America. We really enjoyed it.

By the evening, we went to the Silver Strand State Beach in San Diego, sitting in the sand and watching the sunset, looking at those bloody colors in the sky and the fire in the sea. I remembered my olden days when I used to sit alone in the sand at Jones Beach looking at the sea and enjoying those mornings of sunrise.

And this time I was not alone and I was enjoying the evening instead of the morning. There was someone to enjoy the same moments the same way with me. Both of us were mesmerized by that beauty. She hugged me. "Honey, darling, I love this moment!"

The breeze was playing with her hair.

"Oh my, my, I envy that wind, that is constantly kissing your face and hugging you all over."

She hugged me and kissed my face.

"Are you happy now?"

"Now I envy you."

"Why?"

"How come you are so sweet?

"You keep smiling, keep smiling, my baby.

The flowers will thrive.

The stars will glow bright.

Keep smiling, my dear lady.

The world will smile with you.

Between us the love will thrive."

'There is a great difference between the sunrise and the sunset. The sunrise is a beginning of a new day with a new hope. The sunset is the end of the day. It is a beginning of the peace. It is the beginning of the love. And that is very important in life.'

And sometimes, all of a sudden, she would be very serious, deep in her thoughts, alone and away from the world. Just herself!

I would say, "Hey, Milly, I am here, dear. Please, don't make romance with your ex."

And she would smile. "I am not with him, my darling Mr. Did Say. I was thinking of how fast things changed for me."

But sometimes she would say, "You don't understand what I had to put up with him. I would never forget him in my life."

"Come on, Milly, your ex maniac is resting in peace. You don't have to be with him."

"No, he is rotting in hell."

And I had to say something to cheer her up.

There was a beautiful rose garden in front of the motel. she smelled those roses. The roses were beautiful. After she finished her appreciation of the flowers, I told her seriously, "I want to warn you strictly, Mil."

"Why?"

"Don't you go so close to flowers? They will steal your smile and then I have to live with smile-less Milly."

We flew to Chihuahua on Wednesday afternoon. We had planned for a delightful stay at hotel Rancho La Estancia. This was a Mexican ranch nestled high above sea level in the Sierra Madre Mountains. My colleague John from the office had praised and recommended Copper Canyon Railroad tour in Mexico. So, we had decided to take the railroad tour.

On Thursday early morning at six, our train started from Chihuahua chugging along the edges of mountains and crossing deep ravines on its bridges. The railroad winds through deep beautiful gorges. The scenery was *"Woah,"* one of the world's most spectacular. I thanked god for inspiring my colleague John to suggest this magnificent tour. We did not complete the whole tour from beginning to the end. That would have taken fifteen hours and we did not have that much time. We went up to Creel, which was the third station from Chihuahua. It took five and a half hours to reach there. We took the train back to Chihuahua and reached there around eight o'clock for scrumptious Mexican dinner at hotel Rancho La Estancia.

On Friday morning, we went for Chihuahua City sightseeing. One of the attractions was to visit Cathedral de Chihuahua. This was also John's suggestion. The cathedral was of Spanish colonial architecture and was simply marvelous.

By Friday evening we reached Tijuana in Baja California in Mexico mainly to watch the bullfights. On Saturday morning we took a sightseeing tour organized by a local company. That was a quick way of seeing the town. We were, mainly Milly, fascinated to eat Mexican food. By the time we finished our tour, there was hardly any time for a good lunch. We had to go and wait in a long line to get tickets for the bullfight and that waiting was in bright, hot sun. We had already bought big Mexican hats, "sombreros." That was a bit of a relief from the heat. Anyway, Milly was getting a good suntan and she looked like a broiled lobster. The people standing in line were talking so loudly that we had no chance to talk to each other. We were just looking around. There were quite a few Americans in the line. Both of us were excited to see a bullfight.

Finally, we got the tickets and we went inside the stand. At least it was cooler inside. They had sprinkled water on the ground to make the area cool and control dust. The whole atmosphere was filled with heavenly fragrance of the earth. I knew this fragrance since I was a little boy. That reminded me of my mother watering our garden and I was playing in mud. I was overwhelmed. I told my feelings to Mil and she hugged me.

The people were wearing colorful clothes with colorful scarves and sombreros. After well past the schedule time, matadors started coming to the ring and going around showing their medals. All the names were mostly Mexican and the announcements were in Spanish. The announcer must have been a comedian because people were bursting out in laughter from time to time. Milly had studied Spanish in school. But she was not able to understand any of this.

She was out of touch and had forgotten her Spanish.

When the actual bullfight started, Milly held her hat in front of her eyes. She had no heart to watch the fight and the killing. I also became nervous and had a strange feeling in my stomach. "I don't think I can see this bloody fight," I said to her. "Should we quit?" she asked me. I said "O.K.," and we left the stadium. I was glad to see that we were not the only people that left. There were a few other quitters too.

It was too early for dinner and we had to do some more shopping. So, we went to the town and bought a few Mexican items. Then we had a dinner at an old-fashioned traditional Mexican restaurant.

We were happy. We had a wonderful vacation like we were in paradise. We came back to earth on Sunday evening.

We celebrated Thanksgiving with Milly's cousins and their children like last year. This year two of her cousins got marriage licenses. They were rewarded by the grandfather. This year I noticed that all her cousins and their families had a softer look at me compared to the last year when almost everyone was looking at me like a show piece in a museum. This year they accepted that I would be there for a long time.

For New Year's Eve, we four (Milly, Julie, and one's darling and the other's honey) advance booked in a very good restaurant. The live music was so loud that we had no chance to break the sound barriers for our conversation. When we had our first drink, John saluted the would-be mother, his honey, Julie. He announced that she was two months' pregnant. From her looks, I knew that was old news for Milly. I toasted and said, "We will celebrate the news by giving them a party next year." We came by a taxi so we had no restrictions on drinking. We drank, danced, and welcomed the New Year 1978. Milly, as exception to her only-one-drink rule, drank three.

Before getting in the taxi Julie said to Milly, "Mil, consider having a baby. It will be wonderful to watch our children growing together."

"It will be wonderful. But I don't know. Not now."

One night, I was thinking of my happiness. I tried to think of happy days with my mother, happy days from childhood. I thought of my heroic college days, and my dream life with Helen, and all my thoughts came back to Milly. My home, sweet home, my dream home, and it was here with Milly. It was finally a reality. All the happiness I wanted was here. My name is Said, a happy man. I really felt I was a happy man.

CHAPTER FOURTEEN

March 22 was the first day of spring. The New Yorkers were waiting for this day as the spring brings the end of the winter and we were close to the summer. The people were excited. Coming home I bought her roses. I wanted to buy red roses, the symbol of American love. The red roses I saw had no fragrance. So, I bought pink ones. I knew as soon as she got the roses in her hand, she would smell them immediately. When I gave her the roses I said, "Happy spring and happy half-year birthday."

"Thank you. Are you going to celebrate my half-year birthdays?"

"No, not really. Today is the first day of the spring and so is your birthday. I bought flowers and it happened to be your monthly birthday." She kissed me thanks.

We cut short our routine, because *Midnight Cowboy* was on TV at eight. Milly could not count how many times she had seen it. Still, she wanted to watch it one more time. I said, "It will be my third time tonight." I was also excited to watch it, because of her interest. And Milly had planned to prepare a special dinner tonight. She cooked chicken piccata. I cooked Arabic-style okra fried and spinach in yogurt. She served dinner in our beloved China set. I opened a bottle of pinot grigio. We rarely had wine for dinner. But I thought chicken piccata was a special dish. It was my favorite and it was her expertise. Pinot grigio was her favorite. "I wish we had enough time for a candlelight dinner." That was my idea. By the time we finished our dinner, it was getting close to movie time. She was rushing to do dishes. I offered my help. But she declined.

"It will be done in a few minutes." So, I came out in the living room and started going through *Time* magazine.

I don't know how and what exactly happened. I heard China dishes falling on the floor. I heard her getting mad and cursing at herself. I ran in the kitchen.

Pieces of china were scattered on the floor. "Don't worry! I will clean it. Just don't move. You will get hurt. I will bring your slippers." I brought her slippers to wear. I held her hand and led her to the living room and then made her sit on the sofa. She was mad at herself. "Take it easy, Mil. Calm down. It is ok. We will buy a new china set." I cleaned the floor. The whole thing took a few minutes.

When I came out, she was still fuming over breaking the dishes. It was our favorite set.

"Why are you so nice to me, Said?" That was her usual way of asking me from time to time. I really had no answer except I loved her. She wanted an answer from me. This time her tone was firm, not casual as before.

I held her hand and sat next to her. "Shouldn't I be nice to you because I love you?" She took her hand away from me and sat in a sofa chair in front of me.

"I do not deserve you." She was irritated. "No, Said, I am not your Lilly. Why do you love me so much? Why? No one ever loved me except my brother. I am a bad girl, according to my mother. In fact, I am a bad girl. Why don't you understand the real me?"

"Why are you saying that?" I did not believe what I heard.

"You are such a wonderful person. You deserve a good wife. You love children. You go away from me and marry some nice and loving girl. That will make me happy. You can establish a paradise.

I don't deserve you."

"I don't think I want children. After the death of Elham, I was miserable, I was distraught. I am afraid things would turn bad and I don't want to go through the same sad experience. I am not ready for children. I want you, Milly. Why are you talking like this? What has happened to you, Mil? You know that I love you from the bottom of my heart. Every drop of my blood loves you and you know it, Milly. And you love me so much you cannot deny that. I am very, very happy. I do not care for anything else in the world. You are my world. You are my paradise. I don't understand how can I convince you? You are the one who brought love in my life. Mil. I love you very much. And I know you love me."

"No, Said, I cannot be part of your life. I am very serious, Said. I mean it. You don't know what kind of girl I was. I did not care for social and moral values of life at the right time. I crossed the line of decency to be called a lady. Love for one night with strangers, weirdos, and sex maniacs; that was my love life. The things some of them said to me, you can never imagine, the same people would never say those word to anybody in real life. They had treated me like dirt, a piece of meat. You would never imagine what kind of girl I was. I used to sell love. I was shame in the name of love. I was a nymphomaniac like a whore, like a prostitute. I felt like an animal and I did nothing to come out of it. I acted helpless like an animal. That is the truth, Said. Why don't you understand, Said? You are too naive to understand the world."

"It is not that. I am my own man. What happened to you in the past has nothing to do with us and nothing to do with me. I only know you as a nice girl. I am very happy, and that is what brings happiness in our lives." I was stunned and beyond the sense of realization. Why was she saying these things? What had gone wrong with her? So far, I was lost in my happiness. I thought she was always very happy with me. I thought that life was bubbling with zest of happiness. I didn't suspect it was boiling deep inside her.

Tears welled in her eyes. She got up. She was looking into my eyes. She stepped forward. "I love you, Said. You taught me a new meaning of love."

For a moment I thought that she was going to hug me, and bursting into tears, she was going to say, 'I am sorry, Said, for starting all this. I love you from the bottom of my heart. I will never leave you. Please, Said, promise me, you will never leave me alone.'

But she stopped. Turned her face away from me, not to show me her tearful eyes. She stepped back and wiped her eyes with the back of her hand. Then she faced me and with determination started speaking to me.

"I am sorry to disappoint you. We shall live separate lives. I know you love me very much. You are such a wonderful person. You know all my past and still never ever hated me for that. Never looked down on me. You never said anything bad to me, even when we fought. I would have accepted it. It would have been very normal to say something hateful. But you are so naive. Anybody else in your place would have made me feel guilty."

She paused, looked at me, into my eyes with a bold look. "Why don't you understand, Said? I was like an animal."

"Mil, please, I beg you. Please don't leave me alone. You are making a mistake. You won't be happy. I told you what happened to you before we met is history and has nothing to do with me."

"No, Said. I am positive. This is the right thing to do. I know your great philosophy, 'Err is nature and correct is human.' You followed it. I acted beyond nature. You never looked down at me. You always respected me. You are beyond love, you are an angel, Said. I am not worth it. I acted beyond human. I hate myself. Every breathe I take hates me. I am not good for anybody. I am not worth living. I wish I could vanish myself from this earth. I got everything in life. I will end my life; I will, if you don't listen to me, Said. I am very serious."

It was a dangerous threat. I was shocked. It was the first time I ever realized that I did not understand her. I didn't know what was going on in her mind. She was completely remote. I was so dazed in confusion that the words she was saying were not registering in my brain.

"Said, I am very serious, if you don't listen to me, I will kill myself."

"Oh, no, please, for god's sake never think like that. This life is such a beautiful thing; it is god's gift; never end it on your own. I will do anything for you. But please don't ever think of ending your own life."

"I promise you; I will never marry again. I am not suitable to marry. I will never go after sex. You gave me ultimate happiness in sex. I don't need any more. I will entertain myself by doing social work. It needs great courage to work with retarded children. I am going to try it and I am sure I can do it.

"I know John, Julie's husband, is on the road at least for the next few days. I will go to stay with Julie. She will be very happy to have me for a few days. That will give you enough time to make your own arrangements."

She made a telephone call to Julie.

She came close to me, put her hand on my shoulder, squeezed it lightly, and said, "Believe me, this is going to be the best for both of us. You will be happy. I will be happy in your happiness. I will always love you. We shall be the best friends."

She packed a few clothes and left the apartment, leaving me alone. I was watching her, waiting to see if she turns back. She did not.

My whole world turned around me so fast. I could not understand. I was holding my head in my hands. I was confused beyond realization. It was like quicksand. I was buried completely so fast I didn't even realize it. I was in paradise and was thrown over a cliff, and there was no end to my scream, my heart wanted to shriek, "I love you, Milly, please don't leave me alone." But my world was hollow. There was no one to listen.

Lightning Source UK Ltd.
Milton Keynes UK
UKHW040805050320
359822UK00002B/470